GOD

Doesn't Make

MISTAKES

*Confessions of a
Transgender Christian*

LAURIE SUZANNE SCOTT

Agent or publisher inquiries should be sent to info@GodDoesntMakeMistakesBook.com

TABLE OF CONTENTS

This book is dedicated to the thousands and thousands of followers

of Christ, who, only because they are transgender,   are ostracized

by the very community of believers with whom they so wish to

worship and serve alongside. It's my prayer this book brings them

hope, that one day they too will feel welcomed and fully a part of

Christ's body.

FOREWORD

Often, the things that are hardest to face are things we simply can't understand. And in those cases, there are two kinds of people in the world: Those who seek to understand and those who refuse to understand.

This is a book for those who want to understand something few people truly understand or can comprehend, because we have no experience on which to base understanding. I was such a person just two years ago. I didn't know a single transgender person. I had never met a transgender person. I didn't understand what it meant to be transgender. In a word, I was ignorant. And I'm a pastor.

One Sunday afternoon, I sat in a meeting at church where a pediatrician friend and a geneticist friend used a whiteboard to explain to us what "gender dysphoria" is and why we as Christians should understand it. What I heard blew my mind. As a relatively well-educated person and as someone who strives to be compassionate to all people, I couldn't imagine why I hadn't known any of this before.

Here's what I learned: There is a difference between sexual orientation and gender identity. Sexual orientation is about who you love, and gender identity is about who you are. I also learned about the growing body of scientific research on gender appearance and gender identity and how these get formed in the womb—usually in ways that are aligned but sometimes in ways that are misaligned. I learned about how anatomy, chromosomes and brain cells must line up like three cherries on a slot machine for most of us to experience unconflicted gender identity.

And then my pediatrician friend said this: "We must believe that even if some people got a lower dose of a chromosome, or an enzyme, or a hormonal effect, that does not mean they got a lower dose of God's image."

Her words echoed in my head and my heart for several days. And then the Spirit moved in me in a way I could not control: I wrote down what I had learned and submitted it to a national news service where I'm a regular columnist. I could not have predicted what those words would unleash, as the column quickly went viral and today has been viewed by more than one million people.

In that column, "Seven Things I'm Learning About Transgender Persons," I confessed that I didn't know any transgender persons. Within hours, my phone began ringing, my email inbox began pinging and Facebook Messenger poured in messages from people around the world saying: "I read that you don't have any transgender friends. I'll be your transgender friend.

"In just two weeks, I engaged in more than 450 personal conversations about the column. And 95 percent of those were positive, many filled with heart-wrenching stories of oppression, confusion, family estrangements and rejection by the church. I heard from transgender persons, from their parents and siblings and coworkers.

And I began meeting face-to-face with some new friends who are transgender. We met for lunch or dinner or coffee and spent hours getting to know one another. They were shocked that a Baptist pastor would sit down to hear from them, and I was shamed to hear their stories of pain and suffering and how difficult it was sometimes just to be able to use the restroom in peace. And I was changed forever.

Every transgender person I have talked with has told me they knew from their earliest awareness, from when they were four, five or six years old, that they were not the gender inside that they appeared to be outside. Most didn't know what to do with this conflict and were afraid to speak it out loud. Many tried to repress it, sometimes through misguided religious strictness. Sometimes they had no words or role models to make sense of who they were. And most of the time, when they finally came to grips with the reality they had known all along, they were rejected by their churches, by their families and certainly by their friends.

Laurie Scott is one of the people I met as a result of that column and the TED Talk that resulted from the column. I have been moved by her story, by her passionate Christian faith and her willingness to step outside her comfort zone to help others find peace in reconciling their faith with who they know they are inside.

Seeking to understand something that previously seemed so outlandish has changed me for good and for good. My prayer is that reading Laurie's compelling story of life into death into life will change you for good and for good.

Mark Wingfield
Dallas, Texas
June 2018

INTRODUCTION

For some of you, this may be a topic with which you're not familiar. As a Christian it may be a topic that makes you uncomfortable. Perhaps it's a topic you have strong feelings about. The fact that you've made it this far says you're at least curious, not in a strange or perverted way, but curious about how it is that someone can be born with one body and think of themselves as belonging with the gender of the opposite body. Perhaps even more curious might be how a person like this can call themselves a follower of Christ?

There may be some reading this who are Christians and are also transgender. You love the Lord, yet feel that Christ's church has made it near impossible to find a place within His body of believers, you feel like an orphan.

Well, this book is for both of you—because I AM both of you. I grew up wondering how it is that I could be born a boy yet feel like I should be a girl, thinking that there must be something wrong with me and I need to find a way to fix it. I also know what it is to be an outcast from family and the Church because I am transgender.

But here's the good news—Jesus, the Son of God died on the cross for ALL humanity and rose from the grave to give us eternal life for those who will believe.

Some people experience a bump in the road when the Good News and transgender paths cross. For others, they just put up a roadblock. In this book, I don't try to prove that you can be both Christian and transgender, because Christ's salvation isn't dependent upon your gender, there is neither male nor female in Christ Jesus (Galatians 3:28). Though we like to make everything complicated, the apostle Luke wrote in Acts 16:31, when his jailers asked him how they could be saved, he said, "Put your entire trust in the Master Jesus. Then you'll live as you were meant to live…" (The Message) The Bible, the very Word of God makes it pretty simple—we humans tend to complicate it. We find "exceptions." We find reasons that allow us to decide in our own minds who is and who is not worthy of God's grace. We decide how people "were meant to live." And that's unfortunate because God didn't leave it to us, even though we may try to find a way to make scripture fall into line with how we believe.

Let me clear up what apparently is a common misconception—being transgender is not about having sex and it's not about being gay. The only reason for there to be a "T" in LGBT is because it's politically expedient for some. One way I've heard the difference between gay and transgender is; gay is who you go to bed with—transgender is who you go to bed as.

Terminology: When I refer to "*the Church*" with a capital C, I'm speaking of Christ's Church, the global body of believers—not any particular church or denomination. When referring to a local body of believers I will call it by name or simply "the church", no uppercase letter c.

6

Transgender is the most generic term currently available to describe those who don't feel their gender matches their body. Do I believe there are people genuinely born with one body and truly feel with every fiber within them that they are the opposite sex? Yes. Do I also believe that due to the popularity in the media these days of a "transgender culture" that some adolescents, either in rebellion or for getting attention will say they are transgender, yet when they grow into adults live comfortably within their own bodies? Yes. The term I recently learned to apply to them is "trans-trenders," and I laughed when I first heard it because it seemed so appropriate.

I can't speak to all things transgender. I can't speak about people who say they feel one gender one day and another gender another day. I can't speak about people who say they don't feel like they are either man or woman. I don't get it just as you probably don't get it. Transgender is an umbrella term that encompasses a wide spectrum and is common in the vernacular today, so that is the word you will see me use predominately in this book. To be more specific, I would be identified as someone who is transsexual— someone who is born with one body but clearly feels in their mind and soul to being the opposite sex (I know—it's weird).

I know it's easy to call things we don't like, that make us uncomfortable, or we don't understand, a sin. And that's when we often go looking to the scriptures to justify via our faith, that it's okay to disapprove of something. We go to the Old Testament, we go to the New Testament—wherever the verses are is where we go to justify our "beliefs" (frankly, I wish there was a verse to justify not liking Brussels sprouts, but I haven't been able to find it yet).

If I thought it was a sin for you to eat bacon, I would quote Deuteronomy 14:8 and tell you to stop eating it. If you ordered a bowl of clam chowder at a restaurant and wanted to know why I was shocked, I would give you Leviticus 11:10. Do you have the fashionable jeans with the horizontal tears? Not if you believe Leviticus 10:6 means what it says. 1 Peter 3:3 could be interpreted women shouldn't be allowed to make themselves more attractive with makeup, hair, and jewelry—and never mind 1 Corinthians 14 and women remaining silent in the church! In fact, if a woman doesn't give birth, she can't be saved—just look at 1 Timothy 2:15!

Those verses are black and white. If you disagree, that must mean you're wrong. They are obvious—what is there to question or debate?

My point is this—there are more to the verses, their context both within the chapter and book and within the culture of the day, as well as the accuracy of the translation itself (all translations are based on various copies of the original texts, because we don't have any of the originals to work from.) We shouldn't be so quick to stand firm on a particular slice of an English translation of the Bible to support our personal biases.

There are studies on the structure of the brain that show that parts of the brain of someone like me, a male-to-female (or M-T-F) transsexual, are much more like someone who is born female than someone who is born male. Research is beginning to show that something happens early on in the womb that changes what would otherwise be the normal development of the male body and brain. I've always said I don't need science to find a cause to justify in my mind that I was born this way—because there is no other explanation. However, a scientific answer may help others, particularly those who feel that this sense of being "in the wrong body" is a sin. Just as it's not a sin to be born deaf or left-handed, it's not a sin to be born transgender. And just like those who are born with a hearing or some other impairment, it may not be immediately evident until later, perhaps much later.

I was compelled to write this book, because I could no longer just idly sit by and listen to Christians in total ignorance talk about how people who are transgender are out to destroy families, attack women and girls in bathrooms, pump children full of hormones and ruin society in general. Nor could I allow Christians who are transgender complain about the "evangelical church" (referring to predominately conservative Christians) and how hateful and un-Christ-like it was. I am a conservative evangelical Christian who is transgender, so I am likewise hurt when I see a similar ignorance displayed toward churches and people with whom I identify.

Some names of people and churches in this book were changed out of respect for them. The stories in the book are as I remember them. Others in the stories may have a different perspective. This is how I remember the events that have shaped my life and brought me to the point of doing what I never thought I would even want to do—write this book. One name I "changed" is that of Satan. Many in the church like to refer to him as "the enemy," but for me, that feels a little too "nice," so you'll find me calling him that "son of a bitch." That's about as close to cursing as I get in my vocabulary—but I think someone who seeks to kill and destroy you deserves nothing less than the strongest language possible. And that son of a bitch has absolutely tried to destroy me, and I am taking it personally.

I start each chapter with scripture and also something I've learned along the way as it applies to that chapter. It was a real learning experience as I was writing, going back and essentially reliving many of the events of my life. I saw patterns that weren't evident at the time. It's like free therapy if you don't mind the months and months you have to put into it, and now that I think about it; therapy might just be cheaper and faster.

1

A LONG TIME AGO IN A FAMILY FAR, FAR AWAY

"For I know the plans and thoughts that I have for you," says the Lord, "plans for peace and well-being and not for disaster to give you a future and a hope. Then you will call on Me and you will come and pray to Me, and I will hear [your voice] and I will listen to you."
Jeremiah 29:11-12 (AMP)

BEING TRANSGENDER: If being transgender was something you could "fix," something you could pray away, something you could tell yourself that you have to "suck it up" and live with, then I would have done so long ago, and this book wouldn't exist. In fact, you might otherwise be spending your time with good friends right now, whether they are your next-door neighbors, or Ben and Jerry. But this book does exist. Being transgender can't be fixed, prayed away, or ignored. I know— because I tried. I tried every way possible. There are people who think something must have happened early in life, some kind of mistreatment to twist an innocent little mind to think they are not what their body says they are. To them, since God doesn't make mistakes, I therefore couldn't possibly have been born this way. Well, He doesn't, and I was. You might be wondering how it's even possible that someone who is transgender claims to be a follower of Christ. The fact that I'm transgender has no bearing on my decision to follow Christ. Why would it? But it took nearly committing suicide, a desperate phone call to a friend, and later hearing God's voice for me to realize it, and be willing to risk losing everything and everyone I cared about in order to truly live.

January 2000. I live in Sacramento, California. Everyone on Earth had just celebrated like they never had before and the "millennium bug" that was supposed to crash computers and make planes drop out of the sky turned out to be the "millennium dud." I had been the caregiver for my 92-year-old adopted grandpa for several years until he passed away at home January fourth. For the last two years of his life, I hadn't been to church. The very small church I previously attended was the first church I ever attended as "Laurie," and when it had to close its doors, I concentrated on taking care of grandpa. But now he was gone, and it was time to move forward and find a church home.

I grew up in large evangelical churches with the conventional choir, hymnals, and pipe organ. I found later that I liked a more "spirit-filled" church with contemporary worship and raising hands in praise. I was also aware that some churches can seem to be at the fringe in their experience, and that's not what I was looking for. I didn't want a church with people shaking in the aisles and falling to the ground when the pastor breathed on them—that wasn't my style either.

By this point in time, most churches had some kind of website, so I began my search for a church using the internet. One caught my eye: Awaken Fellowship. They offered a free video about the church. The video wasn't long, maybe five minutes, but it did give me a good feel for the church. Family-focused, worship focused, and most importantly, Bible-focused. It appeared lively with a fresh, youthful feel to it, so I made plans to go the next Sunday.

As I arrived, I saw it wasn't a big building. From the rounded front it looked like at some point in time it might have been a free-standing movie theater. There was a vacant lot across the street for parking. Inside, it had the old maroon plush theater-style chairs with thick cushions and wood backs. It even had a small balcony. I took a seat toward the back half of the main floor.

The worship and the music were of a high standard. People worshiped with their hands in the air. I saw people come out from their seats to the area between the platform and the front row to worship, in what was almost like a Christian mosh pit. These people weren't here to be entertained, they were here to worship God! It was an amazing thing to behold. God's spirit was clearly in this place and in these people.

I had been to enough churches in my life that I'm always on guard when visiting a new church. I didn't want to hear only a single verse read from the Bible and then a 30-minute unrelated discourse on the beauty of trees in God's world. I didn't want to hear if we had faith in our FAITH that God would bless us. I didn't want to hear that if we gave $100 to the ministry that

God would give us ten times back that amount. I didn't want to hear that God promised us material wealth if we only believe (the "name it and claim it crowd").

I wanted to hear the genuine Word of God taught. I wanted to hear how God's Word can apply to our life today. What Jesus did for us on the cross, and what we're called to do as His followers.

The pastor's message was good, very good. He was passionate in a deep, heartfelt way, and he taught from a solid biblical basis. The pastor's name was Frank, and he announced that since it was the first Sunday of the month, he and his wife invite any visitors to their home that evening to get better acquainted and ask questions they may have about the church. I thought this was an amazing thing to do, and so I went to their home that evening to learn more.

It was nice getting to meet the "person" Frank (not the "pastor" Frank) and his wife Beverly. I was impressed with how genuine and real they both were. I began to go to Awaken every week. Shortly after that I attended their four-week church membership class—what they believe, how it's structured, etc. I made new friends and enjoyed getting to know other members

I also let them know that I had a background in music and sound engineering with churches and music groups, and would love to serve if they needed me. They wasted no time connecting me with the gentleman in charge of the media folks (sound, video—all of it) and just like that, I was up in the balcony getting acquainted with their audio system. It was nice being involved in a church again, being able to contribute, being able to serve.

A few weeks later, I received a letter with the Awaken logo on it. It was from the pastor inviting me to leadership training offered by the church. One Sunday evening a month, selected members of the church would gather for additional teaching from the pastors.

I panicked. Me? Some kind of leader at the church? I'm happy with the way things are! Just me, the church, and a few friends. It's all good at this point, and I don't want to mess that up. They wouldn't want someone who was transgender, how can I say yes to this?

Then I calmed down. I figured the church probably sent this out to everyone who finished the membership class. I was no one special. It was nothing more than bulk mail from the church based on the sole accomplishment of attending four weeks of a membership class. I convinced myself that saying no to this would be easy.

And just to prove how smart I was in figuring it out, I called the church office and asked the church secretary if they sent that letter to everyone who completed the membership class.

"Oh no, not at all," she said. "The pastors and staff discuss and pray carefully over who these go out to."

My mind screamed, "Oh, crap!" and I went back into a mild mode of panic.

What am I supposed to do now? How do I say no to this? I felt honored that they saw something in me that made them want to include me. They prayed about me over this. They felt God's leading about this. Who am I to question it? I couldn't take this lightly!

But I couldn't dive into this and have things blow up both in my life and at the church sometime later because I'm transgender.

That would be bad for me, and it would be bad for the church—neither of which I wanted. If I was going to say yes to this, I needed to have an open and honest discussion with the pastor. Now you have to understand; I didn't WANT to have an open and honest discussion with him. I would have much preferred a casual conversation over a taco from Taco Bell discussing upgrading the church's sound system, or making CDs rather than cassettes of each Sunday's message. But I didn't see any way around this door but to walk through it. I'm not going to leave a church I love, I'm not going to say no to leadership training if they actually prayed, so I had to let Pastor Frank know about my background.

The next day, I called the church back and asked for a meeting with Pastor Frank and Beverly, and I got on his schedule for the following week.

A few days before our meeting, at the end of the Saturday evening service, Pastor Frank said if anyone needed prayer, to come up and be prayed over. I was worried about our upcoming meeting and went to the front. Beverly came over to me, laid her hands on me, and started to pray. At the same time, I started to cry. The reality of what I was going to divulge to them suddenly overwhelmed me and I couldn't help it. After another moment, she finished praying and looked me in the eye and said the Lord had told her that He loves me, he knew my pain, and was going to use me for His church. I hugged her and thanked her. She said, "We'll see you in a couple of days, right?" I looked at her with my watering and probably red eyes, nodded yes, smiled and left. Neither of us had any clue at the time what the Lord had in mind for me, nor how He was going to use me for His Church years later.

So, Tuesday arrives, and I pull into the church parking lot. I took a big breath and went into the church offices. Pastor wasn't quite ready for me, and I had to take a seat for a short time. Those were nervous minutes for me.

Beverly then walked into the room, greeted me with a big smile, gave me a hug, and said, "Let's go in."

We walked into Pastor's office, and I took a seat on the small sofa in his office. I asked rather sheepishly if it would be okay if we closed the door. Beverly got up to close it, and I took one last big, deep breath.

This was it, a pivotal point for the very direction of my life, my relationship with God and His Church. I was about to reveal to my pastor and his wife that I was a woman who had been born male, and I didn't know what was going to happen when I tell them.

In 1957 in Los Angeles, California, at a hospital that is now nothing more than a parking lot, Robert and Marie had their first child. The birth certificate said it right there in black and white: Congratulations! It's a boy! I can only imagine the hopes and dreams they had for their firstborn—for me.

It was around the second grade I began to notice "feminine" things. Not having any sisters, nor any girls my age in my neighborhood to play with, I was pretty much on my own to figure things out. I probably would have taken notice much earlier in life had there been girls around—after all, it's hard to play "dress up" when there's no one to play dress up with. At the foot of my bed was a large, wooden chest where my mom kept all kinds of stuff. One day I looked inside and in there was a yellow skirt with brown trimming around the edges—I remember it vividly, very 50's. I pulled it on and realized how wonderful it was. I liked how it swished, and I liked how it looked on me. And yet I somehow knew that I couldn't let anyone know how much I enjoyed it. I mean, these were girl's clothes.

Girls at school wore skirts, and I was curious. I wanted to wear a skirt and fit in with the girls too, but it's not something you say: "Hey, Mom, can we go to the store and buy me a nice skirt to wear to school? I want to look like the other girls."

There was something about our family dynamic—no way to fully explain how I knew, but I knew this had to remain my secret. This was when I knew I was a girl inside and that everything I felt made sense to me.

Even being surrounded by all things male (my dad, brothers, and the neighborhood boys) there was one thing I always wanted that was considered taboo, at least for normal boys. It was the Kenner Easy Bake Oven. Things like being able to bake a tiny cake with a lightbulb sounded like fun to me; almost magic. I identified with the girls in the commercials, not because I wanted to bake therefore I must be a girl, but I wanted to bake just like my mom and grandma because I wanted to be like them. Even to this day, as much as I've cooked and baked things in real ovens, that silly little Easy Bake Oven still intrigues me as something the little girl in me never got to do.

The next few years during elementary school were a time of discovery for me. It was during this time, I would play with my mom's lipstick in the bathroom because it made me feel more like a girl—she liked to wear pink. I remember wiping it off at least one time with a washcloth. Looking back, I wonder if she didn't notice when doing the laundry, or if she just didn't say anything. Then, there was the time I thought it would be fun to wear nail polish. I put it on the nails (mostly) of my left hand, and I'm sure it was a sloppy mess between missing part of my nail and getting it on the cuticle and skin near my nails. Then, I went outside to the front yard, trying to admire it without being too obvious. There wasn't anybody else around in the neighborhood as far as I could tell. If one of the kids in the neighborhood were to come by, I would simply put my hands in my pockets. But at least for a few minutes, I got to be like a girl.

It was when I went back inside that I learned an entirely new and important lesson—how hard it is to remove nail polish. Much to my shock and dismay, it doesn't rub off, and it doesn't wash off. I'm sure my mom had nail polish remover somewhere, but I didn't know at the time about the existence of such a mystical and magical substance. What was I going to do? I couldn't sit down at the dinner table later with pink fingernails. That would not go over well.

So, I went into my room and got a pocket knife, and then back to the bathroom carefully scraping it off my nails. It was a slow process, and fortunately, I didn't cut off a finger while doing it. Going to the hospital with pink fingernails, whether they were physically attached to my hand or not, wouldn't win me any sympathy points with my family.

In an amazing twist of unintended irony, one Halloween, my mom dressed up my youngest brother Allen as a girl. He was around five years old and was crying and crying. He didn't want to be a girl. I think it was a black dress with polka dots on it with a bow at the waist he was wearing. I wished it was me being dressed up. I was the one who wanted to be the girl! My most common prayer as I went to bed was "God, please make me a girl." Because surely if God didn't turn me into a girl, there is no way possible I could be, right? I can't tell you how many times I woke up sad that I was still a boy.

Having a dad who was a barber meant my hair was cut for free—it also meant we didn't have any say in how it got cut. Of course, my dad's haircut of choice was the most unfeminine haircut possible, a crew cut. I hated crew cuts. I used to cry when getting my hair cut, but at some point, in helpless submission, I surrendered my protests and would quietly sit there and take it. I wanted long hair; girls have long hair. But this was the 60's. Only hippies and druggies had long hair; good boys didn't.

When I was in the fourth grade, my teacher would choose someone to stand at the front of the class and give a three-minute speech on a topic of his choosing. It was always unannounced, and one lucky day it got to be my turn. I was already nervous talking in front of people, but then he gave me my topic: the advantages of having a crew cut.

All I could do was stand up there and cry. I couldn't think of a single advantage of having a crew cut, not one. I didn't like crew cuts. It had been forced upon me just as a lack of privacy is forced upon a jailed prisoner. And I was a prisoner, a prisoner of my own body and circumstance. The teacher let me stand there, saying nothing with tears coming down my cheeks, for the full three minutes. When my three minutes were up, he said, "Ok," and I was allowed to sit down.

That same year, our grandfather had given a trumpet to my middle brother Vince. But Vince was only in the second grade, and took lessons for just a few weeks; he hated it. Music wasn't his thing. One evening my dad walked into my bedroom holding the trumpet and said, "Vince doesn't want to play it anymore. You want to give it a try?"

"Sure," I said, and I took right to it. I thought it was fun, and I liked making music. I had already learned a few chords on my dad's guitar—my dad had been taking me to an evening beginning guitar class for adults. (I guess I had an ear, because I seemed to be the only one on a room full of adults capable of tuning my own guitar). I took quickly to the trumpet and liked it more than the guitar. I didn't know it at the time, but music would impact the direction of my life in ways to this day I'm amazed to look back on.

I wasn't all that interested in normal "boy" stuff, but when one tries to fit in and be normal, one does what one can.

I was in Cub Scouts for a year. I clearly wasn't that enamored with it, because I remember virtually nothing about my time in it aside from wearing the uniform to school once a week. I was also involved in Little League baseball, specifically the minor league of the Little League. I was pretty good. I was the best pitcher on the team and even hit a couple of home runs. But one year was enough for me. When I didn't sign up the next year to play, the coach called my parents asking why, so of course I ended up playing another year. When that season was over, that was it. No more baseball—and I never missed it.

During fifth grade, we started to attend a large Baptist church. That summer, I went to the church's week-long summer camp in the mountains of southern California. It was at this camp that I accepted Christ into my life. It was a Friday evening, and we were all around a big fire pit, singing songs. Then one of the ministers from church spoke, and he asked those who wanted to accept Christ to stand up and pray a prayer along with him. I did and so did several others. A few months later, I was baptized at church.

In the sixth grade, I noticed that some girls were starting to develop. This was another sad reminder that I couldn't be one of them. Across the street lived a high school girl who was a flag twirler. When her flag team would practice in her front yard, I would hang out in my front yard and watch them. It looked like fun, but I didn't get to have that kind of fun. I was expected to have boy kind of fun with her little brother who was my age.

Junior high was pivotal for me in a few ways. I was getting pretty good on the trumpet, and I loved playing in the band. It was in my first year of band that I knew that I wanted to be a band director. Band was absolutely my favorite class.

Since this was now the late 60's, my dad began to let my hair grow out—a little. Longer hair was becoming more common on guys, and it wasn't a day too soon for me. One day my mom said to me, "Your hair is so straight, we could give you a perm and put some waves in your hair." I loudly objected, because a perm? That's what girls do! Inwardly, I so wished I could say yes, but I was afraid that somehow my secret would be discovered. I wouldn't have been able to hide how much I liked it.

But the worst thing to have ever happened to me was what happens to all boys eventually. Most boys welcome the production of testosterone as their entry to manhood. To me, it might as well have been poison. Something about this reality made the dream of being a girl seem all the more impossible.

But as was the custom in my family, there was no discussion about what my body was doing, what it all meant. There was never a talk about the birds and the bees. Oddly enough, since my dad was a barber, not even a discussion about shaving. I was beginning to get a few hairs on my face, and it was a friend of the family at church that gave me a shaving kit. Looking back, that does seem a little messed up. So, like everything else in life, I pretty much had to figure it out on my own. I didn't want to shave. It seemed an admission that my body was unavoidably and permanently changing in ways I didn't want. But I couldn't deny what was happening to me, and I was powerless to do anything about it.

A day didn't go by when I didn't know what I wanted. I just never thought it would be possible, and I didn't know what I could do about it. I wanted to dress like the girls. I wanted to be with the girls. I wanted to BE a girl. Every day this would be what I wanted, and all I could do was try to act like a normal boy.

My family thought I was a homebody. Whenever the family headed out somewhere, if I thought I could get away with it, I would stay home. This was so I could play with my mom's makeup and clothes. Vince's bedroom was at the other end of the house up next to the driveway, so I would dress up and then lay on his bed and enjoy "being a girl" for the brief time I had—all the while keeping an eagle eye out the window so I could quickly get out of the clothes when I saw them pull into the driveway. By the time they would be back in the house, I was usually in the bathroom at my end of the house getting my own clothes on and/or taking off makeup. For some reason, they never thought it strange to always come home with me in the bathroom. No one ever asked if I was feeling sick or anything. Go figure.

In high school, I did well in band, but around my sophomore year, there was this guy who played baritone horn (think of a baby tuba—the horn, not the guy) who felt like he needed to bully me verbally. I worked at school during lunch in a lunch trailer (for a whopping $1.35/hr.), so I was excused from band about 10 minutes early each day to get ready before the rest of the school got out for lunch. I don't know how he managed to get away with it, but for a couple of weeks, he would follow a short distance behind me, calling me a sissy and taunting me. I tried to ignore him, as he wasn't dumb enough to start a fight in the middle of the school.

One day, a senior who played French horn named Sue had to leave class early right after I did. She heard him calling me names, and she immediately came to my defense and took him down (not physically), telling him that if he didn't stop she would turn him in to the principal. Just like that, I never heard from him again. I don't know what it was that made him want to pick on me. Generally speaking, I spent my life trying to fit in, but clearly, he saw something. I suppose whatever it was, Sue saw it enough to come to my defense. I wasn't a wimp, but I wasn't one to pick a fight or even get goaded into one. I'm sure it's not an occasion she would remember, but it's one of those things in my life that I wish I could go back and tell her "thank you."

By the early 70's, thankfully, longer hair on guys was pretty normal. I was so happy because mine had finally reached a length that if I was home alone long enough, I could play with my mom's curling iron. I liked it when I could put some curls in my hair, but before anyone got home, I'd put water on my hair and comb it straight again. No one could ever, ever know my secret. But one Saturday, my secret almost came to an end—and at sixteen years old, I thought my life as well.

2

THE TRUTH SHALL MAKE YOU
WISH YOU WERE DEAD

"Whoever acknowledges me before others, I will also acknowledge before my Father in heaven. But whoever disowns me before others, I will disown before my Father in heaven."

Matthew 10:32-33 (NIV)

MY CHRISTIAN CONFLICTION: This verse was a great source of guilt for me. Now, I would never disavow my Lord and Savior, but my relationship with God was something quite personal to me. After all, He knew all that I was going through, He knew how I felt, and for reasons I'm sure psychologists have lots of theories over, I kept it all to myself. I didn't talk about being a Christian openly very much away from church. Oh, I pretty well lived as a Christian should, but talking about it was near impossible. It was deep-down securely locked in the same room in my heart as my deepest secret—that I was transgender, that I wanted to be a girl. I didn't know how to tell people that Jesus loved them without risking my transgender secret becoming known. I was so afraid that if I did tell someone about Jesus and they later found out that I was transgender, it would nullify anything I told them. That I was some kind of freak, and it would totally destroy and invalidate what I had said about Jesus. I was spiritually neutered, and my fear made me shrink off into the background.

My dad was a barber, and like most in his profession, he worked on Saturdays and took Sundays and Mondays off. Since it was Saturday and I didn't have to get ready for school, I decided I would sneak into the bathroom, put on some mascara, and then go back to bed. I would lay in bed facing the wall, and for a brief while, at least feel a little more like a girl. It was a little risky since everyone else was home, but the short few feet back to the bathroom door made me feel pretty safe. I had done it before and got away with it each time.

I put on the mascara and admired my eyes in the mirror for a moment and then flushed the toilet—you don't do that and THEN put on makeup, because people would start to wonder why it took so long from flush to exit—right? These are all the planning and thinking steps one goes through when hiding a secret like mine.

So, I open the bathroom door and take two steps toward my bedroom when suddenly, my parent's bedroom door opens behind me. Our bedroom doors faced each other, and the bathroom door was to the side in between the two.

Uh oh! It's my dad about to head out to work. I keep walking into my room and my dad calls my name. It's hard to pretend you don't hear someone who's only five feet behind you, so I acknowledged him with a "yes?" but kept going with my back to him, headed toward my bed, then laid down, pulled up my covers, and faced the wall.

This was not going to be good. I was burned. I was caught dead to rights, and I didn't have a single way to explain my way out of this. With all the thinking I put into it, getting caught was something I neglected in the planning process (clearly my planning skills needed some work).

Not surprisingly, my dad wasn't happy with me having my back to him, so he said rather directly, "Will you turn around?"

This is it, possibly my last moment on Earth. Now, my dad was strict but wasn't in any way violent. I never thought he'd harm me (my last spanking was when I was twelve years old,) but when your biggest, deepest, darkest secret in life is about to be revealed to the last person on earth you would want it revealed to—it feels like your world is about to end.

I have no idea what he actually wanted to say or talk to me about; I'm sure he doesn't remember either, because as soon as I rolled over in bed toward him, he said, "What is that on your face?"

Have you ever been caught so off-guard that your best and only answer was a soft and embarrassed "um…" accompanied by a shrug? I mean, what could I say? He knew what it was. There was no place for me to go wither off and die. I was trapped. If I said anything at all, I don't remember what it was.

My dad said to me "Go take that off" and said something about discussing it later.

I went back into the bathroom, closed the door behind me, and thanked God I was still alive. I took a few minutes to allow my racing heart rate to get back to something resembling normal.

While washing off the mascara, I tried to think of how I was going to explain this. What am I going to do? What lie could I possibly come up with that would be even remotely believable? I wasn't into theater at school, so I wasn't getting ready for a role I was playing. It was the early 70s; the only males on the planet wearing makeup at all were David Bowie and a band called the New York Dolls—neither of which I was in to, so I wasn't going to be able to sell it as crazy fan worship.

I did know that this wasn't going to go away, that today was going to be a day of reckoning. The phrase "tomorrow is promised to no one" never meant more to me than it did this day. If there was a tomorrow for me, I didn't know what that tomorrow would look like.

I washed the mascara off (fortunately my mom didn't use waterproof mascara). Then, I sat on the toilet until I was sure my dad had left for work and it was safe to leave the bathroom. I opened the door, went to my room, closed the door behind me, and crawled back into bed.

This is when I began to pray for a nuclear attack from the Soviet Union, or for the San Andreas Fault to finally drop California into the Pacific. That might be enough to distract my parents from my wandering into the world of makeup, but even then, I couldn't be sure.

Eventually, I got out of bed, got dressed, and did what I have spent a lifetime learning how to do: pretend everything was normal. I have breakfast, and everything seems normal with Mom, maybe

Dad didn't say anything to her. I'm sure my brothers are clueless. So, until my dad gets home, it appears that it's condition green—all clear.

Now, my dad coming home was never something I looked forward to. Usually, I was greeted with "What have you accomplished today?" I had an endless chore list of things like pulling weeds, sweeping the pool, cleaning the garage, and trimming the huge hedges along the front, side, and back of the house. It had been this way since I was young and probably explains my aversion today to gardening or yard work. I never did it for joy; it was done to stay out of trouble (but hey, when the rest of my life gets sorted out, I'll still have this to talk about with Roma, my therapist).

Since it appeared as if the day was going to be free of drama, I relaxed a little. After lunch, my mom wanted me to go to the supermarket with her. I was fine with that. My brothers were home, and I had taken enough risks for one day. We got into that huge brown station wagon of ours and not more than ten seconds out of the driveway, Mom says, "Dad told me about this morning."

That immediately snapped my spine straight! I didn't expect to have this talk with my mom, in the car and on the way to the store. And then at that moment—the heavens opened. Bright light beamed down on me. An angelic chorus began to sing as my mom said what I considered a blessing from the good Lord Himself, "You were just experimenting, right? This was the first time, right?"

I could have driven a pair of 18-wheel trucks through the door that had opened for me. Just experimenting? The first time? What else could I say but... "Yes, it was."

Did I tell a lie? Yes. Was it a big lie? Yes. But when I'm thinking an attack on my country by the second-greatest nuclear power on the planet is what it might take to avoid having this discussion with my father that evening, then you bet I'm going to lie!

Here's the crazy part: it was never spoken of again. Ever. By anyone. Not even when my dad came home (I guess Mom had spoken with him in the afternoon). It was our family's version of the "three wise monkeys": see no evil, hear no evil, speak no evil. After covering our eyes, ears, and mouths, my parents added a black hood so as to never even think of it again, because apparently, they didn't.

I didn't have much in the way of girlfriends in high school and wanting to appear "normal," I couldn't have girlfriends like the girls would have girlfriends. I did have a good friend who was a girl, Janice. She didn't go to my school, but we went to the same Baptist church. Janice also sang and played the piano. We would sit together up in the balcony and sing the harmonies in the hymnal at the evening service (we were Baptists, so we went to church twice on Sundays!) Janice and I never "dated," but she WAS my date to Disneyland after graduation for Grad Night.

In southern California, that's what a lot of schools did for graduating seniors, an all-nighter at Disneyland following the graduation ceremony. We'd toss our caps and gowns, get on buses and head to "The Happiest Place on Earth." Even in college, Janice and I would sometimes get together and play tennis followed by a lavish meal at Taco Bell. Because nothing is too good, and price is no object for two college students. The cool thing is that to this day we are still good friends. The difference is that now she calls me Laurie and she is a pastor in the Lutheran Church. My friendship with Janice played a big part years later in my finding the help I needed in figuring out the rest of my life.

In college, my passion for music and intention to become a music teacher continued, so I became a music major. I went to the local junior college and wow, did I hit the jackpot, because it happened to have one of the finest music programs around, particularly jazz.

I did have a girlfriend there. She had a job with a burger chain locally, and they were opening a new Mexican food division (similar to a Taco Bell but a little nicer) and they needed employees. She put in a good word for me, and I was hired to work evenings and weekends for minimum wage, which back then was around $2.30 an hour (but gas was only a buck a gallon, so it wasn't so bad, plus I was still living at home). Over the next couple of years, I worked my way up to assistant manager.

During this time, I was still going to the Baptist church I grew up in and was still involved in music. I was the lead trumpet player in the band that accompanied the small group of college-age singers that did more contemporary songs. At that time, most churches (at least those that I knew of) were still rather traditional, choirs, hymnals, and if you were lucky, a pipe organ) This smaller group had 12 singers with individual microphones and a 20-piece jazz band.

It was a lot of fun to play in the group, but two things were always difficult for me. The first one was that for performances, we got broken into two groups: the boys and the girls, each with our own outfits. At rehearsals, it didn't bother me as much because everyone was in street clothes. But when we performed in our outfits, in my heart, I simply wanted to be one of the girls, to be wearing what they were wearing, to be what they were.

It was even harder at the end of each performance. We were doing more than performing; we were using music as a way

31

to introduce people to Jesus. Many of our performances were outdoors and drew people who had perhaps never heard of Jesus before or even been inside a church before.

During the rehearsal each week, the director would take time to do a brief Bible study to help us grow in Christ and understand why we believed what we did. Whenever we performed, she encouraged us to go out and talk to those in the audience at the end. Most of those in the group would go out and talk to people, but for me—I couldn't do it. I would find ANY excuse, so I didn't have to talk to people out there, especially about God or Jesus. I would take my time packing up my horns. I would gather all my music together. I would help unplug microphone cables and carefully wind them correctly (there's a technique to it you know—and it's not going around your elbow). I would fold up music stands, help take down speakers—anything! Anything but talk to people.

My relationship with Jesus was personal, deep, and very much tied up with my secret about being transgender, though I didn't know the word for it at the time. So, I didn't talk about Jesus. I was at church every Sunday morning and evening and involved in the music group. But talk about it at a personal level? Nope. To quote President Bush 41, "Not gonna do it." Ever.

Music continued to influence my life in positive ways. My best friend in junior college, Mark, was the lead trumpet player of the jazz band. He transferred to the state university in the Valley (in southern California "the Valley" means only one thing: the San Fernando Valley, birthplace of the "Valley Girl"). This was one of the best music schools on the west coast, so I applied and transferred there the following year.

I know that today we live in a world of scholarships or school loans, but that's not how I grew up. Back then, we paid for what we bought. When I went to the university, another friend and I rented a guest house in the backyard of a home a couple of miles from school. For each of us, it was about $80 a month, and in that first year, my parents paid my rent. I bought my books and paid for my classes, food, bills, gas, etc., working. As an assistant manager in the restaurant chain, I was able to transfer to a store about 30 minutes away from my school (it was southern California—driving to work for 30 minutes was no big deal).

This is where I first lived apart from my parents and brothers. This is where I worked on getting my bachelor's degree, so I could go into teaching. And this is where, both for better and worse, things began to happen that would change my life forever.

3

TILL DEATH DO US PART

"A woman is bound to her husband as long as he lives. But if her husband dies, she is free to marry anyone she wishes, but he must belong to the Lord."

1 Corinthians 7:39 (NIV)

TRYING NOT TO BE TRANSGENDER: When I was young, being gay wasn't talked about in a positive way, and you can forget about someone who was transgender (back then, transgender wasn't even a word). So people like me dealing with being transgender tried very hard to be "normal." Transitioning wasn't even considered an option. You don't hear about it as much these days, but it wasn't uncommon for males who were transgender to join the armed forces—you know, to make "men" out of them. I didn't go the military route. For me, my last desperate attempt was to get married. She wasn't just someone I wanted to be with, she was someone I wanted to be like. She was musical, tall, and beautiful. Maybe that would be enough, to somehow live life vicariously through another. As I found out, it doesn't work that way. You can't live your life through another person. Parents can't (though some try to) live their lives through their children, and being transgender, you can't live your life through a spouse. It doesn't change who you are, no matter how hard you try—you are who you are and have to live your own life.

Throughout my life, I fought wanting to be a girl—I fought it. Because I thought it was wrong unless (when I was younger) God would magically turn me into a girl. That there must be something wrong with me. I was still trying to be "normal." I was still hoping there was some magic that might make me a normal guy leading a normal, happy life. What was wrong with a good Christian thinking that?

After that year in the guest house, my roommate and I moved into a two-bedroom apartment across the street from the school, and two others joined us so between the four of us it wasn't too expensive. The university was a long hour from my parents' home and a solid hour from my church. Though I would attend a church now and then in the Valley, I still would drive out each Tuesday evening to my old church for rehearsals in the music group that I still loved being a part of. And that's when things got even more complicated for me, if that was even possible.

Being a college-aged group, it naturally had turnover among the singers. One Tuesday evening I came to rehearsal and there she was—a new singer in the group. Jan had just graduated from college and was working part-time at the church helping in the music area with children. She was tall, she was blonde, she was talented, and she was beautiful. She was everything I wanted to be, and I couldn't help but look at her.

I was in college and 22 years old. I thought having a girlfriend might help with my feelings of wanting to be a girl, that being close to femininity might somehow "be enough" to help me cope with it all (though it never seemed to help in the past). When you are first attracted to someone, it's hard to NOT look at them, and pretty soon they notice it. Now if they like the fact you're looking at them and are looking back at you, you're going to get together—and well, we did.

It was probably a good thing that she lived near the church an hour away. I hate to think what would have happened to my work at school if we had been close enough to get together every day.

I graduated from college and was now working on my teaching credential.

We had been dating for about nine months when the music group had a tour in Hawaii. Following an afternoon performance, we had the evening off, so Jan and I walked down to the beach on Waikiki. It was perfect Hawaii weather, comfortably warm with a gentle breeze. On a grassy area before the sandy beach, we relaxed under a palm tree, and we looked at the stars as the waves gently came in and the palm leaves rustled in the breeze. It. Was. Perfect.

I had planned on proposing to her on a hike to Sacred Falls later that week, but it was an impulsive moment, and I asked her right there. She said yes. We agreed that it would probably be best if we kept it to ourselves for the remainder of the tour, but we did confide with the minister who traveled with the group and spoke at our concerts. He respected our choice to keep it confidential and gave us some valuable pre-marriage advice.

When we flew back home, a bus brought us back to the church where everyone met us. We managed to keep our secret until we could tell our parents at home that evening. But it seemed pretty much everyone in the group knew or wasn't surprised by the news—we were together all the time in Hawaii, and though we didn't say anything on tour, I suppose it was obvious.

Did being engaged make my desire to be female go away? No. Did I hope that being married would make it all go away? You bet. If being married, having a woman in my life, sharing our life together didn't take away the feeling that I was female, then I didn't know what I was going to do. I didn't know what else I could do. I had been keeping my secret my whole life. Was it going to get easier or harder to do? I didn't know.

But getting married did make me think about our financial future more. As I was finishing up my teaching credential work, I didn't see much of a career path as a music teacher. But working in the restaurant, I saw the district manager come by now and then in her company car. She had her boss and he had his boss, and each had a nicer car—management paid pretty well, and the perks were good also.

My district manager had been half-jokingly asking me for at least a year, "When are you going to stop with this silly idea of teaching and go into management?" They really wanted me. I knew her well enough that she wasn't just saying it; she thought I could do well in the company. It was a young division that was growing, and I could see the opportunities there.

One day, I contacted her and said (as if holding out my arms to be handcuffed), "Okay, you got me. Take me into management."

And within two weeks, I had left the teaching program at school, secured an apartment down in Anaheim, and was working as a manager trainee in the company's highest-volume store.

A couple of months later, I had finished the training program and was promoted to manage a nearby restaurant. And a couple of months after that, I was training new manager trainees and making a nice salary—no one questioned my decision not to teach music.

We pushed forward with our wedding plans. With both of us being musicians, we had certain requirements. Being a trumpet player, I wanted brass players. Jan was a singer and pianist and wanted (surprise) singers. And we both wanted a church with a great pipe organ. Fortunately, the church that was across the street from our church had great acoustics and an amazing pipe organ—so that's where we got married.

For the brass players, my trumpet teacher, who sometimes performed with the L.A. Philharmonic and was part of a professional brass quintet, offered the quintet at a ridiculously cheap cost (pretty much a wedding present). I had a friend from school arrange the Wagner wedding processional for brass quintet and pipe organ—it was pretty amazing.

We also had a vocal octet made up of professional and semi-professional singers who were friends to perform with Pinkham Wedding Cantata—high-level stuff. Oh, and by the way, the bride and groom did get hitched during this musical extravaganza. This fairy tale wedding was exactly what we wanted, though I'm sure for some who attended it was boring and too long—tough!

While we were engaged, Jan got a job teaching in south Orange County at a private Christian school; so when we married, we got an apartment in that area so her drive would be easy. But now it was a bit too far to keep going to our old church. A friend from our old music group was now at a large church in Orange County, so we checked it out and loved it. The pastor was great and nationally known. They had a great music program and a full orchestra that often played. It was a great fit for us, so we got involved, and I became the lead trumpet player in the orchestra. In 1985, our church's music director was the music director for the 10-day Billy Graham Crusade at Anaheim Stadium, and I was the lead trumpet player in the brass choir right there on the platform with Billy Graham himself—it was pretty cool!

How much better could life get for someone? A beautiful spouse, a great job, and a musical outlet through a great church we loved. When Jan's job was eliminated a year later, we decided to look for a home to buy closer to where we both grew up. We ended up buying a home close to my parents and my old high-school, and only a few miles from her parents. A young couple in their mid-twenties, owning a home where they grew up, close to family—the American dream continued.

At our church, Jan met a couple of other gals who were great singers, and they formed a vocal group. They were very good. They sang either a capella or to recorded instrumental tracks. There were a couple of songs they wanted to sing, but no tracks were available. So we gathered a group of talented friends who were excellent musicians to record the instrumental tracks the trio could use in performances. We hired a recording studio, a friend wrote the arrangements, and I produced the tracks for the songs. It was a fun time and where I first met the guitarist in the session, Frank, who later became my best friend.

The girls were also a part of a young-adult contemporary group at the church. They had someone running sound for them, but there were often minor issues, feedback, etc. I was usually around during performances because Jan was there. One day I went up to the director and mentioned that if they pulled down a certain frequency on their equalizer, it would get rid of most of the ringing and feedback they were hearing. I guess he did because it seemed to help, and a few weeks later he asked if I would be willing to run sound for them going forward, which I accepted. This was my first time running sound for a group larger than the three girls with a recorded track, and it got me more interested in audio engineering.

One time the girls had a performance, and since it was a bit of a drive, Jan and I picked up the other two and I drove them all to the location. In the car, they were talking about normal girl stuff as if I weren't there. All I could think of while I listened to them was how I wished I could be one of them, one of the girls, BE a part of the conversation. I ached inside. And that's when I realized that being married wasn't making any of what I was feeling any better.

But I WAS married and now feeling (in a way) stuck. I promised to love her for better or for worse and was torn. I did love her, but does worse include death? Does worse include wanting to kill myself because of the torment of who I knew I was inside, who I was supposed to be, unable to do anything about it?

We were married about four years, and she was feeling the need to start a family. To say I wasn't feeling it would be an understatement, but what could I do? I wasn't capable of speaking up about it. The thought of being a father to a child, a father I knew I could never be, paralyzed me. I couldn't fake it that long.

After around a year of "trying," she didn't get pregnant, and so Jan went in for fertility testing. When all the tests came back negative, it was my turn to see what was going on, if anything.

Laurie Suzanne Scott

I went in for a testicular biopsy so they could figure out how much sperm I had. It took several days to get the results. When the results came back it was a bit of a surprise—I was sterile; I couldn't father any children.

Jan got the call with the results and was in tears when she told me, in part because she felt bad for me, but this was her dream, and she was seeing that dream dashed by this single phone call. To be honest, I can't remember how I outwardly reacted, except that perhaps she was so devastated herself and projected that devastation onto me, that she didn't recognize my lack of agony or pain as an issue. We hugged, and I assured her that everything would be ok. As it turns out, I was right about the future, but not how she expected it—and frankly, nor I.

Since everything was physically fine with her, Jan later talked about artificial insemination. She wanted to give birth to a child of her own—something I could never blame her for. It's a natural desire of a woman, and I completely understood. I'm sure she assumed I would want to be a father just as much.

What I didn't know how to handle or explain, was that I knew I wasn't capable of being a true father to a child, whether a boy or girl. I've faked being happy as a male all my life, but I knew I couldn't pull off the role of being a father to a child. How do you fake that? This is when I truly understood the phrase of being between a rock and a hard place.

As the days and weeks passed, my brain began to feel as if it had short-circuited and there was only a buzzing noise going on in my head. How could I possibly tell her that I couldn't be a father to the children she so badly wanted? What, other than the truth, would be an adequate reason? I didn't know what to do and how not to be forced into the situation of being a father to someone who deserved a real father, someone I couldn't be.

Finally, I could take the pressure no more—it was consuming me. After maybe a couple of months, she was talking about making the appointment to have the procedure done. If she did become pregnant, she would be so excited. How would I be able to hide my internal fear and terror? I was in a panic. I had to tell her; she needed to know, it was the right thing to do, but I was scared out of my mind at the same time.

One evening, she had a rehearsal at church, and so I made my plans to tell her. I decided I was going to tell her everything. And I was also sure I would chicken out and not be able to tell her if we were simply sitting at the kitchen table or on the sofa. She needed to hear the truth, and there was only one way I knew how to do it so I wouldn't be able to back out at the last minute.

While she was away at rehearsal, I took a bath and I shaved my legs. Then I began to get dressed—but not in my normal clothes. I put on a dress that I had bought and kept hidden. I put on makeup and topped it off with a wig, another secret purchase. To say I was nervous is an understatement. This was the first time I was voluntarily blowing up whatever life I had.

I knew what time to expect her home, and I made darn sure I was ready before then. I had a glass of wine (okay, maybe two) before she got home to steady my nerves. I sat on a chair in our family room and waited. My heart was beating hard, and all I could do was try to breathe, breathe—in and out.

Eventually, she came home. I heard the car door close out front. My heartbeat began to go off the charts. I was about to expose a lifetime secret, and I hadn't left myself a way out. This was it. The moment I never in my entire life wanted to have happen. And it was about to happen. "Oh God, what am I about to do?"

She came in the front door and announced herself saying, "Hello."

I simply said, "I'm back here." I could feel my face getting flushed. Jan walked through the kitchen into the family room where she saw a woman in a dress sitting in a chair with her legs crossed; I imagine her first fleeting thought was that I had another woman in the house. It took her only seconds, and then she realized it was me. When she asked me what I was doing, well, that's when it all began to fall apart—that's when my not being normal first seriously impacted my life, not to mention hers.

To be honest, the rest of the evening is a blurry memory. I don't remember the words I used to answer her questions, but they amounted to "This is what I've wanted to be for my entire life."

She asked me to put my own clothes back on and take off the makeup. She asked questions, and I did my best to answer them. I'm sure she was hoping this was just a phase I was going through.

No doubt her world was completely shaken at that moment. We were both good kids growing up in good Christian homes, we were both the oldest in our families, the first to get married, the first to buy a home, and we were active and involved in our church. One friend described us as Barbie and Ken—everything seems perfect and hunky dory, the only thing missing was the white picket fence. This wasn't the kind of thing that happens to people like us from families like ours.

As the days went by, I found myself thinking (and probably hoping) what I've since learned others in a similar situation have thought: That maybe my wife would be okay with me dressing up and at least being a "part-time girl." That's what you call desperate and probably even delusional optimism. She had her dream when we got married, and having a husband who wanted to be a woman was never a part of that dream. I did try to test that water, though. I kept my legs shaved, but that didn't go over well either.

In hindsight, it's probably a good thing that Jan wanted to go with artificial insemination, because that forced me into telling her. I couldn't bring a child into the world knowing that I couldn't be the kind of father that the child should have.

Eventually, it got too hard for her, and she asked me to sleep in the other bedroom. When it became clear that I wouldn't be able to change, she later asked me to move out and she filed for divorce. I never argued with her over it. How could I? She deserved the life she hoped for when we were married, and I couldn't give it to her. I didn't even hire an attorney; I gave her whatever she wanted and sadly signed the papers. I had, in her mind, killed the man she thought she married.

Once the divorce was final, I think for each of us it was, "Now what happens with my life?" The single greatest regret in my life is that Jan's life got intertwined with the mess that was mine. But God is good, and He is faithful. I am ever so thankful to the Lord that today she is happily remarried with two daughters of her own.

I moved in with my brother Vince, who owned a home a few miles away—and soon after that, the house that Jan and I had once lived in was sold. All I ever told my family and friends about the divorce was, "Things just didn't work out." Most people correctly interpreted that as, "I don't want to talk about it." I was okay with leaving it to their imagination and certainly my family at least never questioned it further, at least to my face.

One day, I got a call from the guitarist Frank, who I had met at the recording session for the trio. He liked how I worked producing the recording for the girls and asked if I was available to mix sound for a Christian band he was in. They had a concert coming up, and he thought of me. I said sure, and from there we became good friends and I became part of the band.

Jan was still going to our church in Orange County, so I decided it best to leave and find a new church. Frank invited me to his. It wasn't a huge church, but it was a growing church and for me, a different kind of church. Growing up Baptist and having recently left a rather conventional evangelical church, going to a Foursquare church with a worship band and people raising their hands in worship was a dramatic change. And I learned something about myself—I liked it. But I didn't immediately jump in with both feet. I can remember standing there for months with my arms down at my sides, seemingly incapable of raising my hands while singing the worship songs.

Then one Sunday, miracle of miracles happened during worship—I discovered that my elbows could bend! Now, they didn't leave my side, but I did get my forearms and hands out in front of me a little, as if I were carrying a small log. It was a step. I was starting at the shallow end for sure.

As I learned these worship songs that I had never heard before, I was able to close my eyes as we sang. I found that when I wasn't looking at others, worried what they would think of me, and allowed myself to enter into God's presence, that it was natural to want to raise my hands to Him. And of course it's natural. When a child sees her daddy come home, doesn't she want to run to him with arms outstretched? Somehow, we forget we're God's children, and it should be natural to want to approach Him with our arms outstretched.

Growing up as I did, God was someone we sang about out of hymnals and studied out of our Bibles. And when told what

Christ did on the cross for us, it was almost an intellectual decision to "accept" Jesus into our life. Now, I'll admit that my own personal issues didn't help with my growth as a Christian, but I was discovering what it was to be in His presence, to still my soul, be able to listen for what He wants to tell me, and also to express my joy and gratitude of having Him in my life.

And this is where I first learned about healing. I, of course, have read about healing in the Bible, but I grew up believing that things like healing and speaking in tongues only happened in the time of Christ and not in current times. This was the first church I had ever belonged to that actively prayed over, and for, the specific healing of one another. Laying hands on someone for healing? This was new for me.

Frank became my best friend. He was a great guitar player, and we both enjoyed talking about music and just hanging out. He was such a good friend that he tried to hook me up with a girl from church that he knew. He introduced us and she was very nice, but unknown to Frank—I was still trying to sort out my life. I was now divorced, feeling like I've already failed, and I wasn't ready to even think about another relationship. I told him I wasn't ready for anything like that, as nice as she was. As it turned out, and what he hadn't told me at the time, was that he liked her too. They started dating and eventually got married— so Frank, you're welcome!

It had been about a year living at my brother's home when he became engaged, and it was time for me to find a place of my own—so I bought a condo in Orange County. I had earlier moved to a new restaurant company and was now working at their corporate office in Orange County. It was a short drive to work and not far from church. I remember my dad coming to visit me one day, so I took him to the office and up to the top floor where my office was, view and all. The son of a barber with a big office and a view of the area from the top floor—he was clearly proud of me.

But my internal struggle continued. Frank was close to another family at church, and since Frank and I were such good friends, eventually I became friends with them too, but mostly with Cindy. Cindy was the mom and is what you call a prayer warrior. This woman knows how to pray, and she prays a lot. I think she also sensed there was something going on with me.

One day, I went over to her house to tell her exactly what was going on with me. That I wanted to be "normal," and I wanted God to fix me. Cindy prayed for me, and prayed for me… and prayed for me.

During the normal course of a day, I might be busy with work or something else, and my gender issue wouldn't be top of mind at a given moment. But sooner or later it would pull at me, as if the emotional pain would flare up out of nowhere. Cindy told me when those times come, to call her, and she would stop and pray for me right there, anytime day or night.

I can't tell you how many times I made that call. Sometimes in the middle of the day and sometimes in the evening.

It was also around this time that I told my friend Frank. He didn't understand it, but he joined Cindy in praying for me. I continued to run sound for the church and Frank's band, and had a wonderful time doing it. Unfortunately, I wasn't playing trumpet much these days—the musicians I knew at my old church dropped out of my life as they learned of my divorce and (I assume) the reason why. I missed performing, but being able to run sound for the most part satisfied my need for musical fulfillment.

My job had me occasionally traveling overseas, one time for six solid weeks over Thanksgiving, Christmas, and New Year's. And then, an opportunity came up that would allow me to stay home more. The company was growing, and presented me with a couple of options: they needed a district manager over some restaurants in southern California. They also needed someone to work with the growing franchise restaurants in northern California. There were stores in the San Francisco Bay area, Sacramento, Stockton, and soon Portland and Reno, and they needed a company representative who lived in northern California.

My boss, the president of the division I was in, and a very smart man whom I respected, pointed out that I would have better visibility and opportunities for advancement if I stayed in southern California. Moving to northern California could put me "out of sight, out of mind."

I gave it some thought. I went into management because of the advancement opportunities. But having spent around 14 years in the restaurant business and watching the politics involved, going to northern California and getting away from that sounded pretty good.

Part of me felt a little bad about moving, because my youngest brother Allen had recently married and moved to Texas, north of Dallas. My middle brother Vince had recently moved with his wife to northern California, about 45 minutes from Sacramento, leaving only my parents and me in southern California. If I moved out of the area, they wouldn't have any of their kids close to home. But I couldn't allow that to be my reason to stay, and I knew I'd be back down every few weeks anyway for business meetings.

So, in spite of my boss's advice, I took the position in northern California. I sold my condo in Orange County, and a new chapter of my life was about to begin. Yet, I had no idea how dramatically different my life would become as a result. I didn't know I would get so close to killing myself, I didn't know I would have God Himself speak to me in the middle of a freeway, nor did I know I would see the "impossible" dream come true.

4

THE BREAKING POINT

"At this point, Lord, you may as well take my life from me, because it would be better for me to die than to live." The Lord responded, "Is your anger a good thing?

Jonah 4:3-4 (CEB)

BEING TRANSGENDER IS NOT A SIN: Something that happens to many well-meaning and otherwise loving Christians, is confusing their personal feelings about something as good or bad, right or wrong, in relation to God's will. I've done it too. I grew up thinking it was a sin to drink ANYTHING with alcohol. I grew up thinking it was a sin to smoke. A Christian who smoked or a Christian who would drink wine (or worse) to me was someone who wasn't really a Christian—I mean how could they be? Just look at them, they're SMOKING! And forget about it if they drank! I remember around high school or maybe my first year or two in college, my dad learned that if you first soaked a fish fillet in white wine, it helps remove the "fishiness" when it's cooked. So he went to the local supermarket to buy a bottle of wine—I know he felt self-conscience standing in line holding a bottle of wine. I'm sure he was wishing he could tell anyone standing near him "oh no, I'm not going to drink it—it's for my fish." Yes, for some people who have a particular weakness, trouble does seem to find them when they drink—and for them, it probably is a sin between them and God to drink. Smoking, well I think it's a bad habit, certainly not good for you, and I'm a bit allergic to the smoke anyway—but I'm sure smoking in and of itself isn't actually a sin. If you're spending your family's last $20 on cigarettes rather than food for your kids, well then maybe it is. That's the kind of environment I grew up in—the kind of thinking that surrounded me. Many people think being transgender must be a sin, because they just don't like or understand it. And as with most things, if you don't like it, you can probably find a verse or two in the Bible to justify your feelings. I didn't even have any verses to think that being transgender is a sin, it's not like I'm choosing it—it's not something I DO, it's something I AM. But it takes quite a while to get from point A to point B when you confuse what YOU think with what GOD knows.

Sacramento, California. A job promotion (with a company car), a new city, an opportunity to finally straighten myself out and get life back on track. The day finally came to move into my new home, and I found my neighbors to be very nice. It was a fairly tight neighborhood, and we even did a progressive dinner each Christmas which was always fun (especially since we could walk from one home to the next). I made it one of my first priorities to look for a new church. I remained close to my friends Frank and Cindy in southern California who were still praying for me and knew my struggle trying to be "normal."

Growing up Baptist, the charismatic church that I had attended in Orange County opened my eyes to another level of worship that I hadn't seen or experienced before, and I liked it—so that's what I sought. There was a non-denominational church I had heard of, so I went for a visit to check it out. I found the people to be nice, the music good, and the teaching what I felt to be on point, so I kept going.

In my continuing attempt to be normal, I dated a girl there at the church a couple of times. She was a single mom with two young girls. One time, she needed help with some things on her property, so I went over to give her a hand. She was a good mom, and as she should be, very protective of her girls. We went on another date and it was clear we liked each other's company, so while we were sitting in the car, I told her about how I had been married before and what caused the divorce, but that it was something I was working on overcoming. Smooth move, eh? Nothing cements a relationship with a woman like telling her "surprise, I used to be married and oh, no big deal but I wanted to be a woman myself—but I'm getting over it." If you're wondering did she leap into my arms at this point, the correct answer would be "uh, no!"

I believe it was after about 10 seconds of stunned silence the next words heard in the car were "I'd like to go home now, please," and no, I wasn't the one saying those words.

Not surprisingly, she talked to one of the pastors at the church about it, who then called me and said that she had talked with him and he asked if I would talk to him after the service on Sunday. I said yes (I mean what else could I say?). I was helping with sound that morning, and he came over and asked me to meet him in one of the rooms when I was finished securing the equipment. When I walked into the room, it wasn't just the one pastor waiting for me, but about five men from the church.

I was a little intimidated at first; maybe they were angry that I had upset their longtime member and friend, and they were going to "make sure" it didn't happen again. Fortunately, that wasn't the case. The pastor said that she was a little rattled by the whole thing, and it was probably best if we not date. I didn't disagree with him. He asked how long I had been dealing with this, and I told him for as long as I can remember. I confirmed that I had been married before and gave a little background into that. Since we hadn't spoken much previously, he asked about my relationship with Christ, when I became a Christian, and that I truly did want to be rid of this "affliction" (for lack of a better term). I told him yes, and all the men gathered around me laid hands on me and started to pray. It went on for several minutes.

At that moment, I did feel "better" (I mean, when people gather around you, lay hands on you and pray for you, you SHOULD feel better—right?) but it didn't have any bearing on my gender identity issue. I continued to go to this church and over the next few months would occasionally meet with the pastor, and people there would pray over me at Bible study—but a peculiar thing was happening. I wasn't getting "better," I was getting "worse." I even fasted for a week over this—I only drank water and iced tea and prayed in my living room, that was it. I was pretty weak by the following Sunday when I went to church. I remember being in the sound booth and feeling light-headed when I stood up. Prayers at the church continued, and the more I sought healing, the more miserable I felt.

I would occasionally call Cindy in southern California when I was hurting with my desire to be female, and she would always stop

what she was doing to pray for me right there over the phone—
she was almost like my own personal "transgender anonymous"
lifeline, and she was my "sponsor" (though she of course wasn't
transgender).

There was a psychologist who attended my church, and the pastor
got me connected with him and we had several appointments
together. I didn't realize it at the time (since I had never talked to
a psychologist before), but he knew pretty much nothing about
transsexuality—whatever he knew he must have read it in a book
right before we first met. He asked me questions about my potty
training, how long was I breastfed, did my mother secretly want
a girl and when changing my diapers say "bad pee-pee, bad pee-
pee".

I know, it seems so ridiculous now but hey, I was trying to get
"better" and he was a REAL psychologist, plus I didn't know any
better. He even allowed me to come dressed as "Laurie" a couple
of times. Maybe he thought I was schizophrenic and wanted to
see if a different personality would come out. Frankly, I didn't
know why he did, but it was me who proposed seeing him as
"Laurie" because I wanted him to see me as a "normal" woman
and not a freak—which is how I thought people like myself were
perceived. As to his questions, since I obviously didn't know the
answers myself, I had to go back to the source, my mom.

Now you have to understand… I really, really didn't want to
tell my own mother that I was struggling with feelings of being
female, but the psychologist had questions, and there was only
one person on the entire Earth who could answer his questions.
So, I drove down to southern California and met with my mom
in the home where I grew up. It was a hard thing to tell my
mother about all that I've been feeling for most of my life, but
I guess what made it palatable for her is that I was trying to

overcome it and was asking for her help. I told her about seeing a psychologist and the questions he had for her. Remember, we never talked about ANYTHING in my family of that kind of private nature—it wasn't in the family DNA. I had never used the words "breastfeed" in front of my mother before. I'm sure I had never heard her use those words before either, and I know for a fact we never talked about my potty training or her changing my diapers.

To say it was an "uncomfortable" conversation is an understatement—squirming and wishing I was on the other side of the world is more like how I was feeling. And guess what?

Surprise! NOTHING unusual came out of this discussion with my mom! No, she didn't secretly wish I had been a girl and somehow unconsciously transmitted that desire to me. Breastfeeding and potty training were apparently what she expected—but of course I was her first, I suppose she talked with other women about it during that time to know what to expect. So, I learned nothing new, and I had to have an uncomfortable conversation with my mom about a lifetime secret.

My next appointment with my psychologist was basically this: I reported "nothing unusual."

His response was, "Well, I've got nothing."

That pretty much ended our professional relationship.

I was starting to hurt at this point in a big way, and I was troubled by the fact that it seemed like the more I sought God, the harder I tried to be "normal," the worse I got. I was beginning to have thoughts that, since there is clearly something wrong with me that even seeking God isn't fixing, and since I can't continue to live this way, that maybe I should just kill myself.

It's a desperate person who thinks these things, and yes, I was desperate. I had cried before God. I had pleaded before Him. I was in such anguish, such torment—and I was about done. I had nothing left inside and saw no future in living.

About a year before I moved to Sacramento, my middle brother Vince had moved from southern California to a town about 45 minutes outside of Sacramento. So, now that I lived in the area, I could visit him and his wife on occasion—it was nice having family a short drive away (of course they knew nothing of my secret). He lived in the Sierra foothills and the roads there all wind back and forth a lot. There is, however, one road as you approach the main highway a few miles from his home that has a fairly straight part, maybe a little less than one-quarter of a mile, then it curves around this huge oak tree as you continue your way toward the highway.

It was at this spot during my return home from one of my visits that I realized that I could probably get quite a head of steam built up in the car. I just had to get it up to between 60 and 80 miles an hour right and drive straight into that big ol' tree. All I would have to do is put my foot all the way down on the gas and NOT turn the wheel when I got to the curve. Simple.

A couple more visits to my brother's home go by, more assessment of the distance and speed. I was sure it would work, but then I realized something, this is the first car I ever owned that had an airbag, and I thought "what if the airbag actually works and I don't die?" How would I explain driving the car (my company's car no less) at high speed into the tree? With no skid marks! What bothered me most of all is how can I even be at this point— how can I be this low when I'm seeking God in all this? I wanted God and yet and I wanted to die. I was incapable of reconciling the incongruity of it all and was the lowest I had ever been in my entire life.

And that's when God showed up.

I had stayed in touch with my dear Christian friend Joy whose father was a pastor. She was still a member of the church in Orange County that Jan and I attended when we were married. One emotional evening, I called Joy crying and told her I didn't know what to do. I had done everything that I "was supposed to do." I've met with pastors, I've been prayed over several times, I saw a Christian counselor, and I was much more of a mess now that I've ever been, and frankly, I was done.

With one simple question, Joy (with the prodding of our Lord no doubt) asked the one question no one had ever asked. The one question that not only did it never occur to me to ask, but even if it had, I would not have dared ask it myself. She said, "Have you talked with a professional who has any experience with this?"

What? What do you mean talk with a professional who has experience with this? Joy wasn't encouraging me to pursue moving forward with sex change surgery or anything like that, just an honest question, if I had talked with someone who had a background and knowledge in what is technically called "gender dysphoria."

But how could I ever entertain such an idea? I'm a Christian, whatever it is I'm feeling is wrong, isn't it? What is there to talk about? I didn't choose to be transgender, but somehow it must be against God's will, right? At that moment as Joy was speaking to me, the Lord was there also. It had never crossed my mind that perhaps my path was something other than what it currently was. That maybe the reason I was getting more and more miserable seeking God's will for me, was that I limited His will to what I thought it was supposed to be. This opened to me the possibility that perhaps I was constraining God, and that His love and grace for me was greater than what I was expecting or willing to receive.

This didn't mean I suddenly thought all my troubles were over, but that it was okay to consider the possibility that in some way, somehow, a professional with experience might be able to help me. This gave me hope. And in that moment, it did strip away any sense of abject desperation and wanting to commit suicide I was feeling. I had hope, maybe for the first time.

So, now what? Where do I start? This is 1990, there is no such thing as an Internet! I was talking with my friend Janice (my grad-night date) who was now a Lutheran minister in St. Paul, Minnesota. I told her about my conversation with Joy, and that now I somehow had to find a therapist who knew about all this. She was aware of a "gender" program at the University of Minnesota and was willing to call and get more information; perhaps a name I could call.

One week later, she had the name of a doctor (psychologist) who was in charge of the program there. So, I called and was able to schedule an appointment with the chief doctor of the program. I arranged for some time off work and drove out there to visit my friend Janice and meet with the doctor. I hadn't seen her in a while, so I was looking forward to catching up.

The day after I arrived was my appointment with the doctor. I drove to the University and found my way to the medical center where his office was. After a short wait filling out paperwork, I was able to see him. He asked for my story, my history and asked additional questions to fill in whatever blanks I had left out. He was nice, genuinely cared, and was interested in helping me. He told me I was lucky, because Lin Fraser was in San Francisco and could be of help to me. He didn't come right out and say "yep, you're transsexual all right," but if he wasn't sure, he knew Lin could figure it out. Lin was (I later learned) an internationally known expert in the field, and I was fortunate to live only 90 miles away from her.

I waited a couple of weeks before calling Lin. It's one thing to go to Minnesota to talk to someone you know you're probably going to see only once in your life; it's another thing when you know that step may change your life in a way that you can't yet fully imagine. It's a little scary, and yes, I was scared.

Finally, I made the call and told her who referred me to her. Another couple of weeks go by and the day of my appointment arrives. One of the advantages of my job as an area supervisor and franchise representative was that I could schedule my visits as I wanted. Since my company had a franchise located in the Mission District of San Francisco, I simply scheduled a visit to that restaurant earlier in the day—it also pretty much eliminated the possibility of traffic making me late for the most important appointment of my life. After wrapping things up at the restaurant, I drove to my first meeting with Lin.

Her office was only three miles away, but this is San Francisco, so it took me 20 minutes to get there. But that wasn't enough. Have you ever tried to PARK in San Francisco? Every space on the main streets has a meter on it, and they're all being used. The side streets may not have meters, but you can only park there for two hours. If you are lucky enough to find a stretch of curb that for some reason no one is parking at, it's because there IS a reason—street sweepers. Depending on what side of the street you're on, you may not be able to park there between 10:00 am and noon on Tuesday, but on the opposite side of the street, it may be Thursdays between 2:00 and 4:00. You have to pay close attention to the signs, or you'll find yourself with a ticket, or worse.

Eventually, I did find a legal place to park. I walked down the street, into Lin's office, and sat down. There was an assortment of magazines there, everything from car magazines to your expected women's magazines like Vogue. I wanted to go for the Vogue, but I didn't want to be the guy sitting in the chair reading Vogue—call it a lifetime of self-imposed conditioning. I had spent my entire life making sure nothing appeared "out of place" to anyone, and I wasn't ready yet to start shattering that illusion, so I opted for a car magazine—after all that WAS the obvious choice, right?

It was 2:00 and right on time, a door by the main entrance squeaked open, and down the hall came a woman in her early-mid 30s (maybe a few years older than me), about 5'4" with shoulder length permed hair, she looked at me and asked "Larry?"

I said "yes" and followed her back to her office. She closed the door behind me and asked me to take a seat. There was a chair and a sofa to sit in, so I go into thinking mode. "Is this a test? Is one choice better than the other? What does it say about me if I choose the chair over the sofa or vice-versa?" I chose the sofa because I was going to be there for a couple of hours and wanted to be comfortable—if that meant I was lazy, so be it (FYI, I sat in it, I didn't lay on it—that just seemed too stereotypical a thing to do). She started off by saying she wanted me to fill out a questionnaire. It was a LONG questionnaire and very detailed, but I guess it was cheaper than spending hours answering those same questions in a regular session. When I finished, I handed it back to her. She glanced through it for a few minutes and then set it down next to her.

She looked at me and said, "So, what's going on?"

I started to tear up, and my face probably got flushed, because that's what happens when I cry—the words were so hard to say out loud. It's an amazing thing how something you've thought about all your life, the very phrase that has gone through your mind thousands of times, can be so hard when you have to activate your vocal chords and make a sound that another person can hear with their ears. I composed myself enough to say, "All my life I've wanted to be a girl, and I can't live like this anymore."

At that point, tears began to roll down my face—these were words of truth for me. I wasn't this emotional with the doctor in Minnesota; I was much more guarded and "in control." Maybe it's because he was a guy, or because I knew he was so far away from where I lived that it was just a one-time visit. But here in Lin's office, it was different. This was playing for keeps with my life, and I needed to know if I was crazy, if what I thought I wanted was in her estimation the right thing for me, and if it was, is it really possible? If it wasn't the right thing for me, then what was? I'd had this within me all my life, and I had tried all the options I could think of on my own to deal with this.

Now came the questions from Lin. She asked for more information about when I first had this feeling that I was a girl inside. What was it like, what was I thinking? There were specific snippets that I remembered growing up. I told her about how at night when I was little I would pray in bed that God would turn me into a girl, and my feeling of disappointment when I would wake up the next morning only to see that I was still a boy. After all, if Santa Clause could go to all the homes of the world in a single night and come down the chimney to deliver toys, and if the tooth fairy could turn a tooth that had come out from my mouth into coins, why couldn't God turn me into a girl? It seemed a simple and innocent enough request to me.

Lin would ask the occasional question, but I was doing all the talking—whatever she wanted to know, I would tell her. It seemed we had just started and I was finally able to open up about things when, "Okay, our time is about up."

I think to myself, "What? Already? But you haven't told me what's wrong with me. You haven't told me how to fix this." I was like a can of warm soda that has been dropped and shaken and ready to spray out my soul when you open the top. We had only started to pop the top on all this and now I have to leave? She told me this was a good start and wanted to know how often I could come in. Since I had four restaurants in the bay area I could schedule around, I told her I could come in a couple of times a week, so we scheduled to start meeting regularly. I thanked her and left her office.

A few short months earlier, I had picked out the tree where I was going to end it all. I was done; there was no hope for me. Living was such internal torture that I preferred death. Then, God planted into that thinking side of my brain the thought that the air-bag just might ruin my plans and save my life. Because He knew I needed to make a phone call first, and that phone called turned out to save my life. But God didn't only use other people to speak to me; He decided soon it would be time for a "person to person" call, or to be more accurate, "almighty creator of the universe to a fragile human being" call.

5

THE REVELATION

"Your own ears will hear Him. Right behind you a voice will say,
"This is the way you should go," whether to the right or to the left."
Isaiah 30:21 (NLT)

WHEN GOD SPEAKS: Christians often talk about hearing from God. When we do, normally we aren't referring to an actual audible voice booming from a burning bush—but perhaps it's a sudden thought that clearly didn't come from us. Sometimes, it may come in the form of a voice of a friend who speaks such truth to us; that only God could know how perfect those words were for you at that moment. It may come from reading His word, not just reading words like those in a magazine but reading with the intent of seeking what it is He wants to teach you at this particular time with those particular words. But it does happen, perhaps rarely and for me only twice in my life when it is as close to an audible voice as can be, but it was His voice AND He was speaking directly to me. And when He did it was literally life changing—and something I'll never, ever forget.

So, my appointment with Lin was over, and as I walked back down the street to the car, my mind was in a bit of a haze. It had been such a whirlwind of emotion, on my drive home I was questioning myself… "Was I doing the right thing? Did I give the right answers? Are there even any right answers? What if she determines I'm NOT transsexual? What does that mean if I'm not?"

All these questions were swirling around in my head as I crossed the Bay Bridge from San Francisco and headed up Interstate 80 toward home, and THAT is where it happened. All those questions were swirling around in my mind, and I was wondering if all this was a mistake, that maybe I was screwed up and had some mental problem that wasn't fixable. I had already destroyed my marriage, and maybe suicide was going to be my only way out, because I surely didn't see any hope of a "normal" life. Then, at 65 miles per hour, I heard these two life-changing words…

"It's okay."

It wasn't audible as if it came out of my stereo, but it was much more than only a thought; it was more than thinking in your mind how someone you know sounds. It was loud. It was clear. And it came out of nowhere… "IT'S OKAY."

And at that exact moment, I suddenly KNEW that I could put all my questions and worries about my gender identity behind me. God had told me in these two words that I was "okay," that this whole process that I was beginning was okay, and that "Laurie" was okay to continue to be who I *really* was, who He created me to be.

I was amazed at what had just happened (it's a miracle I didn't cause an accident). And then peace, pure peace fell over me—and suddenly I was fine. I was beyond fine. I realized that this is the time and place that marked a new beginning for me—that no matter what may come along on this journey, I was going to be okay.

Remember when you were little and maybe you wanted something so bad at the store you couldn't stand it, so you ask your mother, "Mama, can I have one, please?"

Your mother looks down at your eager face and sees that you would like to have it, but it's a little expensive, so she tells you, "Go ask your father, and if he says okay, then you can have it."

So, you run to your father and ask him, "Daddy, can I have one, please, please, please, please?"

Then your father looks at you with a straight face for a few seconds, then breaks out into a smile, laughs and says, "Of course you can," and you're so happy that your father said it was okay.

That's how I felt the remainder of my way home that day. All I could do the entire time was smile and thank God. My Father in Heaven knew my heart, and that it had been a prayer of mine for my entire life, and on this day, He told me, "okay." So this began a process that would lead to a life I had only dared dream about and at the same time, feared. Can I actually do this? HOW do you do this?

At first, I was driving from Sacramento to San Francisco to see Lin twice a week. Lots of talking the next several months. Some of it my history, some of it about family, church, friends, work and the actual process of transitioning itself. I mean, how do you deal with all that, especially when your entire life is contained within a rather conservative environment and you're not used to talking about anything?

Without a doubt, the hardest part for me in the process was letting people know—but I didn't immediately start telling people because frankly, I simply didn't know how. I didn't know for sure, but rejection from my family wouldn't have come as a huge surprise if it happened, I say that because I grew up with them, I knew them, and even though they loved me, I suspected this might be more than they could comprehend and accept—I would have to see. But my friends, and work! What about work? This is not an inexpensive process, the therapy, the hormones (yet another doctor bill), electrolysis for facial hair and the surgery itself—it's crazy expensive (like $50,000 expensive). So many things involved—it can overwhelm you.

Because I wasn't seeing a therapist "within" my insurance company's plan, I had to pay for 50% of my therapy (actually, all of it, and I would be reimbursed for half,) but that meant my insurance company was paying for the other half. Lin started out the billing with a diagnosis of depression (or something related to that—I wasn't paying much attention to the diagnostic codes on the piece of paper, and I never knew what they meant anyway). Later she added the diagnostic code for "gender dysphoria," a clinical term for someone whose gender identity (whether it be male or female) doesn't match their physical body. So, now we had two items on the paper I was submitting to the insurance company: depression, and gender dysphoria. And when the time came, the insurance company paid for my prescription hormones. We were building a history with the insurance company with the hope they would cover my surgery—only time would tell.

Planning was now a big part of my life. For me to see the finish line, I needed to see and deal with as many of the hurdles I would face as possible. For my own peace of mind, I had to have a plan. Before starting the "real life test" (more about that later), I knew that I would at times need to leave my home dressed as Laurie. The first time was when I drove down to see Lin dressed as Laurie. This meant leaving my home in broad daylight and returning home in broad daylight—oy vey!

Here's how I did it.

The first thing I did was back my car into the garage the night before, so I could pull straight out, hit the garage door opener as I left the driveway and keep on going. At the same time, praying there were no neighbors who might see me leave. The morning arrives and I get up—I'm really feeling the nerves. Oh, I've snuck out after dark a time or two dressed, but I had the dark of night to help me keep my secret, no one was going to see more than a silhouette. But this was going to be right out there in the middle of the day, and I was going to have to walk over a block from my car to Lin's office, mid-day in the center of San-freaking-cisco.

I got up and took a shower. The shower did not take away any of my nervousness, and then I spent the next two hours getting ready. Yes—two full hours. Keep in mind that my hair was relatively short as one would expect of a male mid-level manager in a large corporation. I had a wig—no prep needed there. I spent two hours working on a close shave and my makeup. You have to remember a few things here, I had no sisters. I didn't grow up around girls, there were no teen or women's magazines around the house for me to sneak peeks at for tips growing up. And we're talking 1990 folks, the Internet (as we even remotely know it) was still several years away—there was no YouTube (I'll tell you something else, I've learned more about putting on makeup the last few years from YouTube than my previous 20-something years as a woman on my own). I lived alone, so shaving my legs was no big deal, but since I had only recently started electrolysis on my face, it took a lot of work to be sure I got as close as possible to a smooth face, so I could then put the makeup to work.

After perhaps the longest two hours of my life, I'm now ready to burst forth into the world as Laurie in broad daylight. That was until my brain starts going to work. What if I get stopped? My driver's license certainly doesn't match up with the woman driving the car. What if I have a flat? Who would I call? How would I explain it? What if I'm in an accident! Oh no! I'll be on the six o'clock news!!! "Lord, if I have an accident, make it a good one and just take me home right there." These are the thoughts that run through your head when faced with 90 miles of driving a northern California interstate highway with no evidence whatsoever that the woman driving the car is, in fact, a woman. It is pretty much a miracle in itself that I didn't have a nervous breakdown right there in my home before ever going into the garage.

But now it's time to go. I put my wallet in my purse, and with my heart beating harder and harder, I safely get in the car (I should add at this point that I had an attached garage and still had seen no daylight—I was a bundle of nerves). So, there I was in my dark garage sitting in my car. I took one last big breath, buckled my seat belt, and started the car (engine works—check!). I reached up and pressed the garage door opener.

The darkness was broken by the sunlight flooding in through the opening door in front of me. I put on my sunglasses (more camouflage), and as soon as there was enough clearance for the top of my car, I pulled out onto my driveway and into the street, pressed the door opener to close the garage while rolling and kept on going. Whew! None of my neighbors were out in their yard at the moment and I was off. Getting out of the neighborhood, I felt like I could relax a little. As I got onto the freeway and took a relaxing deep breath I suddenly remembered: "Oh crap, the toll booth!"

You only pay a toll on the Bay Bridge when going westbound on Interstate 80 entering San Francisco. There's no getting around it unless I want to take the long way into the city and come in from the north via the Golden Gate Bridge. But for one thing, I hadn't allowed enough time for that, and secondly, it was just a stupid idea. I was eventually going to have to face people (like strangers) up close if I was going to go through with all this, so I spent the next 90 minutes preparing myself for the encounter. I reached in and grabbed a dollar bill from inside my purse. If you ever drove across the Bay Bridge back then, you knew that even though there must be fifteen or more toll lanes, there were always long lines of cars, and that day was no different.

As I approach the toll plaza, I see what seems like thousands of cars. Oh great! So, I choose a lane and gradually come to a stop as we all creep our way toward the toll booth. I'm looking straight ahead, because surely everyone in their cars within 100 feet of me is looking and staring at me. I wouldn't have been surprised had there been a television news helicopter flying overhead announcing to the SHOCK of the citizens of San Francisco that a man dressed as a woman was about to enter their fair city. "Hello, citizens of San Francisco. A man dressed as a woman is about to enter the city via the Bay Bridge. Place your children in a secure and safe place. We will inform you when it is safe to come out again." You see how crazed one can be when you're in the process of turning your life upside down (albeit for the better).

Of course, no one was looking and no one cared. You forget in moments (or hours) like this that people have their own lives to live, their own worries, their own concerns, and just their own stuff on their mind—a crying child, a meeting to get to, a meal to plan. All I could imagine is that they had NOTHING better to do with their time waiting to get to the toll booth than to look around for men who might be dressed as women driving a car near them (yeah well, that's what I thought).

As my car crawled closer and closer to the toll booth, my heart began to beat even harder. I made sure I had that one-dollar bill that I needed firmly in my grasp, because there was no way I was going to fumble around looking for it with the guy in the booth staring back at me.

Two cars ahead of me, I see the window go down. An arm extends out to hand the gentleman a buck. They pull onto the bridge and the car in front of me does the same thing. Window down, arm out, arm in, drive away. Now it's my turn to pull up. What should I say? Should I say anything? I don't know. What have I said (if anything) in the past? Maybe "hello", maybe "hi", maybe "good afternoon" would be better. The decision was simple—say nothing! I rolled down my window and pulled up to the tollbooth, and as gracefully as possible handed him the dollar bill and tried to give him a smile as I drove off.

I'm sure he didn't see or think anything about our encounter. It's San Francisco after all. Imagine the different kinds of people you must see sitting all day in a toll booth leading into San Francisco. I'm sure all he saw at most was perhaps a somewhat nervous woman—but more likely he saw nothing. Most likely he was thinking about how much longer until his shift was over and what would be for dinner when he got home.

Okay, one barrier passed. Now all I had to do was find a place to park near Lin's office. If you've never driven in San Francisco, let's just say parking anywhere near where you want to be can be quite the challenge. Getting within one block of Lin's office is considered a good day, and thank the good Lord I find a spot down the street one block and around the corner. Now all I have to do is WALK—something I've been doing since I was around a year old. It sounds so simple, but I was very nervous—I had to get out of my car and close the door without getting my dress caught in the door. Whew! Step one—complete, door closed successfully with no fabric connected to it.

Now a simple walk for a block and a half on the sidewalk of a fairly busy street in San Francisco in the middle of the day. A piece of cake unless you've never done it fully dressed as a female and this is your first time. I tried to stand up straight and walk like I had somewhere to go, not in a hurried way but with purpose. And oh, I wasn't wearing clunky men's dress shoes. These were heels. Granted they were low heels, but they were holding up a very nervous, self-conscience woman. Eye contact with passersby? Out of the question. I hadn't learned how to play poker yet, but I knew you could tell a lot about a person by looking at their expression, and I don't know what I looked like, but I know how I felt.

It was so much easier to walk looking straight ahead toward my destination and pretend there were two people on Earth at the time, just Lin and me. I finally reached her building after what was now the longest walk of my life, walked up those 20 or so steep steps from the street, through the door, and down the hall into the waiting area. So, there I sat in that same wicker chair I always sat in trying to look all normal. Of course, having arrived early, I had to sit there as other patients of the other therapists came and went as well as the therapists themselves. It was so easy to think that they must be worried about the freak in the waiting room—but of course, once again, this IS San Francisco, AND this was a good part of her practice. I wasn't the first transsexual to grace the waiting area.

Finally, it was time, and Lin is nothing if not prompt. Her door opens, she walks down the hall, and with a big smile says, "Aw," telling me with that expression that I look fine. I walked into her office, she closed the door behind us and said: "Don't you look lovely." Lin isn't the type to say "Don't you look lovely" if you probably don't look at least fine—which was all I needed to hear. She asked about my experience, so I told her about the adventure I had (in my mind) coming to the appointment. Of course, I still had my trip home, but one uneventful drive into the city made it easier to take the drive out of the city and back to Sacramento.

Ah yes, the trip back home—simple and direct with two exceptions. The street I lived on was a U-shaped street, and I was at the top of the loop. Normally when coming home, I would come up the same side, which also happens to be the side that I knew most of those neighbors, but this time I came up the other side so at least it was less likely anyone might see me or recognize my car. My plan was the reverse of when I left home—get close, open the garage door, get past the door as quickly as possible, and close the door behind me. Four simple steps, I've got it all figured out—now all I have to do is execute.

I drive up my street (on the far side) and prepare to pull into my driveway and into my garage, I reach up and press the garage door opener, and… nothing. Since I don't normally pull into my driveway from this direction, I didn't know that the opener didn't work as well from this particular angle. So now I'm physically in front of my home, pulling into the short driveway, and poking the opener again and again saying to myself, "C'mon, c'mon, c'mon," when finally, the door opens. I had to briefly stop in the driveway before the door was high enough to enter. I did peek to my left as I pulled into my garage and wouldn't you know it, one of my neighbors a couple of doors down was out in front of his house. Maybe he didn't see anything, maybe all he saw was the car—he would know it was mine and wouldn't have to confirm it by looking to see who was actually behind the wheel. Dark grey Taurus, a typical boring company car, nothing to see here people (I hoped).

That evening, all was quiet, no phone calls from the neighbor, no one knocking on my door, seems like all is well and life goes on in our merry little neighborhood. That is until a couple of days later. I was out in my front yard, my neighbor saw me and came over to tell me he saw a woman pull into my garage driving my car the other day.

"Okay, think," I'm telling myself, "and think fast."

He said a woman was driving my car; he didn't ask why I was dressed up as a woman. He said "a woman."

That told me he naturally assumed it was, that's right—a woman in my car. So, I leaped at that assumption and said: "Oh, my brother and sister-in-law were in town, he wanted to go to some places down here, but she wanted to shop at others, so they came by and I let her use my car."

Part of me thinks I should feel guilty for being able to come up with such a good lie off the top of my head, but controlling this entire situation as best I could among the people in my life was the only way I could continue moving forward without having my life blow-up in my face.

This was something I was committed to doing. It was something I had to do for my own survival. And it all came into being by hearing His voice on Interstate 80 say those two simple words… "It's okay."

6

I KILLED SOMEONE, BUT IT WAS HIM OR ME

"My father and mother may abandon me, but the LORD will take care of me."

Psalm 27:10 (GNB)

THE LOSS OF FAMILY: One thing I've learned in my life is that it's almost impossible for "normal" people to wrap their heads around someone being transsexual. You're either a male or female, a man or a woman. I've just described 99.7% of the human race, including you who are reading this right now. But if you are part of the .3% whose body doesn't match your sense of who you are, well then welcome to my world. There is just no way to fully explain it in a way that someone can internalize and fully understand. Just as a man knows he's a man and a woman knows she's a woman, a person who is transsexual knows their body is wrong and may not know what to call it—but they know. However, some folks, including Christians, refuse to accept that it's possible to truly be transgender (I'll add that 2,000 years ago many Christians also refused to accept that the world was round—I'm just sayin'). And when it comes to family, they may experience intense pain and hurt at the "loss" of the person they've always known. Now truth be told, they haven't lost anyone, but the failure to accept the person they've always known and loved as someone who may now look different, and has maybe even taken on a new name, is why they feel they've "lost" that person. This "new" person isn't allowed into their lives. To them, their loved one might as well be dead. They grieve their loss, and they may even feel anger—anger at the person who killed their loved one. They don't see the same person, they see two different people even though that's not the truth, and the transgender person who transitions is often treated as if dead.

One thing my near-brief disaster taught me was that I didn't want to try to handle my transition to Laurie here in the same neighborhood—it's hard enough without trying to explain yourself to friends and acquaintances who LIVE next to you and whom you see on an almost daily basis. And besides, I didn't want to be known as the neighborhood "tranny" and have parents pull their kids off the street when I was walking my dog.

My neighbor Kim lived three doors down. Even though I was in the restaurant business, I had always been a little geeky and was pretty good with computers, so when she had a problem, I'd go over there and fix it. I saw her Bible on the end table, so I talked to her about church and God, and we connected at that level. I was friends with both her and her husband, but I was closer to Kim. They never saw a girl over at my house and as it turns out they thought I was possibly gay (wrong). I guess my being single and alone most of the time gave the neighborhood something to talk about.

There was a time when Kim was over at my house and used my restroom and apparently, there was a long hair from my wig on the floor that she saw so, "Ah ha! He has a girlfriend after all!" Wrong again, but now something new for the neighbors to speculate about—people just love to talk don't they? Since she was such a good friend and there were going to be big changes in my life that I couldn't deny, AND I didn't want to lose her as a friend—I went over to her house one day and told her my story. This... was... hard. I hadn't told anyone prior to this that I was actually going to move forward with living out my life as Laurie, surgery and all.

It's very difficult to have the "I'm going to live as a woman" discussion with people BEFORE you transition; because not only can they not wrap their head around the concept of you feeling you are not the gender of the person they see before them (especially if you've strived hard to hide that fact from them), but they are now trying to picture you as someone of the opposite sex, which is almost as hard. Imagine your own brother, your father, or your son telling you that he is going to spend the rest of his life as a woman. Picture that in your mind, and well, there you go. Telling people you know, when you've lived your entire life doing anything and everything to hide it from them as I did, makes it even harder for them to understand.

Fortunately, my friend Kim (whom I love to this day) was "curious" enough about my single existence to have formulated theories about my life. Once I got through the tears and the long build-up of telling her how I always knew I was different, how I had sought God in all this, and how I had wanted to kill myself not 30 miles away from where we lived—it all made sense to her. Being single, not having a girlfriend, finding the hair in my restroom. Her response was, "It doesn't matter—you are who God made you to be and if that's Laurie, then okay."

This relatively "easy" conversation with Kim behind me launched a series of difficult phone calls to friends: my friend Joy who saved my life with her one simple question, my friend Scott who had known me since I was in Jr. High school, and others. One of the most difficult calls was to my best friend, Frank. My phone call to him, I fear, broke his heart. He was clearly hurt, and I don't know—maybe he thought I hadn't done enough before God, maybe he thought I was totally deceived by that son of a bitch Satan and was a lost cause. All I know is that this was the last conversation I ever had with my friend, and I miss him to this day.

But absolutely, the hardest conversation was with my mom on the phone. I was in northern California, she was in southern California, and even though I was down there every couple of months for work, I couldn't tell her in person—I knew it would deeply hurt her. I didn't want to see the pain it would cause her, and I didn't want to see her cry. She already knew I had struggled with this because of our earlier conversation the Christian therapist had put me in the position of having with her. I told her that I had tried, I had prayed, and I had been prayed over. I told her that I came close to killing myself on a road home from Vince's house, that God had led me to a Christian friend, how I heard from God, and that I was going to have surgery and live out my life as a woman. I could hear the hurt in her voice as she said: "Oh, Larry." Being Baptists where having God speak to you is not really mentioned much, my hearing from Him probably sounded like something shy of insanity.

All I had to say was, "I know, Mom, it hurts—and I wish there were another way, but it's who I am and always have been, I'm sorry I couldn't have told you sooner." I can only imagine how my mom must have just sat and cried after hanging up the phone. I was her firstborn, there was a special love there, and it must have felt like I had thrust a large knife into her heart. It hurt me even to tell her, but the time for excuses and lies had passed.

I left it to her to tell Dad. I couldn't begin to know how to have that conversation. When it came to my brothers, I called my sisters-in-law and talked with each of them at a time when I figured my brothers would not be around. To my brothers and probably my dad, this was REAL news because, I'm sure my mom told no one about this months earlier when I was trying to "fix" myself. I asked my sisters-in-law how they thought my brothers would take it and when would be a good time (if any) to tell them.

They both said the same thing: "Let me tell him." And so that's what I did. As it happened, it wasn't too long after those conversations with my sisters-in-law that I got a call from each of my brothers. They were confused, and they were angry.

I tried to explain it to them, but they had a lifetime of me being their big brother, and this was not something they would understand, were going to accept, would like, participate in, or agree to in any way. I remember laying on my bed when I was talking to Vince. Maybe it was his way of trying to talk me out of it, but he told me in something between a pleading voice and a shout, "You're going to wind up homeless and living in the gutters in San Francisco." Well, that went peachy.

But that didn't live up to what Allen had to say. I should add at this point that I had recently been out there to visit him, his wife, and my two young nephews. We had a very nice time when I was there—so I'm having to guess there was a strong sense of betrayal and perhaps anger, at feeling he had been lied to all these years and especially in my recent visit. It was a short conversation with

Allen, he told me if I ever showed up (implying as a woman) on his doorstep, he would shoot me right there, and I believe the next sound I heard was the "click" of the phone hanging up. To this day, my brothers have never spoken to me.

But back to living in my neighborhood. I didn't want to deal with my transition in my neighborhood, so I decided I would rent an apartment somewhere across town in preparation and later buy a new home as "Laurie." But of course, I had to sell my home first. Enter—GOD!

My next-door neighbor had been trying to sell their home for four months, while a few doors down they had been trying to sell their home for almost three months. I had no idea how long it would take to sell my home. My floorplan was the smallest in the neighborhood—about 1,100 square feet, so I figured it would take an eternity to sell.

Since I was going to move to an apartment and my crazy huge and loud audio system had no place in an apartment, I decided to sell my equipment. But at the same time—I could NOT go without something to replace it—so I went to a local stereo store. I was talking to a nice salesman and told him I was looking for something small and compact that sounded clean and accurate (those are the terms we audio geeks use). When I told him what I was replacing, he looked at me rather confused and he said, "Why are you getting rid of all that?" He knew exactly what I was getting rid of and couldn't believe it.

I told him I was selling my home to move into an apartment and simply didn't have space for it all. He asked me, "So, where is your home? I told him where I lived and as it turned out, he was looking for a home in my area. "How much are you asking for it?" he said. My home wasn't even on the market. I hadn't even talked with a real estate agent. He asked if he could come by and look at it.

"Sure, why not?" I said. So, I told him to come over that evening if he wanted. As for me, I RACED home to tidy things up a bit. Since I wasn't expecting anyone to come over and poke around my entire home, it wasn't exactly what you would call "show ready." After two hours of madly putting all the dirty dishes in the dishwasher, the oven, and anywhere else I could hide them, hiding the dirty clothes in dresser drawers, mopping the kitchen floor, and running the vacuum cleaner real quick over the carpet—voilà! I was ready for a home tour.

He and his wife came by as planned. When he walked in, he immediately commented on my current stereo setup (it was impossible to miss), and after a brief demonstration (he insisted—all I wanted to do was sell my home), he and his wife walked through my little house. I told them to take their time, look around, and feel free to ask any questions. I knew what my neighbors were asking for their larger homes, so I used that as a guide for mine (even though I knew nothing about real estate or how to determine the value of a home).

When they were done walking through the house and had seen the yards, they asked how much I was asking. When I gave them a number, the husband and wife softly talked for a minute and said, "That's good—we'll take it."

What? Who sells a house like this? I went to a stereo store in the afternoon and several hours later my home was sold? This just doesn't happen! We got the papers we needed to fill out, got a title company we agreed on to handle the paperwork, and a month later my home was sold. It had never been on the market—I had NEVER even spoken with a real estate agent about selling it—and it was done! And even more proof God was all over this, two of my neighbors—both with larger homes than mine, did eventually sell months later, and both for less than what I got for my home, and I didn't pay a real estate commission. It truly was God being there the whole time.

With the house sold, I moved across town from my home into an apartment north of downtown. But before I tell you about life in the apartment, let me introduce you to the "Real-Life Test."

As badly as I wanted to be able to live as a female, I likewise didn't want to make what would literally be a life-long mistake. There was what was called the "Standards of Care" for transsexual patients seeking surgery. These were standards that any reputable professional, whether it is a psychologist, psychiatrist, or surgeon would adhere to. In a nutshell, it required living full-time in the expected gender for one year—NO CHEATING! But that wasn't enough—after living a full year, you needed a letter of recommendation from at least two professionals (in my case my therapist and psychiatrist) before a surgeon would agree to perform the surgery. The purpose, of course, was not just so the professionals felt sure you were ready and able, but for you to be sure as well. There's no way of hiding it from your friends, family, work or church. If you can't make it a year living full time, then surgery certainly isn't going to make it better. At that point, it's time to consider some type of "plan B." The real-life test is kind of a high-dive into a swimming pool before you go cliff-diving in Mexico.

So, I'm in the apartment. This was the time for me to get my plans made and prepare to start living full-time as Laurie. Not only did I NOT make an effort to get to know my neighbors around me—I made an effort to be every bit the stranger. These people weren't my past and they weren't my future. If someone saw me going out as a woman and pegged me as being the guy that lived in that apartment—so be it. This was a level of risk, and even ridicule if it came to it, that I was willing to withstand. Say what you want about paranoia, it does tend to make you prepare for things whether they are real or not.

As I got settled in, I started to see what life as "Laurie" would be like. One of the first things I did was invite my friend Kim over for lunch. I didn't want to hijack things, so I asked her if it was okay that I be "Laurie" when she came over. She had never seen me dressed as a woman, so at this point in time "Laurie" was a person in her imagination, and reality was about to push her imagination aside one way or another. I can't tell you who was more nervous, Kim or me. I know I was nervous, and I recently asked her what was going through her mind before we met that day. She told me she was a little unsettled not knowing what to expect—in hindsight I probably should have had a nice picture of me taken to show her BEFORE having her come over to see me in person. It certainly would have made it easier for her. So, here she comes to meet her former neighbor who, when she last saw him, he was a guy, and now she was going to meet her as a woman. She didn't know how she would react—what if I wasn't very attractive at all? What if I looked like a guy in a dress? I was wondering; would she be gracious? Would she tell me the truth?" (I know today she certainly would tell me the truth, Kim doesn't hold back—THAT's a friend!)

She arrives at my apartment and I open the door, I try to smile with a "well, here I am!" kind of look. Now, I don't remember her exact words, but here is what she told me she was thinking back then – "Damn, she looks better than me!" (I have to say, even 25 years later it feels pretty good to be able to write that). Kim and I would go out now and then, so I got more practice going out in public in broad daylight. She also would, when necessary, break me of a lifetime of learned habits, you know—the things I was "expected" to do as a normal guy.

One time we were going to lunch, maybe a Denny's or something like that. I was in front of her and opened the door for her, she put her hand in the middle of my back and pushed me in front of her through the open door. She laughed saying, "You don't need to open the door for another woman, just go in." That was a sign that I was getting comfortable with myself in public, and when that happens then ingrained habits kick in, because I'm not thinking about every little step I take. So now I have to pay attention, so that I would learn a new set of habits—today, I make it a point to always go into a store or restaurant ahead of Kim just to show her I learned my lesson very well all those years ago.

With the decision made to transition, one of the things on the "checklist" was hormones. Whether you're transitioning from male-to-female or female-to-male, before you have surgery, physiology is going to want to be in control of your body, meaning if you're born male then testosterone is going to want to be in charge. If you're hoping to develop breasts and have your body appear a little more feminine, then overriding testosterone required a higher dose of estrogen and progesterone prior to surgery (after surgery, you only need a much lower dose). I started to see an endocrinologist who prescribed and monitored my hormone level. They do advise you that prolonged use of female hormones in males can lead to sterility, but clearly that wasn't a concern of mine, because as I learned when I was married, I was already sterile.

It was a unique and frankly wonderful feeling once I got my prescription. Up to this point it had all been emotional, yes, but still an academic and theoretical dream. Taking those pills for the first time brought a palpable sense of reality to my life. I wasn't scared, I wasn't doubting for a moment, all I could do was say to myself, "It has begun." Now, this wasn't "the point of no return" but it was the beginning of my physical changes other than makeup and clothes. But the next day, after starting the hormones, you won't believe what I noticed about my breasts! That's right! Absolutely nothing! It's a slow process and it takes many months and even a couple of years. If you're a woman or have a daughter you know this. But I also admit, I had to take a look just to see (and if you're a transgender woman you have to confess—you did it too).

While I'm talking about things changing with hormones, one thing that doesn't change is beard growth. Once testosterone gets those little hairs going, they don't want to stop, so welcome to the world of electrolysis. If you don't know what's involved, an electrologist puts a small probe (like a needle) into the pore where the hair is and sends an electrical current to destroy the root of the hair—and just like that, you've killed one single solitary hair. Now let's do it again, and again, and again, and again. Hundreds of hours of this are necessary to clear your face. If you have hair on your chest, well, you go there too. And in case you're wondering—yes, it hurts. About an hour at a time was all I could stand. The lengths we gals go too to be beautiful, and in my case, less hirsute (make that your new word of the day).

Oh, and one more thing to work on—my voice. I didn't have a terribly deep voice, but when I did sing in church choir, I sang baritone. And NO, hormones don't change that when you're going from male to female. When testosterone (that demon drug) does what it does to your body, it's really not reversible (for female to male individuals, taking testosterone DOES help deepen their voice and promote the growth of facial hair, and like it or not—male pattern hair loss if it's in the family). A deep voice comes across rather strange when you're in a dress, so for a few weeks I also went to a vocal coach who had experience helping people like me soften it up and modulate the pitch, enough that even though I may on occasion get called sir over the telephone or over one of those high quality top-of-the-line speakers found at any fast food restaurant—I've developed such a habit that my voice now is simply my voice, and in person I don't have any problems. I would have to make an effort to let my voice drop and let it sound like I used to, and since I have no desire to do so—I don't. Singers would call it your "chest voice," and I just don't go there anymore, I pretty much live in my "head voice" and it seems to work for me.

Another barrier I was going to have to cross was church (no pun intended). I once again turned to my friend Janice in Minnesota and asked her if she was aware of a church in Sacramento that might be open to someone like me attending. This was 1991 and I wasn't aware of ANY church being open to someone who was transgender or anything in the neighborhood of that. Janice didn't know anyone personally, but once again came to my aide and asked around her denomination in Sacramento. She got me in touch with a pastor at a Lutheran church near downtown. I met with her as my male self originally and we talked. I talked about my life, what I was planning, where I was at, and asked if it would be ok if I came as "Laurie." We decided to meet again, with me as "Laurie" this time—I think this was to give her a little peace of mind about my appearance—again, a photo would have been helpful (Note to Self—if I ever come back and have to live through this again, be sure to have a picture to show people what you will look like). When she saw I didn't look like the Frankenstein monster in a dress, she didn't have a problem with me attending. So, for the better part of that year, I would attend the services dressed as a female. Being so liturgical, it wasn't what I was used to and not my cup of tea, but being able to attend church as a woman with no issues was a stepping stone for me.

This was pretty much my year in the apartment. Going to work as male but moving more toward living as a female outside of work became my life. As time got closer for the next step, I started to look for a new home. I still had the job with my company, and I wanted to take every advantage of my status as a paid employee in order to move into a home as "Laurie." There was a new development in the area a half mile north of where I first lived in Sacramento. It used to be nothing but empty fields, but now they were building homes—most of them "starter" homes for young couples and entry-level home buyers. There was a perfect, yet-to-be-built, three bedroom, two bath home at the end of a cul-de-sac that I was able to buy. Since when I put my deposit down I was still several months away from having a fully built, ready to move into home, that provided me the time, and yes, a definite timetable to get ready for the beginning of my "real-life test" and the rest of my life.

Part of the fun part of buying a new home is that you get to choose what you want in the way of carpet, tile, counter-tops, etc., in your new home. I was moving into this home as a woman; I wanted it "girly," so yes, I wanted pink carpet. My friend Kim went with me when I went to the design center to choose my interior, and while I was choosing the color of my carpet (it was light pink, almost a light rose color—nothing glaring), Kim leaned over and whispered to me "you're showing."

I didn't know what she was talking about, so I said "what?"

"You're showing through your shirt." Since I was still presenting myself as a guy, I suddenly realized that the hormones I had been on for several months were actually working. These are things you may not notice on a day-to-day basis, but when a friend who hasn't seen you in several weeks says something, NOW you pay attention. I began to be self-conscience about how I looked in my job when I went to the various restaurants. Obviously, I wasn't going to wear a bra, but it wasn't anything a tight t-shirt couldn't solve, at least for now.

I had told my friends, I had told my family. For better or for worse, I had told the people closest to me and I cared the most about. I was now in escrow to buy a new home. But work—how do I handle work? I can't go and become unemployed over this. I wasn't raised not to have a job as an adult, I certainly had no clue how to live off the government for help or support—so I gave it a LOT of thought before calling a meeting with my boss and a human resources person whom I also knew. I was a week away from closing on my new home, and I couldn't have the sudden loss of a job mess this up. I drove down to southern California. The next morning, I went to the corporate offices, saw my boss waiting for me (totally clueless as to why I wanted to meet with him and HR), and the three of us sat down in a conference room. They sat there and looked at me with a "so why are we all here?" look on their face.

This was the most REAL moment of what I was going to do—I was about to jeopardize my livelihood for living my life as a female. I simply started saying, "This is how I've felt for all of my life—this isn't anything new." I started to cry, and the gal from HR reached out to hand me a tissue, my boss, being a bit of a "manly man" was probably confused as to why this guy who works for him was crying. I kept it short. I told them that for all my life, I had always felt like a woman inside, and that I had gotten to the point of killing myself and couldn't live like this anymore, and that I WAS going to start living as a woman in the next few weeks. I shared just a little about my life and going to therapy before finishing up saying that I knew it might be hard for employees in the restaurants to deal with, or for that matter the customers, but it was something I had to do.

There was a pause in the room, and the HR gal said, "Okay, why don't you take paid time off the rest of the week and we'll discuss this and get back to you in a few days."

I drove back home to Sacramento. The parent company of the restaurant was based out of North Carolina, and I imagine the company phone lines within HR were all abuzz during my drive home about the franchise rep who was going to have a sex change and wanted to stay in the company (it was the early 90's, and this wasn't exactly something you heard about often). Now, if you've been paying attention up to this point, you've noticed I have an aversion to rejection and are probably wondering why I would subject myself to it with my job. I wasn't sure what they were going to do, but I was pretty sure they wouldn't want to see me back in the restaurants as a woman. This was where I was kind of hoping they would think the worse of what I might look like as a woman, to perhaps find another position for me, or perhaps transfer me to a different division of the company.

It only took them a couple of days to get back to me. The local HR rep for another division of the company contacted me and asked to meet, which we did. He was very matter of fact and didn't get into the details of why we were meeting (my transition), but told me the company agreed with me that it could be difficult not just for the customers and employees but also for me if I remained, and they wanted to offer me a severance package. It was pretty generous, basically a year's salary plus one year of COBRA health insurance. He asked me to get back to him within a couple of days.

The unemployment rate in Sacramento was over eleven percent at the time, so finding a new job wasn't going to be easy. I contacted him, mentioned that my two concerns were the high unemployment rate and that my surgery would be at the very least one year away (the real-life test awaited me). I asked that the amount they were offering be AFTER taxes, not before, and also for the maximum eighteen months of COBRA to ensure my medical expenses would be covered during this time. I also asked for a letter of recommendation in my new name and that my personnel file reflect my new name should someone call for a reference. He said he'd convey my request and get back to me as soon as he had an answer. The next day, I got a call and the company agreed to all my requests (I'm thinking they REALLY didn't want me to stick around and would have probably given me anything I wanted to NOT come back). I was VERY satisfied with the agreement, and the company probably felt like they dodged a bullet—in other words, a win-win. I met with him a few days later; he had papers for me to sign saying I was voluntarily leaving, with the details of the severance package. He had a nice check and my letter of recommendation—and with that, we shook hands, he wished me good luck, and we said goodbye. And just like that—I was unemployed.

A few days later, it was the big day—moving day. I wasn't moving any of my male clothes with me, I had boxed up pretty much everything except what was on my back and donated it to the Lutheran church that helped me through that year. This life change was for good, and yes, I was burning that bridge. I was all packed and had movers take my things from my apartment to my new home across town. This was literally the first day of the rest of my new life. I started this day as my male self for the very last time. When the movers had finished loading the truck, I explained to them that I had to head into San Francisco on business, but that "my sister" would be at the house in an hour and a half to meet them (they were going to break for lunch, so the timing was perfect). I had held back a suitcase for me, and as soon as they had left, I said goodbye to "Larry" and introduced the world to Laurie. I changed, got my makeup on, and headed over to the house as the truck arrived. I introduced myself and told them what went where, and when the day was over—Laurie was home!

7

GOOD MORNING ALICE

"He will wipe every tear from their eyes. There won't be any more death. There won't be any grief, crying, or pain, because the first things have disappeared."

Rev. 21:4 (GW)

DETAILS, DETAILS: The life of someone who is transgender is seldom simple. When you're younger and before transitioning (if you ever do), your greatest fear is being found out. At some point, you may decide you must transition or die (it certainly was for me). Transitioning can be a personal, emotional, not to mention legal, nightmare. Losing old friends can be painful, and starting to live as the other gender requires learning all kinds of things you never had to before. Things most people don't think about—how you walk, how you talk. And every state is different when it comes to the legal stuff—

driver's licenses, birth certificates. Then, there are bank accounts, car registration, all kinds of stuff involving going to places and talking to strangers who work for the government and can make your life easy or difficult. But you do it—you endure it because in the end, it IS worth whatever you have to go through; it is a matter of survival.

It was early June in 1992, and one of the first things I think of as I wake up my first day in my new home is, "Only 365 days until I can have surgery—thank you God!" I felt like Alice in Wonderland, or maybe even more like Dorothy realizing she wasn't in Kansas anymore when the world goes from black and white into color. There was a sense of wonder and excitement as I woke up to my new life in a new neighborhood, how I would make new friends who only knew me as Laurie, and how I looked forward to what my life would become. What I had only dreamed of for most of my life had come true.

While I figured out what I was going to do for income, I concentrated on some of the necessary administrative tasks. Step one was to get a new driver's license. All I needed was a letter from my doctor stating that I was being treated for gender dysphoria and as a result was living full time prior to having surgery in a year. I walked into the DMV with my letter and when I got to the counter, said I needed a new driver's license and handed the letter to the clerk.

She read it and said, "Okay, fill this out then go to that window over there and they'll take care of you."

I filled out the form, handed it to the person at the window, they typed some things into their computer and said, "Go stand over there and I'll take your picture." And just like that, I had a new license with my name Laurie Suzanne Scott, sex-Female.

Now that I had my driver's license, my next stop was to the Social Security office to get a new card in my name. They were satisfied with my having the driver's license and issued me a new card. Two down. My next job was to get my home into my new name, because "Laurie" didn't exist in the credit reporting agencies yet, so my old name was all over the documents to the home. I went to the title company that handled the transaction and the gal there was sweet and helpful. She figured a way to quit-claim the home to myself in my new name, so I went through that process and soon enough the home was now in MY name.

A legal name change is just a little more involved, but not much. Where it gets a little tricky is when you add a change to your birth certificate. I learned that in California you could take the standard name change form, and in cases like mine add an extra sentence, something to the effect of having the Los Angeles Department of Public Health issue me a new birth certificate indicating my new name and sex, and having my old birth certificate sealed—only to be opened by court order. I thought that was pretty cool—the only hitch was that I was going to have to wait until AFTER my surgery, because I would need a notarized letter from a doctor stating that I had already undergone the surgery. OK, I can wait a year for that.

Most of the neighbors had all moved into the neighborhood by the time I did—my lot was the smallest on the street and one of the last to sell, but it was perfect. It was at the end of a cul-de-sac, so no traffic, and it made for a little better sense of a neighborhood. I was getting to know my neighbors; many were couples with children of various ages, meaning there was always some kind of activity on the street, which was nice. Of course, I was still driving down to see Lin every week, I mean, this is a BIG step. I was pleased to report to her that I was very, very happy and getting along just fine meeting my neighbors and simply being "Laurie."

But being Laurie was a learning process for me. For one thing, I had to learn how to take care of a wig because my hair was still too short to make it look in any way feminine. I also learned that wearing a wig during a Sacramento summer day can get extremely warm, especially on the fourth of July when the neighbors decide to close off the street in the afternoon and have a block party. It wasn't even a particularly hot day that year, but a couple of hours in the sun can certainly make one's brow moist with perspiration. But it was a fun time getting to know the neighbors better, sharing food, and capping it off with fireworks. Everybody chipped in, and we gave the money to the guys and sent them off to buy whatever they wanted.

This was my first time sitting around with other women, AS a woman, and I guess I was a little nervous because I was new at this whole gals getting together thing. I discovered that when answering a question, women will "probe" further with another woman if the answer doesn't seem complete, or if there are details you're leaving out, whereas with guys whatever you answer is more than they are really interested in hearing anyway. This is where I first had to figure out how to answer questions like "were you married before?" As a guy, I could answer that question with "yes, but it didn't work out" and that would pretty much be that, since no guy actually cares or even wants to hear about the details beyond that. They've had their obligatory moment of compassion and now it's time to break out the beer.

But as a woman, with other women, I quickly learned it then continues with, "Oh, what happened?" "Did he cheat on you?" Lots and lots of probing questions. Then, I would have to come up with something to the effect of, "Well, it just wasn't meant to be," and they could tell at that point by my response and my (granted faked) sad tone of voice that I didn't want to talk about it.

I mean, what would I say anyway? "Oh, well you see my WIFE couldn't handle me going through a sex change—she didn't want to be married to a woman, go figure!" I got pretty good at sending the "I don't want to talk about it" message without having to say it. On a rare occasion, I would have to be a little more blunt and spell it out for someone that I REALLY didn't want to talk about it, but for the most part I developed the skill of diverting the conversation and avoiding the question, kind of like a politician (just typing the word politician makes my skin crawl—I guess I could have found a better analogy).

I was still getting used to life as Laurie, and I didn't think I was ready to jump into a church at this time. It had been a few months since I moved in and Kim had recently left her job. She had a friend who was a real estate broker who asked her about becoming an agent. Kim asked me to attend their real estate school with her, and I thought "why not?" So, we went to school together, and as soon as it had finished, I signed up to take the license exam.

Now, if there is one thing the government doesn't care about, it's your privacy. Within three days of signing up to take the test, I was getting all kinds of junk in the mail about studying for the test, how to pass the test, etc., and of course they all wanted money. Since I wanted to PASS the test, I did sign up for a video course. Today, we would log onto a website, pay online, and have a code sent via email to log in with and be watching them within minutes. However, this was 1992, the closest thing to a public Internet was CompuServe and AOL, and we were using dial-up modems at a blazing 56 kilobytes per second. Imagine the slowest Internet you've ever had and then make it ten times slower, and that's what this was. There was no watching video on your computer this way—you couldn't even listen to music this way. Nope, what you got instead were VHS tapes with worksheets sent to you through the US mail. It wasn't so bad, you go into your living room, pop in the tape and, sit back on your sofa—not a bad way to learn. So, I watched the tapes, worked the worksheets, and later took and passed the state's test.

Kim hadn't gotten around to taking the test yet, and not knowing any better, I assumed I would be working for the broker that Kim knew, but I had forgotten how much the state cared about my privacy. No sooner had I found out that I passed the test than I started to get all kinds of mail from real estate brokers all over town saying join us, we care, and you'll love us. They were just letters on stationary and didn't say much about the people, not even pictures, just words—all except for one. The broker for a Century 21 office in town sent a similar letter, but she included her business card and on the card was her photo. She struck me as a nice person in her photo, so I called and made an appointment to talk to her.

I walked into the office and saw it was busy with several people working and a few on the phone at the time. The receptionist opened up with "hello", a big smile and asked how she could help me.

I said, "Hi, I'm Laurie Scott and I have an appointment with Patty about being an agent."

She just gave a bigger smile and said: "Oh great, let me tell her you're here." The gal was a happy person and was the perfect person to be the first you see when you walk into the office.

Patty came out of her office and with a handshake and a smile said: "Hi, come on back here with me." It was the same smile I saw on her business card. Her office was in the back corner; the walls were glass with aluminum blinds. There was a large desk in her office, and across from it against the blinds, were two chairs for guests. She sat behind her desk, I sat in one of those chairs, and we started to talk.

I didn't know much more about real estate than what I learned in the classes to prepare you for the test—and the problem with that is that passing the test doesn't do much to help you actually be a good real estate agent. I talked about my various jobs in the restaurant business and that I was ready for a change. She explained the program the company had to help new agents find their footing and, well, we just hit it off. I said, "I'm in if you'll take me." With a big smile, she said yes and then pulled out some paperwork for me to fill out, some for her, and some for the state. She showed me to a desk where I could fill out the paperwork right then and there (hey, it's not like I had a job to run off to—my life's calendar was pretty open these days). All the forms were pretty run of the mill stuff except for one question on one form... "Have you been known by any other names?"

Really? You have to ask THAT question? With my elbow on the desk, I put my head on my palm thinking, "What am I supposed to do with this?" Here I am going after my first job months after making a life-changing move, and I have to answer THIS question? And it was on an official State of California form with some long number next to it—it was official all right. I didn't want to be publicly perp-walked into court someday for lying on a government form, so I gulped, stood up, walked over to her office door, and said, "Patty, can I talk to you a second about this form?"

I walked in and asked if I could close the door. She looked confused as to why someone would need to close the door to ask a question about a form a hundred or more people have filled out, with not one person stopping to ask her a question about it. I sat down and looked at the bewilderment on her face. I grabbed a tissue because I was feeling the tears coming on, as I explained this was a difficult question for me to answer, partly because I don't know where it goes, who sees it, or even if anyone would—because I may not be welcomed if they found out. I told her the problem was that until a few months ago, I was known as Larry, and that I would be having surgery the following year, but that I had already changed my driver's license and social security information, while the surgery timeline was dictated by the doctors.

She said, "Oh," a little surprised as you might expect but not shocked either—to my surprise she took it pretty much in stride. She told me to go ahead and put my previous name down on it, that she's required to have it filled out but keeps them herself in her office; it doesn't go to the state and no one else sees it. "So, are we good?" she said.

I sniffled and smiled and said, "Yes."

On my way out she said, "And oh, by the way, I wouldn't have known." I smiled and went back to the desk to finish the paperwork. I enjoyed real estate, the freedom of doing business on my terms and schedule, not to mention not having to sweat the whole gender thing in a corporate environment.

The New Year arrived, and I continued to do pretty well in my real estate business into spring. My weekly trips into San Francisco to see Lin continued, and my hair was finally long enough that I thankfully didn't need to wear a wig any longer. The gal doing my hair permed it and insisted I needed to go blond, so it was quite a change from the rather straight brown wig I had been wearing. I simply told folks I felt it was time for a change (truer words were never spoken!).

Everything was now leading up toward my surgery, and it was time to get all my ducks in a row. We had spent the last two years building a case with the insurance company toward having them pay for my surgery. The day came when I had to make the call and tell the insurance company what I was going to do, to ensure it was covered. To my surprise, the gal on the other end of the phone who pulled up my records said, "Oh yes, we anticipated this and it will be covered. There has been one previous to you." THAT surprised me! Back then before there was social media and 24/7 news, people like me felt like we were the only ones. I was astonished to learn that I wasn't the first to be covered by the insurance company.

My surgeon had learned under Dr. Biber, who was practically the godfather of these surgeries, so I had confidence in him. Lin knew him and felt confident referring me to him. We did the initial consult over the phone, and of course, he wanted the letter from Lin and my psychiatrist, which wasn't a problem, and we scheduled it for July. My surgery was to take place in Portland, so I had another agent at the real estate office cover my business the weeks I would be out. My story to people was that it was "female issues," which wasn't a lie, and that I had family there to take care of me after surgery—and yes, that WAS a lie.

As a male adult, breasts don't develop with female hormones as much as you would have had you been actually born female. The rule of thumb is a size smaller than a sister or your mother. My development was small but since breast augmentation surgery even for someone transsexual was considered cosmetic by the insurance company, it wasn't covered, and I had to pay for that part myself.

It was morning the day before my surgery—Kim came to pick me up at home and drive me to the airport. When we got to the airport, she gave me a hug for good luck, and I was off. Sacramento to Portland is a quick flight. The doctor's staff had a good system set up for people like me traveling there with no one to take care of them. There was a gal named Denise who had surgery years earlier who lived there, so for a nominal charge, she would not only meet me at the airport and schlep me to the hospital, but she also would put me up at her place and fix my meals. I mean—she was doing it much more so out of compassion than for money, because she couldn't have been doing much better than break even on her expenses.

From the airport, we went straight to the hospital, where I met with my doctor and his staff. He did a physical examination and wanted to be sure to answer any questions I might have. He handed me the paperwork to fill out and directed me to the hospital's financial office to finish up any insurance work and to pay for my cost.

On the way to Denise's home from the hospital, we had to stop by the drug store, and then Denise took me to her place and got me set up in my room. There was one extremely unpleasant experience in this whole "adventure"—when they are going to be operating on you anywhere near your intestines/colon, surgeons want you to be CLEAN just in case of a nick. And oh my! To be "clean," you have to drink the most vile, disgusting, nasty, and obnoxious aqueous substance known to man. The purpose of this delightful ambrosia is to make you go to the bathroom, and go to the bathroom a LOT! And of course, you can't go to the bathroom a lot unless you drink this stuff a lot. I think it was about half a gallon, but you would think it was five gallons. Honestly—this was by far the worst part of the entire process. It took me probably an hour and a half to choke down this stuff, it was so awful. It makes the cod liver oil we would get as kids when we didn't eat our vegetables seem like Hawaiian Punch. I tried to sleep that night, but bodily functions kept me racing to the bathroom (without question the stuff worked—that's for sure).

The next morning (no breakfast of course), we went to the hospital. My surgery was scheduled for 10:00 am, but while I was in my gown getting ready in pre-op, the doctor was called to help with a girl who was badly burned in a car accident—so they moved me to a room and a bed until the doctor was available. Around 1:00, a nurse came into my room and announced: "Ok, it's time to go."

She made me sit in a wheelchair (because apparently, the gown has magic powers that disable the muscles in your legs) and wheeled me back to the pre-op area where I sat on a gurney. My doctor came in with a black Sharpie and started to draw lines and semi-circles around what breast tissue I did have. Then, he asked me "what size do you want to be?"

"Huh?" I said. In all this time, I never had given it much thought as to what size I wanted to be. I said, "I'm not sure."

He said, "we'll see what we can do with the tissue we have to work with." He explained that they were saline implants (during this period of time, silicone implants weren't allowed because the government can be stupid). So, when he was done making it look like someone had played "connect the dots" on me, he said, "See you in a little bit," and he headed off to get ready.

Then, the staff had me lay down on the gurney. That's when the anesthesiologist came in and gave me the rundown of what he was going to do, etc., and that he was going to get me started with a mild "cocktail" via IV to relax me. I don't know what was in it, but he was one outstanding bartender, because I almost immediately began to feel "relaxed." If you've ever had surgery, then you know how strange it can be to feel "relaxed" via legal pharmaceuticals, lying on your back being wheeled down a hospital hall, looking up while white fluorescent lights swirl all around overhead. It's not something you experience in the course of a normal day, at least not for me.

As they wheeled me into the operating room, my doctor said, "Hello Laurie, are you ready?"

And feeling relaxed thanks to my bartender, I was like, "Yep, let's get this party started!" They moved me from the gurney to the operating table, and I remember there being country music in the background, and the anesthesiologist telling me that I was going to sleep now and when I wake up it would be all over. He asked me to start counting backward from 100. So, I started... "one hundred, ninety-nine, ninety-eight, ninety—" and that's the last thing I remember (I don't know why they don't have you just start with ten).

After six hours of surgery, the first thing I remember was momentarily waking up in post-op and then waking up again in my hospital room. In my room, I remember feeling like a big dog was laying on my chest, I looked down but couldn't see past my chest because I was rather taped up at this point, but there was definitely more "there" there. As far as down below, it was pretty much gauze and tubes between my legs. The first thing I did when my head was somewhat clear was to call my mom and tell her that the surgery was over, and I was ok. I could hear the mixed emotions in her voice. The happiness in the fact that I was safe and fine following a long surgery—but definitely the sadness that something she could have never imagined in her baby's life had happened. Of course, I didn't want to hurt my mother—I hadn't seen her since I told her of my decision to live full-time and have surgery, but I don't know that there was a way to have that conversation and not have her feeling hurt. I'm sure there was a sense of finality to it in her mind—I have no doubt she had been quietly hoping that I would "change my mind" about going through with the surgery.

One interesting thing did happen in the couple of days I was in the hospital: two weeks before my surgery date, I had to stop taking my hormones because taking estrogen increases the chance of blood clots, which you certainly don't want in surgery. But something surprising happens when your body is used to a particular estrogen level, and then it drops to a very low level—it's called menopause. Yep, there I was in my hospital bed and suddenly I was getting hot flashes, then they would go away and I'd ask for more blankets, then it would happen again. I sometimes get kidded by my girlfriends for never having had to endure periods or (for some of them who are old enough) menopause—and I have to leap to my defense saying, "Hey, for two weeks I had hot flashes, so there!" And no, not one of them has ever felt sorry for me.

After a couple of days in the hospital, I was finally able to gingerly go back to Denise's home for another five days of recuperation. Each day I got better, and the last day I went back to see the doctor for a follow-up before heading home. He was satisfied with my healing progress and gave me the green light to return home. Thank the Lord they had told me I would want a "donut" to sit on for my trip home, which would have been an uncomfortable flight had I not had one (people around me must have thought I had seriously bad hemorrhoids).

When Kim picked me up at the airport, her first question was "how are you?" Then she gave me a hug. I was walking a little slower than normal, we got my suitcase, and she drove me home (yes, sitting on my donut in her car as well). To her, I looked the same as the day I left, but she knew what I had been through and it made no difference to her one bit—I was Laurie a week ago when she took me to the airport and I was that same Laurie when I landed back in Sacramento that day. Anything that had changed wasn't visible, but she was so sweet and sensitive to help make the drive home "gentle," since I was still in a healing mode.

I had cooked plenty of food for meals before I left and placed them in the freezer, so I could take it easy when first back at home. After several weeks, I was back up and running and working. I met with the gal who monitored my business for me, so I was back up to speed and jumped back in. Everyone at the real estate office was glad to see me back. Some of my listings had expired while I was out and, of course, I didn't have any new ones—it was almost like starting over. But Laurie was back, better than ever!

People have commented to me since then how "brave" and "courageous" I was to go through with transition and the surgery. But this was something I not only had wanted all my life, but with God's blessing, what I needed for my own survival going forward.

8

THERE'S A NEW GIRL IN TOWN

"For the winter is past, the rain is over and gone. The flowers are springing up and the time of the singing of birds has come. Yes, spring is here."

Song of Solomon 2:11-12 (TLB)

IT'S A NEW WORLD: Many who travel the same road as I up to this point can be a little self-absorbed. When your body and soul are in disagreement, it's a difficult thing to ignore and a difficult thing to resolve. Most of my life, I was trying to figure out how to live with it—it was a total fail. Then, living full-time for a year as a female yet not physically female, well that keeps you busy trying to appear normal. Part of you feels "released"— able to be yourself for the first time, relating to the world in what feels completely normal. But part of you feels paranoid that at any moment someone might "read" you as not being an actual woman, and that your new secret might be revealed. But after having surgery that pretty much goes away. You've successfully lived a year as a woman, and there are no more physical reminders of the discontinuity of your life. Finally, you have the chance to live life fully for the first time. And it makes it easier to focus on other people rather than yourself. When for the first time in your life you are comfortable in your own skin, the world begins to open up in an almost miraculous way.

Yes, spring is here. Not literally, because it was closer to the end of summer, but I was now outwardly female in my body to match that part of my being that had always been female. I had achieved what growing up I certainly didn't think was possible and even fought for years. Having done that, it was now time to live life—no more landmark goals related to my gender identity, it was time to get back to work.

One real estate listing in particular following my surgery, had a huge impact on the direction of my life as it turns out. Early each morning, I would drop off literature about myself at the homes of listings that had expired with other agents the day before. I explained they would be getting lots of calls that day, and that I'd call in the evening.

One evening, as I was making my phone calls, a gentleman with an accent answered the phone. I couldn't place the accent, but he had been waiting for my call, liked what I had dropped off, and was going to talk with two others but wanted to talk with me as well.

The next day, I went to see him. He was a cute older gentleman in his 80's, and as it turns out his accent was Dutch. His wife had died a couple of years earlier, and he was moving to Florida where his oldest daughter was going to retire, and they could be close. As it happened, I got the listing. There were a few small things I wanted to tweak to have it ready for sale, but in a couple of days, it was done and on the market. I wanted to make sure the house always looked good in the event potential buyers came through, so every few days, I would swing by and check on things. Every time I did, he would be sitting in his recliner watching tennis—he seemed lonely, and I felt sorry for him.

Each morning he would go out and play tennis with friends at the local park, but for the rest of the day, he sat there at home alone. So, I started to come by more often, and after a couple of weeks it was pretty much every day. Sometimes, I would sit down and talk with him. He was a pilot in the Pacific during World War II, flying P-51 Mustangs and had so many fascinating stories to tell (he was a genuine World War II flying ace!)

Eventually, an offer came in on his home. To celebrate, he wanted to take me to dinner. I said sure—he was such a sweet old man, I wasn't going to say no, and he clearly enjoyed being around people (and yes, I know he "liked" me but he was more like a grandfather in my eyes). His eyes lit up at the restaurant. He was having a lot of fun with the server (a girl of course) and he was so full of life, I could see how he was probably a bit of a ladies man in his day.

During this time prior to the move, there were some things of his that he wanted to sell, particularly furniture that he didn't want to take to Florida, so we arranged a yard sale. A nice young couple expecting their first child came by to look at some things. They liked a bed and also his treadmill. We were talking, and they mentioned the little church that they went to, so I asked them about it, because (what a coincidence) I happened to be at the point in my new life that I was ready to find a church. The church was in the next city not 15 minutes from my home. The couple was very nice, so I asked about the when and where their church met. The when was Sunday morning, and the where was a children's day-care. Being rather tall (almost six foot three), I was envisioning sitting in little chairs designed for four-year-olds with my knees up near my chin, but I decided to give it a try anyway.

Sunday came and as I got ready, I felt a little nervous yet excited about going to church fully as Laurie. It was a SMALL church, maybe 30 people or so, and thankfully, they had chairs designed for actual grown-ups. Needless to say, it wasn't necessary for them to ask, "Is there anyone here for the first time" because everyone knew everyone else. As I hadn't been there before, my anonymity didn't last much past when I first walked through the door.

There was a gentleman with a dark beard playing guitar leading the worship and a young gal high school age singing beside him. He had a nice enough voice and the songs were genuinely heartfelt, he wasn't just going through the motions. When the singing was over, another gentleman came to the front to give the announcements. "Oh, he must be the pastor," I thought to myself as I'm trying to figure out who was who. After the announcements and offering, the man with the beard came back to the front with a Bible and starting teaching. Oh, HE'S the pastor. I was rather impressed that the pastor of this little church was also a talented musician. For some reason I felt comfortable and safe at this small church, the people were friendly, and Pastor Jeff's message was very good. I went back and met more people there over the next several weeks.

I was getting more involved; they didn't have anyone who knew anything about sound systems, so I helped run it and record the messages. I also trained someone, so I didn't have to sit back there every week. We also had a weekly Bible study at a family's home which was a great way to get to know each other better.

This was the early 90's, and one year there was a lot of rain and some heavy flooding in northern California, including the neighborhood and home where we held our Bible study. Even President Clinton came out and toured that neighborhood. They showed him on the local news walking around the area, and I remember on television a woman in the crowd screaming "Oh, he's so handsome!" and I couldn't help but think that this was the mentality that put him in office in the first place, but I digress. Fortunately, the flood damage in the home wasn't too severe, but there was damage along the bottom foot of their walls, requiring a lot of work to fix along with the flooring. Between insurance and others at the church, their home was soon repaired.

As the close of escrow on Grandpa's home approached, his youngest daughter Wilhelmina (Wil for short), who was also Dutch but currently living in Houston, flew out to help him pack. She was just as sweet as her dad and we all went out for dinner. I told Wil that her dad was like a grandfather to me, that I thought he was sweet and special, and that I was glad I was able to help him. In November the sale closed, and he was off to Florida to move into his home in Tampa. I'd call him now and then to see how he was doing. He sounded sad—he didn't know anyone and just sat at home all day.

Early December, he asked if I would come out and help him get some furniture for his new home and decorate for Christmas. He had a second bedroom at his little place and even a bed in it, and since he was paying for it and real estate was slow—I said ok. It was the week before Christmas when I was there. Have you ever tried to buy a Christmas tree, in Florida, the week before

Christmas? They don't exist (at least in Tampa that year). We finally found something that was about three feet tall and looked like it came out of "A Charlie Brown Christmas." And it was NOT cheap! I had bought him a couple of little gifts so that there was something to put under the tree. While I was there, we found him a cute dining table and chairs and a comfortable chair to sit in for watching television. I also hooked up his VCR, so he could watch tapes that he had. I stayed through Christmas, so he didn't have to spend it alone—then I returned home. I would call him every month or so to keep tabs on him. His older daughter eventually had a change in plans and didn't retire in Florida, which left him on his own and alone; not a great thing for someone in their eighties who loved being around people.

The great momentum that I had in real estate before my surgery was never fully regained afterward. The real estate market was at a serious low. Sure, I sold Grandpa's home and a few others, but it wasn't enough to make ends meet, and my cushion from when I left the restaurant business almost two years earlier was starting to shrink. Real estate didn't look like it would improve anytime soon, and as far as I know, I was the only person in my office that was relying completely on one single income from real estate. There were some married couples who were both in real estate together, or they had a working spouse, or they had supplemental income due to retiring from another job. I needed to find a "real" job where I had a regular, steady income. I looked through the newspaper (that's what we did back then, kids, before there was an Internet) and found a small, computer-based company that was looking for someone to manage their customer support department. Hey, I'd always been good with computers, and I had tons of management experience from the restaurant business, so I decided to give it a try.

It was a company that helped people start their own electronic medical billing business, and they were looking for a manager over their four-person technical support group. They must have liked me, because they hired me right away. Once a month or so they would have training for people who signed up for the business opportunity, and I would do a session on the software and how to use a modem to download files from our support department. It was, however, a somewhat strange environment to work within. For one, the owner, and those (I assume) running the company were Hare Krishna. As a result, they were vegetarian and didn't allow meat products in the office. This meant that (since I wasn't going to give up meat in my sandwiches) I had to go out and eat in my car for lunch (a cooler was all I needed to avoid poisoning myself from food left in a hot car).

It had now been over a year since Grandpa had moved to Florida, we still talked once a month or so. Either I would call him, or he would call me. On one particular occasion, I asked him how he was doing, and he expressed how unhappy he was there. He was alone and miserable. So, I asked him, "Why don't you come back to Sacramento? You've got friends here, people you know, places you know." I also said, "If you don't want to buy a home, you don't have to, you can rent somewhere or if you want, I have an extra room, and you can live here at my house."

He said "Oh, I don't know" and I didn't mention it again, but I wanted him to know that he didn't have to be all alone and in Florida. About a month and a half later, he called me and said in his cute Dutch accent: "Laurie if it's okay, I would like to come back and live with you at your house."

I called his daughter Wil, who had now moved back to the Netherlands, and told her that her dad wanted to come back, that it was okay with me, and I wanted to know how she felt about him moving again. She understood how miserable he was there and was fine with him moving back into my home—so

I called the agent who sold him the home and said it needed to go back on the market. She went to see him and get all the paperwork filled out. She called a few days later saying he had fallen at home, and she'd taken him to the emergency room to get patched up for a couple of cuts. Apparently, in his loneliness, he had been drinking at home, and drinking a lot.

A few weeks later, she calls me again to say they have accepted an offer on the home, but that I shouldn't wait for it to close. He was still drinking a lot, and she was worried he might not live long if he keeps it up. I called him and made him promise that he wouldn't drink until I got there (he was the kind of man who would keep his promise). So, I arranged to take time off work and went to Florida to help get him packed up and bring him home. He was a bit of a mess when I arrived, sitting in his chair, and his place needed some cleaning. The home was sold furnished, so only his personal items needed to be packed, and what couldn't go into three suitcases went into boxes and were shipped back to California along with his car (yes he was still driving, oy vey!).

We arrived home and got him settled in; this began a pretty standard routine for me. Get up, go to work, come home, change clothes, go play tennis with Grandpa for about an hour (yes, he still loved to play tennis at 86 years old), and then we would go somewhere for dinner—I ended up almost never cooking except on weekends. He had a favorite restaurant we went to probably four times a week—I think he had a thing for one of the servers there. Eventually, I would just ask for us to be seated in her section. She was always extra nice to Grandpa, and he always left her a good tip. If being home alone in Florida was misery, being out and about and able to talk to people (and flirt with servers) was heaven for him—he would light up with a smile and a gleam in his eye. It was the same thing at the supermarket, another place we'd frequent even when we didn't really need anything.

Again, he loved being out, and at the supermarket, he would never go through a checkout line with a guy working it. He felt men should be working outdoors doing the hard work. He had a favorite gal at the supermarket, and he would insist we get in her line—no matter if it was the longest line or not. We were going to be in her line just so he could flirt with her, and of course she flirted back which made it all the more fun for him.

In the mornings after I left for work, he would visit his friends he used to play tennis with down at the same park, then come home, fix himself a sandwich for lunch, and wait for me to come home. A couple of Sundays I got him to come to church with me. I never nagged him, but at least twice he did come. He felt a little out of place, even though he would sit with me back at the sound board. He was agnostic and happy that way. When I asked another time if he wanted to come and he said no, I didn't pursue it. If he wasn't ready to come to Jesus, Jesus was going to have to come to him. He called me his "guardian angel." One thing I always told him as I tucked him into bed was, "God loves you, and I do too."

The church pastor and his wife invited me to their home to share their meals during the holidays. This is where I learned his wife worked for a large tech company in the area. I told her about the little company I worked for and what I did. She knew I was a bit of a computer geek, and I think that without me knowing it, a seed was planted in her mind.

One Sunday morning, the pastor's wife told me that they were doing some hiring in the internal support center, that she knew the manager of the department, and asked was I interested. I told her sure, and later that week I got a call from a temp agency saying that the company had asked them to give me an interview. In this department you started as a temp and if you were good enough and the openings were there, you could get hired on later as an employee with the additional perks that go with it. We scheduled the interview and I went into the temp agency. After my second interview, by the time I got home, I had a job offer on my answer machine. I took it, and six months later went from a temp to a corporate employee.

I soon found my niche crunching numbers and doing data analysis on my group's performance, and that expanded into other areas that led to a nice career that made me happy. I had regular hours and was able to take care of Grandpa.

After a couple of years though, there were moments of odd behavior from him. One time we were driving in the car at night, and he was convinced that oncoming cars had bombs in them, then ten minutes later it would pass, and he was fine (luckily he never tried to grab the wheel to veer the car off the road). On another occasion late at night, he had gone next door and was pounding on their door for some reason—the ruckus woke me up. The neighbor had already called 911, and when the paramedics tried to calm him down, he took a swing at one and cut the guy's lip (he was a tough old man, I'll tell ya!). They finally got him restrained and took him to the hospital where they did some tests, but he was fine by then, so after a few hours I was able to bring him home.

Then on one Saturday morning a couple of months later, Grandpa and I were sitting in our chairs in the living room, and his hand started to shake. He looked at me rather strangely and said, "It's coming."

I saw his hand but was confused—I said, "What's coming?"

He slowly said in an ominous sounding voice… "Death."

116

And at that moment, he began to shake violently all over—he was having a seizure. I grabbed his hand and got him to the floor and immediately called 911. By the time they arrived the seizure was over, but they took him to the hospital. I knew he had been sneaking alcohol in the house (we're talking bottles of vodka in his bedroom closet, I learned, not a chilled chardonnay in the refrigerator), and I had pretty much put a stop to that. A glass of wine with dinner I had no problem with, but I wasn't going to let him drink himself to death either.

In giving background information to the doctor, I told him about the alcohol, and the doctor found it interesting because he had NO alcohol in his blood, the doctor surmised it was a withdrawal symptom of not having any alcohol in his system. He was in the hospital for a few days and then was sent to a rehabilitation center to regain his strength. He was there for almost six weeks, but by the time he came home he was probably 90%, and after that made it to about 95% of where he was before the seizure.

It was during this time, one Sunday at church, everything went pretty normal, our young singer did a beautiful solo to a recorded track as a special song, but other than that it was all normal… until after the message, when pastor Jeff announced that this would be our last Sunday together. After much thought and prayer with the leaders, it was decided that the church had fulfilled its purpose for the Lord and it was time to close the doors. Everyone who didn't know, including me, sat quietly stunned, I teared up. I didn't know how to react. We all hugged each other and of course thanked pastor Jeff and his wife. Since Grandpa was coming home and needed more attention than before, I didn't start to look for a new church at this time.

With Grandpa home, we started to play a little tennis again, but not for as long. It was good for him physically as well as emotionally to be out doing things and being active, and yes, he was still driving in the mornings when I would go to work (oh boy). This did begin a slow but gradual decline in his health, however.

One time he had gone to the supermarket before I got home, and the next thing I knew there was a knock on the door. It was a county sheriff with Grandpa—he couldn't find his car in the parking lot of the supermarket, and couldn't describe it to the officer. Sadly, I had to take away his keys and that put an end to his driving days. I got permission from my company to work from home most days, so I could keep a closer eye on him.

He was starting to sleep more and over time, and he did get more and more dependent on my help. First, I installed heavy-duty safety grab bars in his bathroom to make it easier for him to get in and out of the shower. Eventually though as he got weaker, it was necessary for me to help him get dressed and yes, undressed when he would take a shower. I wasn't familiar with the term caregiver at the time, and when he moved into my home, I guess I didn't give much thought to what might happen in the future. But he was family to me, I was going to help him as much as I could for as long as I could, and it just evolved into a caregiver role. I was his family too in Sacramento, and I wasn't going to let anyone hurt him. Finally, in 1999, he had degraded to the point where he couldn't speak well. One night as I tucked him into his bed I said, "God loves you, and I do too," as I had hundreds of times before.

He reached out his hand toward me and said slowly in that cute Dutch accent of his, "You are my angel."

I then quietly said, "Now do you believe there is a God?"

And in one word, he simply replied, "Yes." I smiled and gave him a kiss on the cheek.

In November, I took a break (my first and only) for a couple of days and had him taken to a nursing home while I got away to Lake Tahoe to refresh and recharge. An ambulance brought him back home when I returned. He was now in a hospital-like bed that adjusted and had rails so he wouldn't fall. He also wasn't able to communicate any longer, though I could tell he was aware and could hear me, and he now needed to be fed through a tube in his stomach. I would talk to him, tell him about work, call his daughter in The Netherlands and hold the phone to his ear so he could hear her voice as she talked to him in Dutch.

He was born in 1907. On New Year's Eve 1999, while the rest of the world was having one big party, I turned the TV on in his room to a station showing the fireworks from cities all over the world celebrating the year 2000. I got down next to him, and into his ear, I softly told him, "You made it, Happy New Year—it's the year 2000."

Just four days later on the fourth of January, I got up like I did any other day. The sun was shining brightly. I took a shower and got dressed. I heard Grandpa coughing as I passed by his room to make breakfast. After finishing breakfast, I went to his room to check on him, feed him, and turn on the television for him. As I pushed his door open, I saw that his color was off, he was still, and he wasn't breathing. I just started to cry—I feared the inevitable day had arrived. I called out his name, walked over to him, and grabbed his hand—the only way I can describe it is, it felt lifeless. He was gone. I didn't call 911 because he never wanted to be resuscitated when the day came. I went into the living room, sat down in my chair, and sobbed. When I was able to compose myself, I called the nurse who had been visiting him every week. She asked a couple of questions about his condition, and I did my best to answer. She then asked if I had called anyone else, the mortuary, etc.

I said no, I didn't know what I was supposed to do. I said, "Do you call the police when someone dies like this at home?"

She said no, his death was natural, it was just his time, and we knew it was coming. She said she would call the mortuary and then come over herself to take care of the death certificate. I was still in the living room when she arrived, she went in to check on him, and shortly after that the mortuary folks arrived. They went back to get him and, before wheeling him out, asked if I wanted to see him. I said no, I didn't want to see him like that. I had seen him alive and well with his big smile and gleaming eyes, and that's how I wanted to remember him—I didn't need to burn that image of him there lifeless in bed into my brain any further. So, they rolled him out in a black bag on a gurney just like you see on television. They brought him through the living room right in front of me and out the front door.

This was certainly the emotionally darkest day of my life, at least up to this point that is. But this was only a warm-up for what was to come.

9

BIRTH OF A NEW FAMILY

"Then King David went in and sat before the Lord, and he said: "Who am I, Sovereign Lord, and what is my family, that you have brought me this far?"

2 Samuel 7:18 (NIV)

DIVULGING MY PAST: My experience in telling people about the fact that I'm transgender has taught me that men have a harder time accepting it than women. I'm not sure exactly why that is, but I do have a couple of theories that I'm happy to share with you, maybe some sociologist or psychologist will study it sometime. Apparently, the average man thinks about sex nineteen times a day (hey—I didn't make it up, Google it). That's a lot of thinking for someone who probably gets accused of not thinking at all at least ten times a day (and yes, I DID make that up). Maybe it's when they understand that I once had male body parts and no longer do, they start to think what that might be like if it were them, and can't fathom getting anywhere near that part of their body with a knife. It makes them want to cross their legs as a matter of protection. Maybe it's that they feel I'm a traitor to "the fraternity" of brothers (a fraternity I might add I never felt comfortable in or a part of). Likewise, maybe that's why women are more accepting, it's as if I've "come to my senses" and they are welcoming me to "the sisterhood." I really don't know, all I DO know is that it was never easy for me to tell friends as we got better acquainted about my "previous life" because no matter why someone might reject me, the fear of rejection was always there.

The passing of my adopted grandpa was hard on me. Taking care of him, particularly for the last year when he needed and appreciated my help gave me a sense of purpose. I knew I was making a difference in another person's life, making it better.

Once all of the details of his passing were taken care of and his family had come and gone, the house was very quiet and very empty, and I felt very, very alone. With the rejection from my own family and the passing of Grandpa, there was a family-size hole in my heart that needed filling. And that's when I found Awaken Fellowship there in Sacramento.

It's now been about six weeks since the membership class had finished and that's about when I get that dang letter in the mail asking me to be a part of leadership training. I had never planned on telling people at Awaken that I was transgender. No one there knew and I was fine with that. I didn't have an expectation that the folks there would be okay with my being transgender.

But that letter threw a wrench into everything, and so now here I am in the pastor's office with him and his wife, Beverly, and as soon as Beverly closed the door Pastor Frank says, "Laurie it's good to see you, we're so happy you're here at Awaken, what can we do for you?"

My arms were slightly crossed, and I started nervously rubbing my forearms back and forth with my hands as my eyes teared up. I wanted to be anywhere else and do almost anything else in the world than what I was about to do. I started to cry and squeaked out, "This is so hard."

Beverly reached over and handed me a box of tissues. I'm sure they've had church members in this office break into tears before, just not for the reason they were about to hear. I had made some notes of what I wanted to say because I was pretty sure I would be a mess, which I was. So points to me for advanced planning.

I composed myself and finally started. "Please forgive the long lead-in and build-up. There's a lot I want to convey before I say what I ultimately need to tell you. I don't want ever to be an embarrassment to Awaken or the church of Jesus Christ. I'm so scared. I love Awaken, and I love you both." I followed that with more crying, I was panic-stricken.

I was fidgeting with the ring on my finger. I told them between my sniffles as I looked down at the ring: "My ring was a gift from Grandpa; he was all the family I had. I don't have any other family. I've been shunned and disowned by them. In the short time I've been here at Awaken, I've begun to feel that I've got a family here, and I don't want to lose that. I've felt physically ill since last week just worrying about this meeting."

I stopped to wipe my eyes and blow my nose. "All that said, my fear of rejection is only exceeded by my wanting to do what is right before the eyes of God. I greatly respect those that God has put into a position of authority."

Beverly interjected with, "Laurie, it's ok—you're in a safe place here."

I nodded and said, "I know," and reached for another tissue (good thing it was a big box). "I've never been asked to be a part of leadership at a church before. When I first got your letter, I asked Jessica (the church secretary) to give me the scoop. Was it a just a form letter or was it "purposed?" I was hoping it was the former; it would have been easier to ignore, forget about, and just go on. When she said that there was specific input from you and the other pastors before letters go out, that's when I felt "squeezed." I can't tell you how much I respect you both. When a form letter arrives, I can write it off, but when church leaders make a conscious choice, then I believe it's God. Regardless of the outcome, He wanted the letter sent. That put me in the position that I'm in. Perhaps God wants me to pursue being a part of leadership at Awaken, perhaps not—we'll know shortly. As I said, I love you and I respect you both as God's chosen leaders for the flock you've been given to lead. I will listen to and respect what you have to say."

I can only imagine what must have been going through their minds at this point. Did she kill someone? Maybe she has a husband in prison? Does she lead a double life as a prostitute? What could possibly be so bad to have her going through all this?

I continued. "I want to serve God. Because of the letter you sent, I felt I need to bring this to your attention, but otherwise, I wouldn't have said a word to you or anyone else. To be honest, I didn't expect to receive a letter like that."

I told pastor and Beverly that I didn't want to be a stumbling block for Christians within Awaken or for non-believers who would look at me, and see just another reason to reject the God who created all that is good and wonderful in the earth and in Heaven above. I explained that my job doesn't know, my neighbors don't know, and most of my friends don't know.

I said, "My very best friend, Kim, knows. She's one of a handful of people who have known me before and after. That's how I like it and how I would like it to stay. I have no desire to make what I've been through an issue. I'm not an activist, and I don't have an agenda. I simply love my God. I am who I am today. The Laurie you know is who I am. No hidden agenda, nothing sinister up my sleeve." Then I started to cry again. "I've lost both my family and some of my very best friends over this. I'd rather you find out now, and we deal with it now, than have you find out later unexpectedly and put you and the church in an awkward position. This is not something I ever want to be made public. Who I am is not about who I was. I know people read about this and see things on TV, but I'm not like what you may hear about on television. Pastor, you said it yourself a couple of weeks ago; men and women are wired differently. I don't know how else to explain it."

I told them that that was the end of my notes, and I'm winging it from here. Finally, I got to the point. I paused for a deep breath and then I said, "I wasn't born a girl, but I've known all my life that I was. Seven years ago, I had surgery, and except for moments like this, I've been happy ever since." And with that, I shut up. I had just brought the elephant into the room.

There was a moment of silence as they internalized what I had just told them. Then pastor broke the silence with, "Okay, let's talk a little bit." He was still processing what I had just said because he slowly and deliberately said, "So… you're saying you were born with a male body, correct?"

I sniffled and nodded yes, and he said okay. There was another brief pause, and he processed what I had just confirmed, that he had heard me correctly.

He then asked questions like why did I feel I needed to do what I did (have surgery, become a woman), was I attracted to men or women (here we go again with the attraction thing. When people can't wrap their heads around this, they always go back to sex and attraction), and did I feel like God was honoring this?

I did my best to answer his questions, and as I did, I was slowly regaining my composure, though I'm sure my eyes were still red from crying.

We talked for almost an hour. Pastor reached for a yellow pad behind him and with a pen drew a line down the middle of it. He didn't write any words on the pad, but he moved the pen from the top to the bottom of the left side of the line as he said, "I'm sure you see a particular future for your life," indicating that whatever those things are for me would be written down on the left side of the line. Then, he did the same thing on the right side of the pad, top to bottom as he said, "And I would see a future for you where you are made whole again as the person God made you to be." I knew what he meant by "the person God made you to be," that he would like to see me "change back."

I told him, "I understand, but this is who I am. I'm not the person you envision in your scenario."

He acknowledged my statement and said, "Well, we still would like to have you be a part of leadership."

I looked up with surprise and said, "Really?"

Wow! I thought for sure I would be told I needed to change or leave. I figured my odds were very low of having them want me to stick around, it was really a "Hail Mary" since I didn't have much to lose at this point.

He said, "Of course we want you."

All I could say was, "Thank you." I dried my eyes and gave them both a hug.

I said, "I guess I'll see you Saturday night" (which was my preferred service, instead of the three Sunday morning ones). I thanked them again and we said goodbye.

I walked back to my car breathing a sigh of relief. Boy, was I glad THAT was over! And then I felt exhilaration. It began to sink in. I had just told the pastor of my church that I was transgender, and they didn't reject me. They didn't tell me to leave and never come back. They didn't tell me I was a sinner and would go to hell because I was transgender. The fact that they wanted me to stay and take part in leadership training meant the world to me and not what I was expecting.

As I settled into the church I made new friends, Jeff and Darla in particular. We just sort of hit it off—I sometimes helped them with their computer and they invited me over to watch movies and for the occasional dinner. We would sit together at the leadership trainings and over time, Darla and I got close.

They had a small guest house in their backyard that they had converted to an awesome prayer room. Darla and I would sometimes go there to talk and/or pray. But as our friendship grew, it began to get a little awkward when it came to talking about my family and more personal things. Do I have any family? Where do they live? Are we very close? Do I see them very often? Had I been married before? Why did we get a divorce? Was "he" unfaithful? The normal questions that come up and should be comfortable and easy to answer as a friendship grows deeper over time, but for me, they were a barrage of unpleasant inquiries into a part of my life I'm not sure it's safe to talk about.

Unfortunately, I was finding it hard to answer those questions. When you're good friends with someone, they feel it's okay to go ahead and ask what happened, to get to the more personal questions—and normally that would be fine. But now I had to lie. I hated this! What was the purpose of being good friends if you couldn't share life with them? Not being able to answer those questions honestly with people I cared about was a painful thing. I didn't want to start building relationships at the church that would lead to withdrawing from them or being deceitful to maintain them.

If I was going to have close, authentic relationships with people, I was realizing that the truth about my life was going to have to be a part of that. So one day I called Darla and asked if I could come over. We went back to the prayer room. She could see I was struggling with something and asked me what was wrong. She told me that whatever it was would stay between just the two of us.

I haven't had much practice at having this conversation with people who know me solely as Laurie, and I had brought my good friend, the "fear of rejection" with me. I made sure I had the tissues nearby, and I began to tell her my story.

Darla was loving and accepting. Of course, she had questions, and I tried to answer them as best I could. We talked for almost two hours, about my family, my life, and our church. She didn't seem to have any major issues with it as we talked.

When we were finishing up, she asked if it was okay if she told Jeff.

Wait a minute! She just told me this would stay between us! I was a little thrown off balance and said, "But you said this was between you and me."

She said, "Well, Jeff's my husband, and I don't keep secrets from him."

I might have felt differently about having that discussion if I had I known this wee little bit of information before I opened up my soul to her, but what was done was done. I hesitantly agreed, since I wasn't going to ask her to keep this from her husband if she felt it wasn't right to do so. The next few days, I was a little concerned as to how he would react. We were all friends, but I was closer to Darla.

One thing I really liked (and was unique) about this church is that about 45 minutes before each service, they had pre-service worship in what was literally an "upper room." It wasn't very big, there were no chairs, and it would be packed with maybe 40 people. A worship leader or pastor would have a set of songs on tape or CD and it was simply an extended and deep time of worship.

Jeff and Darla were usually there, and for the first time in my life, I asked God to give me a sign. I asked that if Jeff was okay with what Darla told him that he would come over to me and give me a hug at the end of the pre-service worship. Jeff wasn't a particularly big hugger.

I didn't mention my prayer to Darla or anyone. It was a full room this particular week, and I wasn't even sure if Jeff and Darla were there. As soon as it was over, out of the blue Jeff appeared and came over to give me a big hug. THAT was a "God thing." There are the times when the Lord shows up to remind you that He is there with you—this was one of those times. Jeff and Darla became even better friends over the next few months. They pretty much welcomed me into their family, had me over for meals, and we would hang out together.

I got more involved at church, helping with the sound and upgrading their technology. When they had a staff "play day" at Six Flags, they invited me to go along even though I wasn't on staff.

As a Christian, I had never grown like I had at Awaken. The weekly teaching was of course great by Pastor Frank, but getting involved in the women's ministry and leadership training just added to it all the more. The women's ministry would occasionally have special events in addition to regular Bible studies. More growth. Once a month there would be special teaching and training for those in the leadership training program, even more growth. My relationship with God was the deepest of my life.

I was busy planning a trip to Europe in the late summer. I had never been there, and Grandpa's family gave me an open invitation to visit and stay with them as a "home base." They live in the very southern tip of The Netherlands—only a few minutes away from both the German and Belgian borders. During my two-week trip, I also went to visit my dear friend Janice who was currently serving as the pastor at the "American Church in Berlin." I was also able to visit Vienna, Antwerp, and Amsterdam. It was a great trip and I was really enjoying using my new digital camera—so I took LOTS of pictures. When I got home, I decided to turn my photos into a movie with music and sub-titles and have a vacation party at my home with my friends, many of them from my church. A couple of gals from church loved the idea so much they offered help decorate my place—and wow they went all out.

The day of the party while getting everything ready, I got a call from the church office saying the pastor asked if I could come in the next morning at 10:00. I said sure and didn't think much about it beyond that—after all, I had a party to host!

The party was a huge success; about 20 people were squeezed in my living room, everyone had a great time and loved the movie I had put together. Even pastor's wife Beverly was there. It was the highpoint of my year that had begun sadly with the death of Grandpa, but now I had a great church with many new friends—I had a new family. I was now surrounded by friends I loved sharing the greatest vacation I had ever had.

Life was great. Everything was settling in. It could only get better—right?

Well, not necessarily.

10

THE COLLAPSE

"You will not be handed over to those whom you fear. I will certainly save you. You will not fall victim to violence. You will escape with your life because you trust in me. I, the Lord, affirm it!"

Jeremiah 39:17b-18 (NET)

GOD DOESN'T MAKE MISTAKES: I don't want to call that the Christian's "lazy" response when they are dealing with someone who is transgender, I suppose it's more of an uninformed response (and yes maybe a statement of denial that someone could possibly be truly transgender). Everyone likes things when they are black or white, yes or no, and yes—male or female with the corresponding man or woman to match. Some people say it's "common sense." But "common sense" doesn't explain a lot in this world. God made me the way He made me. Am I perfectly made? Nope. But I am wonderfully made. So many people are born with birth defects of varying degrees, some babies die moments after birth, some die before ever being born—did

God make a mistake? My cousin and several friends have Multiple Sclerosis—did God make a mistake? A friend has a daughter that was born nearly deaf and I saw someone on television who was born deaf—did God make a mistake? My friend with MS LOOKS normal, you don't see any external symptoms, yet she at times has terrible pain. I can't SEE the pain—I simply take her word for it. I can't measure her pain—if she says it hurts a little then I believe her, if she says she hurts a lot, I believe her, why wouldn't I? Men and women are wired differently, we know who we are, and we go on with life. But there are a few who are born as one gender, and for reasons no one is yet scientifically able to completely answer, the body doesn't match. It's not a physical pain, but it can result in horrible emotional pain from the mind and soul being out of sync with the body. Being transgender isn't the only condition that science has no answers for; there are thousands of conditions (like Parkinson's to name one) that we don't know what causes them, but we know they exist because we see the symptoms. Because the symptoms of someone who is transgender can't be seen, the easy (and uninformed assumption) is to look at them on the outside and expect them to act and think accordingly, regardless of who they truly are inside.

It was a cool fall morning when I got in my car for my meeting with Pastor Frank. It was a beautiful day. I was in a really good mood following last night's vacation party, and I was going to meet with the pastor of the church I loved—life was good.

I go through the doors at the church and up the stairs to pastor's office just like I had nine months earlier, and surprise, Beverly was there too. But this time I was a little caught off guard. The big smile I saw on her at that meeting months earlier was replaced with a much milder one. Suddenly I got the sense that this wasn't a meeting to talk about the sound or the website or some other ministry at the church, but a meeting to talk TO me. The vibe was different, the loving and cheerful embrace was replaced with a more somber and reserved. "Hello, Laurie. Won't you come in and sit down?"

Why did I feel like I had been called into the principal's office? What did I do wrong? The feeling in the room totally mystified me.

Pastor then said, "Laurie, we love you" (uh oh, those are never good words when you're the invitee to a meeting—those words sound like I'm at some kind of intervention). He continued, "When we first sat down months ago, you remember I had seen a different path for you than the one you've chosen."

I nodded and said, "Yes, but that wasn't something I was going to be able to do. I told you that."

Pastor continued, "We feel that even though you've already had the surgery, that you technically are still male. You were born with a male body and you still have that DNA, and the fact that you've had surgery doesn't change that."

I'm sitting in my chair in stunned silence, wondering, "Where is all this going?" What is he trying to say? What does he expect me to say?

"We feel since you were born male, it's not appropriate that you use the women's restroom."

My mind is beginning to spin, and my shocked and snarky attitude began to well up inside. Was I supposed to use the men's room? "Oh, pardon me boys, don't pay any attention to me. I've seen it all before, it's just been several years that's all. Excuse me while I lift my skirt and sit on the toilet." I didn't say those words because my body was paralyzed. I finally got out something profound like "Um…" followed by a confused look. "So exactly what am I supposed to do? You don't expect me to use the men's room?"

He said "No, downstairs there is a staff restroom. We'll give you a key, and when you need to use it, you can."

Stunned is the only way I can describe what I felt. All these months, the thank yous I was given, the responsibilities I was given, the trust that was shown me, the LOVE that was shown me—all of it now didn't make any sense with what I was hearing. But this was my church, I loved this church. I loved my pastor. This place had become my family. I was too dazed to have much to say beyond a reluctant "okay."

Then, he said something that in my stunned state didn't register at that moment. "We're on a collision course here." If he thought that was true then why say it, and why prolong the inevitable "collision"? Did he think I'd even consider actually "changing"?

I just nodded and left.

My mind was buzzing on my way home. If this was what they needed to ensure peace and tranquility at the church, I guess I could go along with it. I wasn't thrilled with it, but I wasn't going to leave the church I love over a stupid bathroom issue. I was still being fed spiritually, I was serving, and I was (I thought) appreciated. What's a little bathroom thing? I can do this.

At least I THOUGHT I could do it. Until about three weeks later I get called in for another "meeting." I didn't have any false optimism about this meeting. This time Beverly wasn't there. It was Pastor John, the men's pastor. I asked if Pastor Frank was going to be here and he said no, that it would just be the two of us. This was a strange twist, but I rolled with it as best I could.

Now, I didn't expect him to say, "You know what, we made a mistake and we're sorry." This meeting was more like, "We're not feeling that there's a change in how you feel, so we need you to know that you can no longer be a part of the women's ministry. And also, we strongly feel that it is inappropriate for you to spend time alone with Darla since it is our opinion that you are still male. If you would like to study the Bible with Jeff (Darla's husband) that would be ok."

If my head could have rotated a full 360 degrees, I'm sure it would have. I then was given the classic phrase that uninformed Christians (and yes, including pastors) say when they don't have anything better to justify their discomfort… "God doesn't make mistakes."

Pastor John continued that my action by continuing to live as a woman (even though my surgery was seven years ago) constitutes sin, whether I thought so or not. Their position was that I was born male, and that's how God intended it. Period—end of discussion. I was rather upset when I left. I was so confused, not about myself but about my church. I didn't know what to do. These were people I not only loved but respected. My pastors were telling me that I was sinning, and continuing as Laurie was to do so in willing disobedience to God. Was my life a sin? Anything I "thought" I heard from God was wrong? Anything I thought about me being a woman inside was wrong? To them, it was black and white—or if you prefer male and female. And to them, I needed to change back.

I went home and immediately called Lin to schedule an appointment as soon as possible. She slotted me in for a couple of days later—normally impossible with her, but she didn't want to go very long with this hanging over me—I wasn't in good shape. At the same time, I called in sick to work. I was so upset I barely slept that night. The next day I cried a lot.

I asked God, "What am I supposed to do?" From the time He spoke to me on the freeway coming home from my first appointment with Lin, I had never, ever doubted for a moment that this wasn't my path. That for better or worse, this was how He made me, this was His will for me and that He had a plan for me—Jeremiah 29:11 was my life verse: "For I know the plans I have for you," declares the LORD, "plans to prosper you and not to harm you, plans to give you hope and a future." I have clung to that verse, and now everything was being turned upside-down. The two most important things to me, my relationship with God and my relationship with my church seemed to be opposed to each other, and I couldn't process it nor have it make any sense. I still didn't doubt my decision, nor that I had heard from the Lord years ago, but my pastor hears from the Lord too—I didn't know how to process it all.

I drove down to the city for my appointment with Lin (another sick day). I couldn't think. I couldn't work. I didn't know what was happening. I was a hot mess!

I cried a lot during our session. I couldn't help it. Lin recognized the signs of depression—I was clueless. She asked if I could take a medical leave of absence, I didn't know because I had never taken one before in my life. She told me to check into it and wanted to meet with me a few days later because she saw what a mess I was.

I couldn't concentrate worth beans. If I had tried to keep on working and "fake it," I probably would have been fired. So I logged onto the company website and found the information about a medical leave. I filled out the paperwork and took it with me to my next appointment with Lin.

She not only filled out her part of the paperwork, she then explained to me about depression in light of what had happened and why my symptoms were classic and what I needed to do. The first thing was to get me back on my feet and functional, so I had to find a psychiatrist in Sacramento who could prescribe anti-depressants. Now with my muddy brain, I was supposed to find a doctor who could prescribe whatever medication I needed to take? I went through my insurance company's list of doctors in the area to find one, preferably a woman, and fortunately, it wasn't too hard.

With the paperwork filled out and approved, I was now officially on a medical leave of absence at work. Then I went to see the psychiatrist, and I learned that there are lots of different anti-depressants, that they act on certain chemicals in the brain, but they act differently on different chemicals in different people, so it was pretty much a hit or miss guess to see what would work for me. That's just great! I'm a mess and we're playing roulette, hoping that maybe we'll land on red, or maybe black. With my luck, I'd miss them both.

So now I'm starting to take anti-depressants. How did I get to the point that I need anti-depressants? Even when I was diagnosed with depression nine years ago because I wanted to kill myself I didn't take anti-depressants (oh yeah, that's because God stepped in and became an instant anti-depressant). But now I'm being torn between my God and my church. So my doctor takes a guess, prescribes two different medications, and off I go to live happily ever after with my recommended pharmaceuticals.

So another couple of weeks go by, I'm being a good girl and taking my medications (I'm not sure they're working, but I was told it could take a month or two), and then Pastor John calls. The men's ministry was having an event, and they needed me to run sound for it. Regardless of the current state of strife between church leadership and myself, I've always been about serving and just figured if they needed someone, I was their best sound person, so of course I'd help.

I get to the event, and everything is already set up for me—sweet! It was a very simple setup, just one microphone for the speaker. Why did they need me? Anyone could run this setup—volume up and volume down. I could have shown a chimpanzee how to do this in two minutes.

This event for the men at the church was addressing the issue of porn in men's lives and speaking very graphically about it. It was really uncomfortable for me to have to sit there and listen to what, yes, men need to hear in their pursuit of living a godly, manly life that honors the Lord. They could have easily had a guy run sound for this event, knowing that it wouldn't be appropriate for a woman to listen to, but apparently they specifically wanted me to be there—maybe thinking being in a room full of testosterone would do some magic voodoo that I guess they didn't trust God to do on His own. Maybe they thought that I would suddenly wake up right there in the room, stand up and shout, "My brothers—I'm back!!!" In reality, it was extremely thoughtless and insensitive of them to put me there in that room on purpose.

Getting through that morning event was the most unsettling thing I've ever done. When it was all over, I realized the bigger picture of their intent, but what was done was done—I couldn't "un-hear" what I heard. I just had to forgive them because "they know not what they do," to quote wisdom beyond anything here on Earth.

Even though I was no longer participating in the women's ministry, I don't think even the leader was aware, as she asked me to help her burn a song from a commercial CD she owned onto a blank CD for a class she was going to teach. She didn't want to mess up playing the wrong song so putting one song on the disc made it foolproof. She was so happy that I could do that little thing for her and help her with her ministry. I felt affirmed at that moment—that I was still able to serve God, even at Awaken and even amongst the turmoil going on in my life.

The week of Thanksgiving was here. I sent a message to Pastor John that I'd like to meet with him and Pastor Frank. I wanted to know the bottom line of where we stand. I'm an emotional mess, I can't work, and I want to know the bottom-line stance of my church in all this, as in "no more meetings after this." We agree on a time, the day before Thanksgiving.

I show up and they both are there. It didn't take long for me to realize that this was basically a "so here we are again" meeting. They weren't going to budge from their position and I certainly couldn't. Changing my position would result in my death—I knew this. "Been there" and came really close to "doing that," and I knew that wasn't of God. Not that I necessarily intended this to be some kind of showdown, but I did want to see if there were any way they would be okay with me as Laurie, or if that was completely incompatible with what they thought.

It turned out to be a continuation of my previous meeting with Pastor John. Only this time they raised the bar higher. First, I could no longer serve on the sound team because I wasn't "obedient" to those God had placed over me, but they went on. I could no longer be considered a member of the church if I didn't "change back." Because they wanted to "help" me, they were now willing to pay for whatever services I needed to do so—as if it were a financial issue for me. And finally, they even offered to pay to send me to a "place" out of state that helped "people like me."

I went from amazed and stunned to OMG-get-me-out-of-here-before-they-kidnap-me, not that I thought they really would—but I needed to get out of there. And that's just what I did. I got up and literally ran out of there down the stairs and straight to my car across the street.

Pastor John followed me. I headed to my car, opened it quickly, got in, closed the door, and locked it. As I started my car, he caught up with me, and with his hand pressed on my driver side window said, "Laurie, wait!" I was in tears at this point. I was in disbelief. I was in fear for my life. Not only did they want me to change back, but they also wanted me to go to some place to "fix" me. I couldn't get out of there fast enough. They wanted me to become what nearly killed me years earlier. Nothing I thought about nor cared about this church mattered at this moment anymore, because whether they knew it or not, what they wanted would kill me. I drove off leaving Pastor John standing there in the parking lot as he watched me drive away.

I felt like I had been a person totally in communion with God, perched high on a cliff with arms outstretched, eyes closed, praising God for His majesty, thanking Him for His grace and love—and out of nowhere a 500-ton freight train at 100 miles an hour appears unseen from the side and smashes into me. That's my best description of how I felt about what happened to me at Awaken.

This was my real introduction to depression. This took me from the edge of the well to the very bottom of the well. I drove away from that church and completely cut myself off from it because as much as I loved it, it was now toxic to me—it would kill me.

I was still on medical leave with my company, but the next day was different. I didn't want to get out of bed. I curled up on my side with the covers pulled tight over my shoulder. I slept until I couldn't sleep any longer, and then I got hungry. So here I am, sad, unavoidably awake and hungry. I dragged myself to the kitchen and fixed myself some breakfast, and since I wasn't sleepy but didn't want to do anything, I laid down on my sofa and watched one of the many, many movies I had on tape. When that movie ended, I put in another. Then another. Then another. Next thing I knew it was late and I was getting sleepy, so I was off to bed.

The next day—the same routine and in no time, this was my pattern. Get out of bed. Then eat something, then lay down on the sofa, watch movies all day so I didn't have to think about the pain in my life until I was tired enough at night that I went back to bed. Next day—repeat.

I was depressed. I couldn't think, I was always tired, and I didn't see any bright lights in my future. People who were my friends at the church now felt like they had to go along with the pastor regarding me, and I was left out in the cold—no phone calls, no "we miss you," no "please come back." Just silence. Not a very happy holiday season at all that year.

I was now officially at the end of my medical leave of absence at work. Once I realized this was a pattern with no end in sight, I went about getting an extension. I was frankly bewildered by all this. Grandpa was gone, my church and church family were gone. I was alone, and that's how I spent my days—alone.

I did have one friend through all this, a friend who was always there, a friend who never questioned my motives or my need to take advantage of them. A friend that no matter what I asked, the answer was always "yes." And that friend was food. Ah, food! If it wasn't something yummy for breakfast, I can assure you it was something yummy for lunch or dinner. Not necessarily nutritious, but yummy. Bacon is a guaranteed winner. At dinner you can't go wrong with Mexican or Italian. Nothing fancy—maybe a couple of burritos, a huge plate of nachos or a pizza (not a slice or two, a whole pizza). Pretty much your ultimate high-carb, high-fat, high-calorie diet. And here's a surprise—I gained weight. And not just a little weight—a LOT of weight.

When you're depressed, do you care about gaining weight? No! When you're depressed, you pretty much don't care about anything. I thought the hurt would never end. I didn't see any future for me. I laid there on my sofa each day just wishing somehow I could die—that the day would end and after going to sleep I wouldn't wake up because there was nothing for me, no future worth holding out for. Neither God nor man had any use or purpose for me. My life no longer had any meaning. I simply existed from day to day, nothing more.

But no matter what, God never abandons us. I had a tradition with my good friend Scott and his wife in southern California of getting together for New Year's, and they invited me down again this year. I figured why not? So, I drove down and spent a few days with them. They knew what had happened and didn't try to say, "Oh, it'll all be ok" or "Don't worry, things will get better—just put on a smile!" They gave me love and the freedom to talk or not talk as I needed.

They had three smallish dogs, and one was just so cute and cuddly that mostly what I did was sit on their sofa and hold this precious little animal in my arms. Giving this cute dog some love somehow made me feel a little better.

I drove back home to Sacramento on New Year's Day. Two days later, my phone rings. It's Scott. The first words out of his mouth are, "Guess what wandered into our yard after you left?"

"I don't know," I said. "What?"

"A sweet little dog who needs a home. She's blonde, weighs about five pounds and nobody is claiming her." He had gone all over his neighborhood asking if anyone knew anything about the owner. He did his due diligence trying to find the owner, but said that frankly, it looked like she had been living on the street for a while. She was pretty scruffy and needed cleaning up, but if I wanted her I could have her.

He sent me a photo of her. Yep, she was pretty scruffy all right (and that was after they cleaned her up a bit), but she was also very cute, and Scott was right—she needed a home.

So, on Saturday, I drove back down to southern California to meet this cute little thing. She was just adorable. A toy poodle mix, white fur with a black nose, black eyes, and a docked tail. She was happy to get human attention, and when she was happy, her little tail would wiggle back and forth about ten times a second, so I named her Wiggles. She slept with me in their guest room that night and the next day, Wiggles and I drove home together. She really was the miracle I needed. She would let me hold her and love her, and she was always so happy. She just unconditionally loved me. She made the days a little easier to get through.

Over the new few weeks, I began to sink low—really low. I had an appointment to see Lin. I had been there so many times I could do the drive from Sacramento to San Francisco with my eyes closed, and considering my mental state at the time, eyes closed wouldn't have been much less safe. I did, however, get to her office. I sat there dazed, nearly catatonic on the plush, soft fabric of the sofa. It felt warm and comforting—it seemed to almost engulf me as if giving me the big hug I needed. All I could do was hold Wiggles (who now went with me everywhere I went) in my arms and unconsciously massage her little head and neck with my fingers through that curly white fur of hers as I stared at the wall.

All I was cognizant of was the physical and emotional numbness of losing the people I loved, and how alone I felt. Lin had known me for ten years, and this was the first time she was genuinely worried about me. There was a deadness in my eyes that greatly concerned her. When she sees that look in people, she worries about thoughts of suicide creeping in. My life had collapsed around me, and I was in such a deep, dark hole that not only didn't I see a way out, I wasn't even looking. My life, my very existence no longer made sense. Just a few months earlier life was the best it had ever been, and now the most important people in my life were gone, and I didn't understand how God had allowed me to get to the point of being this low with no visibility or hope of a future.

A couple of months go by, and perhaps the medication was helping (having Wiggles definitely did), perhaps my therapy sessions with Lin were helping, maybe it was just time passing and I was running out of movies to watch, but I was starting to feel almost human again. I thought I could return to work, so I let my company know and with Lin's permission, I returned to work.

At the same time, I was starting to feel the emptiness of not having a church and church family where I belonged. I so wanted to, but the thought of going to any church paralyzed me. My friend Kim was going to a church not too far away, and the pastor of my little church from three years ago when I had Grandpa with me was now on staff there—so I gave it a try, mainly because Kim would be there.

We showed up a little early. It was a good size church, maybe 1,500 people. The music was nice, the teaching was nice, and overall, I would say it was, well, "nice." Nothing to really fault it, but it didn't shout "Laurie, this is the place for you" either. Awaken had set the bar very high for what I was looking for in a church—except for that whole "you need to change back to a man" thing.

So, the hunt for a church was on once again, and I turned to what is now my old standby—the Internet. I had found one called Shadowridge a few miles farther from home than Awaken, but even in my head, I didn't know how I could make that trip and go in the building on my own. I told this to my psychiatrist (who primarily was only monitoring how I was handling the medications, I did most of my talking with Lin), but she had a brilliant idea—try driving to this church, a practice run if you will. Make the drive to church a day early, drive to it and pull into the parking lot when it's empty, drive around it and then come back home.

I was struck by how great an idea this was. THIS I could do! THIS was brilliant! No risk, no obligation, no pressure, and most importantly, no people. So, on a Saturday (this church didn't have a Saturday service), I did it. There were a few butterflies in my stomach, but I drove to the church and pulled into the parking lot. Piece of cake. I then drove around the parking lot a couple of times. I saw where the two sets of glass double-doors were up the concrete steps, and then I pulled out of the parking lot and headed for home. I can do this! I can do this!

Now all I had to do was actually do it the next morning when it would really count, and at this point, I still wasn't sure I'd be able to pull it off when the time came.

11

THE REBOUND

"I was pushed back and about to fall, but the Lord helped me. The Lord is my strength and my defense; he has become my salvation."
Psalm 118:13-14 (NIV)

GOD'S CHURCH IS NOT GOD: One thing that I've learned, and it's an important learning, is that the Church is not God. While most people would find it easy to agree with that statement, I find in fact that when people get hurt by the Church (be it in their local church or by a larger organization) that many times they feel that God has let them down. I see this frequently within the transgender community. Christians who are transgender want to be a part of Christ's family, have communion with His people, and yet they are rejected by the Church, called sinful, and told they need to change. The result is these people forever walking away from the community they so badly want to be a part of and losing their faith in God. We need to be sure that if our churches say, "all are welcome" and "come as you are" that we mean it. Being transgender is how they are, 'nuff said.

A dreary winter has passed, and it's a beautiful spring Sunday morning, the sun is shining brightly, and the sky is blue. Having made the "dry-run" drive to Shadowridge Church yesterday, today's trip was pretty easy and I'm feeling pretty good. I pull into the parking lot just like I did yesterday, this time there are lots of cars with people coming and going up and down the concrete steps. Some of the people are dressed nice, others are casual—my kind of church, come as you are! As I walked up the steps people coming out would smile or say hello. The double glass doors were propped open and I'm greeted as I walked in. The room was pretty good size and very tall, it looked as though it was designed to also serve as a full-size basketball court, though it had a concrete floor, not wood and no bleachers. In addition to the lights, there were large windows that went all around near the ceiling that brought in lots of natural light, so it was relatively bright inside. I sat toward the back of the middle section. There were probably 300 or so people there at the time as others came in. The worship band had been playing a soft instrumental song as people got situated. The worship leader introduced himself as Bob, welcomed everyone and they started to play.

Here we go again—what kind of church is this? The type and style of worship can tell you a lot about a church. Were they going to bring out the tambourines and run up and down the isles with banners? Would they publicly be speaking in tongues?

It turns out it was a pretty normal and mainstream church. My standard for a great worship experience was, alas—Awaken. This particular Sunday at this particular service, almost no one was raising their hands but for one woman sitting near the front to the music. It was obvious she was into the worship, her hands held high as she slowly swayed back and forth. The message from the pastor was good as well—overall, I enjoyed the service. When it was over, I went to the woman who had been so into her worship experience and introduced myself. I told her that I was visiting, but it was good to see her worshipping as she did. She introduced herself as Wanda and that her husband was the bass player in the band. She had a big smile, and after the service her husband came over and she introduced him to me.

The next week I came back and sat up with Wanda, and we both got into the worship. Don't get me wrong, it's ok to stand and clap along to the music while you sing, and some songs are perfect for that. But when the words get to my heart, I want to close my eyes and raise my hands in worship. It's a different experience than singing along with the words on a screen (or in a hymnal like the Baptist church I grew up in). After a few weeks, I introduced myself to Bob, told him I had experience running sound and could we have lunch to talk more about the church. We got together, and I shared that I had run sound for a few churches, wanted to make Shadowridge home, and did they have a spot for me. He was happy to plug me into the team.

Music became my refuge and security blanket at the church following Awaken. I was extremely cautious about getting too close to people, and being behind the mixing board in the booth was a safe place for me. I didn't have to talk to anyone else and yet I could serve by contributing to the worship experience. Yes, it was avoidance, but it was also a sanctuary.

In no time I became the leader of the sound team (and at that time the ONLY member as the previous person needed to take some extended time off). I noticed one gal named Andrea on the worship team had a good ear from hearing her sing. The church had enough singers so that they would rotate in and out from week to week, and sometimes Andrea had the week off. I motioned to her at the end of worship one Sunday as she was leaving the platform. She came over, and I told her that I thought she had a good ear, and would she like to learn how to run sound. A big grin came over her face and she said "Sure, would love to!" So, on weeks when Andrea wasn't singing, she was back learning the ins and outs (and do's and don'ts) of running sound at church. Her boyfriend was the keyboard player in a band, so I think she was excited to have a better understanding of how it all worked, because she already saw it happen when she would go hear his band play. Over time I enlisted the help of a couple of others to serve on occasion, so we had a "team," but Andrea and I bonded like sisters.

After a few months, a new associate pastor came to the church, her name was Sharon. She was in charge of counseling, anything creative and pretty much everything either the senior pastor or worship pastor (Bob) wasn't doing (other than the children's pastor).

One day, I swung by the church to see Bob about something, and he introduced me to Sharon. I loved talking to her. She was so smart, not in a "know-it-all" kind of way, but in a wise "I've lived life" sort of way. When she spoke, there was a lot of wisdom behind it, there was truth in her words—no fluff. One time we were talking, and she asked me, "So how long have you been going to Shadowridge?"

I told her "Since the spring, not a long time". She seemed a little surprised since I was so involved at the church.

"Oh! Did you attend somewhere before coming to Shadowridge?" she said.

I had gone several months with no one asking me that question. I HATED that question. I didn't want to talk about it, I was still taking anti-depressants to keep me above water, and the only person I wanted to discuss it with was Lin. So, I gave her a vague, ambiguous answer like, "Yeah, another church cross-town, but I was ready for a change."

Sharon wasn't just smart, she was perceptive. She could tell there was a story there that I wasn't telling, but she let it go. She knew if I wanted to talk about it with her I would. Well, truth be told I DID want to tell her. I was still hurting from what had happened at Awaken, was afraid to tell anyone at church about my history, but at the same time, I needed to KNOW that what had happened to me wasn't going to be a story repeated time and time again in my future. The pain of that experience wasn't something I felt could survive again.

I tried telling her on a few occasions, mostly over the phone. I would start some kind of conversation that was pretty much a nothing conversation; she knew there was something I wanted to talk to her about, I chickened out every time. I would call, say hello but never get to it. Finally, one time after a couple of glasses of wine (or liquid courage as it's sometimes known), I called her and started again with the usual nothing conversation, and she said "Laurie, whatever it is, it's okay. You can tell me."

I was now terrified. I thought to myself, "What if she hates me after I tell her?" I said, "I can't—you'll think it's terrible!"

She then said, "Laurie, I think I already know what it is, why don't you just tell me?" At this point, I was crying.

I then blurted out "I wasn't born a girl."

Sharon's response was—"So?" As in no big deal. She wasn't familiar with people who were transgender, but she was of the love first, figure it out later mindset, and that's what she did. It didn't affect my relationship with her, and to her, it CERTAINLY didn't affect my relationship with God. She saw me as one of His children, period, with no qualification necessary at all. No need for "special counseling" at this point, no need to sit down and discuss this in detail, no special "path" for my life, just "so?" THEN, I went into all that happened at Awaken, the pain, the hurt, the depression and she assured me that, "That was then, and you're here now." Sharon was showing nothing more than the simple love of Jesus toward me.

I was pretty much speechless. Okay, I've spilled the beans—NOW what do I do? She didn't wait for me even to ask the question, she said: "Would you like to get together and talk some more?"

"Yes, of course," I said. Being able to talk about what had happened, about my life and all that I was feeling, WITH A PASTOR, was like breathing cool fresh air after being underwater for two minutes. She still didn't fully understand the whole transgender thing, but that wasn't what she focused on. She was focused on me and my relationship with Christ. Obviously, she wanted to be sure I was happy being female and this wasn't perhaps some desperate cry for help, but once that was settled (took maybe one minute at the most), all she cared about was my well-being and how she could help me continue to grow in Christ.

As time passed, I found it hard to connect with people. After what had happened at Awaken, I was afraid to get too close to people. Of course, there was Pastor Sharon, and there was Andrea, and there was one more exception to that, and that was Martha. Martha sang on the worship team and had such an amazing voice. We became good friends; we'd hang out, have lunch together. As I got to be good friends with both Andrea and Martha, it became harder to not talk about my history; it was starting to get strange that I didn't talk about my family or much of anything other than church and work. Finally, I asked them both over to my house for dinner and shared my history with them. I got two embracing yet different reactions.

Andrea was pretty much like, "So? Makes no difference to me—I love you."

Martha was okay with it too, but her response was, "Why are you telling me?" I took her question to mean she wasn't comfortable knowing this about me, but at the same time wasn't going to abandon me as a friend either. I never questioned her as to why she asked that particular question that way, and, it didn't seem to affect our relationship, so I let it go.

Even with three people at church who knew me well and were good friends, I still took comfort in the safety afforded me by sitting in the sound booth. I was uncomfortable in social settings at church, and so I didn't participate much outside of serving during church and going to worship team rehearsals. Being around musicians was a comfortable place to be, because there was always plenty to talk about without having to get into personal details, and if the conversation did go there, I had many avenues with which to change the subject, instruments, sound issues, song choices, etc.

Late in the year, Andrea ran across rough times and needed a place to stay. Since I had an empty room I opened it up to her. It was nice having my "sister" around through the holidays and into the next year. We had this great tradition of recording Alias on Sunday night, and then we would watch it together on Monday night with a big plate of nachos between our recliners (I know, it's a silly thing to remember, but oddly enough, it's one of my favorite memories). Even when her circumstances improved, and Andrea was able to get her own place, she still came over for our Monday night tradition. Her love and friendship during this time did more for me than any anti-depressants. Which now that I've mentioned it, weren't helping very much.

It had been two years since being diagnosed with depression after Awaken, and despite my doctor fiddling with various combinations of anti-depressants, nothing was working that well. I suppose I was "better" in so far as I wasn't curled up in the fetal position waiting for the day to end. But after putting on my smile, pumping myself up and seeming "okay" at both my work and at church, it took a lot of effort, and by the end of each day, I was drained.

I was feeling increasingly restless at my church. I didn't feel like I was growing the way I wanted (of course MY not growing was the fault of my church—not), but I wanted something more like Awaken—but without the pain. My current church wasn't that, and yet I knew I couldn't go to another church like that either. I felt this strong need to move on to something else, to something I didn't know what, but something else. I needed a change. I'm realizing now that after two years at this church, I was making additional friends, but I didn't think it was safe to tell them, and it was easier to leave than face potential rejection (have I mentioned life being transgender is complicated?)

In November, I found another church. It was further away from home (almost to the corporate office where I worked), and quite a bit smaller. Maybe 50 people or so, but small enough that just like the small church I had attended around six years earlier, it was impossible to be a stranger. EVERYONE knows you're a visitor in a church that small, but at the same time because they know, it's easy to make you feel welcomed.

Having gone to churches with thousands of members, I know there is no way for someone to know you're a visitor unless you tell them. You could go to a church like that for years and still have never met the people sitting next to you on a given Sunday morning. There was something about this church I liked. There was a spirit about it; there was a passion about it. The worship wasn't as "polished" as I've experienced in the past; the worship leader (Melissa) was quite good, the overall musicianship of the team was what one might expect from a church of 50 people. But that didn't matter to me, because it was evident they all deeply loved the Lord and it came across—the sincerity, the passion, the love. It came across as a family, gathering together to worship— and something was compelling about that to me.

Over the next year, I helped enhance the level of their technology, purchased a nice wireless headset mic for the pastor, and I was part of the family. At first, it was easy not to mention anything about my past since well, I was new and there was nothing good to come from my speaking up. But as time went on, I continued to be haunted by what happened at Awaken, and slowly getting closer to people here began to cause feelings of stress. How do you tell people you're close to something that in the past had led to the end of relationships? I was beginning to feel like I was playing Russian roulette—I open up to someone and maybe it's okay. I open up to another person and it's okay. I open up to a third and maybe it blows up in my face.

In addition, I was now driving six days a week from my home, the 45 minutes it takes to get to work and now church, and I'm beginning to tire of the commute, so I start to consider moving closer to where most of my life away from home is being spent. This would also get me out of the house I was living in that had memories of Grandpa and also of my time at Awaken—I was beginning to feel the need for a change. I started to look for a new home, but surprise, the closer I got to work and church, the more expensive the homes were. In fact, there was NOTHING there that I could afford on my salary—nothing! Not even older, fixer uppers—zip, zero, nada.

My friend and former boss Anne who briefly lived in Philadelphia had recently moved to Austin, Texas and invited me to visit her. It sounded like fun, and I had never been to Austin, so I took some vacation time at work to visit her. I like to joke that when I saw where we were landing, I thought I was on the wrong flight. Everything I saw was green. I saw lakes. Where was the dust? Where were the tumbleweeds? Where were the cowboys? It was beautiful and much like the Sacramento I had just flown from— the only thing missing were mountains like the Sierras. This wasn't the Texas I was expecting.

I got a tour of the town and a taste of a few of Austin's restaurants. I was struck by the amount of new home construction going on in her area, and I asked her about home prices in Austin compared to California—she started to laugh.

"Much, much cheaper," she said.

"Hmmm," I said. I WAS thinking about moving closer to work, but I was starting to think that MAYBE I could work from Austin if homes were that much cheaper. So, Anne offered to call her real estate agent Catherine. Catherine came over, picked me up and showed me a few places that I might like in my price range. I was amazed by what you could get for your money. So for the rest of my stay, I poked around online looking at homes while visiting with Anne.

When I got back home, I was liking the idea of getting out of Sacramento altogether. I was still feeling the pain from the last few years, and I was beginning to feel smothered by it. When I thought of Austin, all I could see was a fresh start, no bad memories, an opportunity to begin again. Now all I had to do was figure out how to get to Austin and keep my job. Fortunately, with my job, I would walk into one building, sit at my desk and from my computer, log onto a server remotely that was located over in the next building. I could connect to that server remotely from ANYWHERE—if there was wi-fi at the Hard Rock Café in Amsterdam, I could work from there while sitting on the patio drinking tea and watching people pass by.

This required some thought. How do I ask my boss if it's okay to move while still keeping my job AND minimize the chance of the request getting turned down? So, this is the question I asked my boss… "Is there any reason why I CAN'T do my job from Austin?"

Since I could do my job from anywhere (and already had a proven track record of working successfully from home), he couldn't think of a reason why not, so I said, "Okay, I'll put my home on the market." I thought it would take at least a month to sell and maybe I'd be in Austin by the end of the year or early January. Nope—it sold in four hours (another home selling miracle!). I got the call from my real estate agent at noon that we had an offer—FULL PRICE! My first thought was wow, that's great! My second thought was wow, I didn't ask enough for my house! I accepted the offer, and rather than moving at the first of the next year, I had to be out by Thanksgiving.

So, the madness begins. I don't have a place to live in Austin— Anne has a big home with an extra room, so she agreed to let me rent the room from them when I arrived while I look for a home to buy. A place to live—check. I had my furniture and recording studio gear, where was I going to put it all? I had heard about those companies that drop off sealed containers that you load yourself and lock with your own locks. They pick it up, take it to your new city and, if needed, they can store it until you're ready. So, that's exactly what I did. I solicited the help of a few friends, and after packing the boxes, we loaded all my stuff into three of those containers and locked them up. The next day they came with a flatbed truck, loaded them up with a big forklift, and drove off.

My "sister" Andrea agreed to drive out to Texas with me. We put the last of my things in the back of my SUV, made a comfy place for Wiggles to lay down in the back seat, and I said goodbye to my home. As I was pulling out of my driveway for the last time, my eyes started to tear up. I suppose I felt like I had lost, that somehow Sacramento had beat me. This is where my dream became a reality and where the future looked oh so promising, and now all I had was the hope that things would be better in a new state and new town.

I imagine this is how the nation of Israel felt as they left Egypt, led by Moses for the Promised Land. Full of hope yet not knowing what was ahead. What they didn't know, and what I likewise didn't know, was that what was ahead was going to be a long and even painful time spent in the wilderness.

12

FACE DOWN IN THE ARENA

"My soul thirsts for God, for the living God. When can I go and meet with God? My tears have been my food day and night, while people say to me all day long, "Where is your God?" These things I remember as I pour out my soul: how I used to go to the house of God under the protection of the Mighty One with shouts of joy and praise among the festive throng."

Psalm 42:2-4 (NIV)

BEATEN, BATTERED, AND BLOODIED: In Brené Brown's book, *Rising Strong*, she refers to a speech given in Paris by Theodore Roosevelt in 1910. Part of the speech is as follows: "It is not the critic who counts; not the man who points out how the strong man stumbles, or where the doer of deeds could have done them better. The credit belongs to the man who is actually in the arena, whose face is marred by dust and sweat and blood…" Brené talks about being in the arena, doing life and at times—getting your butt kicked. It's not in the cheap seats that we learn to be stronger; it's being in the middle of it all, getting knocked down time and time again, and getting back up time and time again. The Rocky movies are a good example of this. Rocky kept getting knocked down and yet he kept getting back up. His opponents would just shake their head in disbelief that he would keep coming back for more punishment. But at the end (spoiler alert you millennials), Rocky, badly beaten, bruised, and bloodied, comes out victorious. Life will try to knock us down time and time again, and that son of a bitch Satan will tell us to "Stay down, stay down—don't get up." But it's when we keep getting up that we get that much closer to being victorious, bruises and all over the stuff in life that's hard.

The drive to Austin was so much better since I had Andrea with me to share the driving. We were going to drive to her parents' home in Flagstaff to share Thanksgiving with them. To get there from Sacramento, we crossed the Hoover Dam. We took the opportunity to toss a 50-cent piece from the car over the dam for good luck, like Selma Hayek in the movie "Fools Rush In." Her character did it for good luck (and we both loved that movie) so why not? Getting to Flagstaff took twelve hours. We visited briefly with her family then I headed to bed.

The next day was Thanksgiving, she had family members there, and it was fun. Flagstaff, if you've never been there, is well up in the mountains of northern Arizona (close to 7,000 feet), and as it had snowed earlier in the week, there was still snow on the ground, and the air was crisp. I don't think Wiggles liked the snow very much; she pranced over it more than walked on it— pretty funny. The dinner with Andrea's family was wonderful, but we had a 15-hour drive ahead of us the next day to get to Austin, so I went to bed early.

We left early the next morning; the goal was to get to Austin and Anne's home by 9:00 PM. The timezone change stole an hour from us but we were determined, and after driving past a lot of nowhere, we finally pulled into Austin. Andrea stayed for a few days, so we could go around town, visit the capitol building, do touristy stuff.

One thing we did was visit a church on Sunday. A well-known Christian artist was the worship leader there, and we were excited to see what it would be like. We got there early, and though we were able to enter the building, the worship center was closed off—I imagine they were finishing up with rehearsal or something. So, we milled around with other people waiting to be allowed into the sanctuary, and to the surprise of both of us, no one seemed friendly. Not a lot of smiling, no "hi, how are you," a hello from Andrea or myself was typically greeted with a nod and slight smile, maybe a "hi." Even once we were inside, during the service it felt "cold." After the service on our way to lunch we talked about how surprising it was that the church didn't seem friendlier—I mean we made a special effort to come to THIS church because of the great songs that had come from the worship leader. Apparently, that heart didn't get transferred to those attending the church—at least not this Sunday.

After a few days of fun seeing the town, I took Andrea to the airport, thanked her for tagging along all the way to Austin, gave her a big hug, and sent her home with a new pair of cowboy boots I bought her.

I began to tear up again as I drove out of the airport, it was official—I was in Austin, alone. I stayed with Anne and her family for a few weeks while finding a house. My real estate agent Catherine and I went all over town, from the south part of Austin, to the cities north and northwest. My company had a couple of offices in town, but mostly I worked from home, so proximity to the office wasn't a big concern. I didn't actively look for a church during this time, since I didn't know what part of town I would land in, I knew that the church Andrea and I had visited was no longer on the list.

After seeing most of Austin with Catherine and being torn between two homes. My decision was made easy when Catherine called to say if I wanted the first home we looked at, I had to race to get there because someone else was on their way to leave a deposit check. Now, I don't know if the agent in the model home ever called that other person to tell them that there was someone else interested and it was going to the first person with a check—but when I pulled up to the model, I left Wiggles in the car with the engine running and ran inside with my purse and checkbook.

Yay! I got there first and got the home. This home was already built and ready to move into—all I had to do was close. To get a tax advantage that year, I had to close in a week. Since it was late Friday when I signed the papers, the title company wasn't going to see anything until Monday morning—and the coming Friday was New Year's Eve. Monday morning I actually got a phone call from the title company—the gal thanked me because she thought she wasn't going to have anything to do that week, but now she had nothing to do but work feverishly on getting my sale closed, loan and all, by the end of the week. Amazingly, she did it, and on December 31, I sat in the title company office and signed the papers to close on my new home.

Getting settled in took a while, but Wiggles was happy as long as Mom was with her. But now it was time to look for a church.

I knew very well what kind of church I wanted, one where the Spirit of the Lord was present, one with good music, friendly people and great teaching (in other words—I wanted everything). After poking around online, I found some I wanted to check out. The first one I went to was pretty good. I liked it and decided to go back. The next week I talked with the guy who was running sound. I mentioned that I had run sound at previous churches and asked if down the road they would need some help.

Surprisingly he said, "We're pretty good here, don't need anyone right now."

What? Don't NEED anyone? I wasn't applying for a job, I was offering to serve! I've been to tiny churches and huge churches and have NEVER heard of a church turning down someone wanting to serve. Also, though folks around me seemed friendly my first week there, this week not as much. I took this as a sign and decided to keep looking for a church.

There was another church closer to home, it was non-denominational and took its name from its location—why not? Sunday morning comes, I'm looking forward to visiting another church and out I go. It was in a small center with other businesses around it, a restaurant, offices, etc. Fortunately, since it was Sunday, there was enough parking—I don't think they could have their whole church meet there during a weekday with all the businesses open.

Walking into the building it clearly wasn't designed to be a church; the ceiling was probably ten feet high, which when you fill a room with seats and try to have a platform feels a little closed in (especially if the pastor is over six feet tall and standing on the platform). I'm guessing it probably sat 300 people. With the low ceiling and perhaps the way it was configured, it seemed a little dark where I was sitting; not a big deal but it was a little hard to read out of my Bible.

The worship was very good and spirit led. There were lots of hands in the air praising and worshipping God, and the musicians were good. The pastor gave a great message. After the service I spoke with a couple of people who were smiling and friendly, welcoming me to Texas. One introduced me to the pastor who likewise warmly welcomed me. I must say I was rather impressed with the service, the pastor, the worship, and the members. As I walked out and got back into my car, I started thinking that maybe this was going to be my new church. And then it happened…

Let me first say, Austin doesn't really care a whole lot WHERE you turn left when driving. You can pretty much do it anywhere you like. And to accommodate the whims of the drivers of my new city, on anything other than a residential street, you will find what in California is called a "suicide lane." You might have two lanes of traffic going one direction and two lanes of traffic going the opposite direction. Separating them is a single lane that ANYONE can enter from ANY direction for the purpose of turning left or making a U-turn at ANY time! When two cars traveling in opposite directions each want to turn left in approximately the same part of the road, things can get exciting.

So, church is over, and I'm basking in the glow that I really, really liked this church. I get in my car, back out of the parking stall and drive toward the street where I'll need to turn left. It is a busy street even on a Sunday and the only way home. Traffic from my left had cleared enough that I could pull into the suicide lane, so I did. Suddenly, I was hit. Not by a car but by an immediate sense of anxiety. My heart started to beat fast, my breathing was shallow, and I was scared to death—and I started to cry. I sat there in the middle of the road—I was having a panic attack (though I didn't know that that is what it was at the time). Realizing that I couldn't just sit there in that center lane, I pulled into traffic and drove home—crying all the way.

As soon as I got home, I let Wiggles go out to do her business in the yard. When she came back in, I picked her up and took her to bed with me where I curled up and laid there. I didn't know what was going on with me, but I was a wreck. I cried until I couldn't cry anymore. I spent the whole afternoon in bed curled up. I turned the TV on, but it was nothing more than noise in the background to break the silence that otherwise left me alone with myself.

The next day, more of the same. After tossing and turning all night, I was overwhelmed with a sense of despair, and I didn't know why—all I knew is that I hurt. Not physically, but emotionally—I HURT. It was a sense of agony, of hopelessness, it felt as if someone close had died. I took a sick day at work. I called Lin to make an appointment; she was able to squeeze me in the next day.

Now that I was in Austin we would talk over the phone. She couldn't see the depression in my face (Skype was so new no one knew about it yet) but she heard it in my voice, and after talking about the last several weeks she put her finger on it immediately and introduced me to a term I had heard of but didn't fully understand... PTSD, post-traumatic stress disorder. The last church that I had visited, the one I liked—when I described it to her she said, "It sounds a little like Awaken." And bingo—that was it! This was the kind of church I wanted—unfortunately it was so much like Awaken that it presented a dilemma I didn't know how to resolve. How do I find a church that I can love that won't be like the church that crushed me?

At this point, I gave up—not on God, not on my Lord and Savior, but on church, and to a degree—Christians. It would have been easier emotionally if I had been able to give up on God because then it wouldn't have bothered me not going to church—but it did. It did so much that I went back into a deep depression. I had to find a new psychiatrist because it was necessary to go back on anti-depressants with the hope that they would at least keep my head above water. I suppose they did, but Sunday after Sunday would come and go, and each week I felt bad, and I felt guilty. Bad because church is where I wanted to be, and guilty because I know that's where God would want me to be, rather than in my bed. In looking back, I suppose it fed the depression, which made me feel bad, which fed the depression—you get how that works.

Depression made it hard to work, what made it bearable is that I was able to work from home. I didn't have the added pressure of being in a cubicle surrounded by people in the event I should suddenly and out of nowhere start to cry. But this became my new normal. Staff meetings were always over the phone—I never needed to go into the office.

After a few years, stress at work began to increase. First, the vice-president of our division decided that working from home was not good for the company. Well, guess what? NO ONE from my group worked in Austin. No one in the group was even in the state of Texas. A few were in the US, and others were scattered in Asia and Europe. So, I went into the office where I was supposed to be, sat down at my desk, and decided that this was a tremendous waste of time. The floor where I sat could house a couple hundred people, and there were maybe five of us, all with different jobs in different divisions—total. They didn't know me, I didn't know them, so I continued to work from home after that.

More pressure came in the way of pending cutbacks at the company—it was announced that no one in the company was guaranteed a position. We had been through this a few years prior, and it was not fun. The cutbacks weren't necessarily performance-based, they were looking at what jobs were no longer necessary, and no one was asking us what we thought. This additional strain on top of my clinging to maintain a functional life was enough to necessitate another medical leave of absence—I wasn't able to function well enough, and I certainly didn't want to give them a reason to let me go. So, another three months on medical leave. This time since I wasn't working the days all melded together. Sunday used to be a non-working day, an opportunity to go to church, and if I didn't go I would feel bad. But now Sunday was becoming just another day—and on the surface, it didn't bother me much to NOT go to church on Sundays—but deep down I was still depressed and wished I could go to church.

Shortly after returning to work, the company wanted me to go to Costa Rica for a couple of weeks to train some employees down there on a new system. Going to Costa Rica was not something I was ready to handle. I was just now getting back to work, still dealing with depression but functional. I didn't want to leave home. Going to Costa Rica was more than I would be able to handle. I told them I wouldn't be able to go. In looking back, I'm not even sure what I told them as the reason WHY I couldn't go, but the additional pressure wasn't helping my state of depression.

For years, I had been helping people with their computers, I was always a bit geeky and loved technology. My first computer was a Commodore 64 when I was married. One day as I was working on my best friend Janine's computer she asked me, "Have you ever considered doing this as a business?"

"What? People would PAY me to do this?" I said.

"Oh, you better believe it," Janine said. She had recently started her own interior design business and was part of a networking group where individuals meet and share referrals to help grow their businesses. She knew of a group on the other side of town with a computer tech and arranged for us to sit down and talk about his business, what he charges, etc. We met for lunch and talked about his business. I was shocked at how much (per hour) people pay for computer support. And you don't even need a degree in computer science or anything—heck I was a music major! You need only two things, a skill at it and being good with people—and I was both.

So, in the spring of 2008, I launched my own business offering computer support to individuals and small businesses in town. I didn't want nor could afford the overhead of a storefront, and I also enjoy driving, so I structured my business with an "I come to you" philosophy.

I joined the networking group that Janine was in, and I was off! Since I was starting out with a client base of ZERO, I thought it premature to leave my regular job—I would need some time to build the business. I thought it might be another nine months before I would leave the company I'd been with for thirteen years. As it turned out, things ramped up pretty quick, and five months later it was all I could do to juggle both, so I gave my two weeks' notice to my employer. As my last day at the company arrived, I bid farewell and good luck to my coworkers. I was now officially "self-unemployed" as I liked to put it, since I was no longer an employee.

Business continued to grow, and one of my new clients was this guy named David who worked out of his home. David was a Christian, funny, hated having to deal with technology, and over time his family and I became close. David is one of those people who is a stranger to no one. He had his struggles and for some reason felt safe sharing them with me, and I would listen. It was easy to be his friend—he was like the brother I didn't have.

One evening, he sent me a message simply saying that he could tell I was holding something in and he wanted to be my friend. I told him he didn't want to be my friend—if he knew me better he wouldn't want to be. David wasn't having any of that. If he decides you're his friend, you're his friend and he is yours. I was crying because Janine was the only person I had told in the last few years, and though Janine was totally fine, I didn't know how David would react. I never know how men are going to react, particularly Christian men—they seem to find it harder to process, perhaps because they see it as "jumping ship to join the other team" or something—a sense of betrayal to the brotherhood.

So, I'm telling David about my life and he stops me and says, "Here's the deal—I love you. I don't care about all that, we're all messed up in some way—my family and I love you." And that's how I got adopted into my "second" family.

About a year later, my poor little dog Wiggles began having seizures. She was thirteen years old, and there would be moments when she would seem to freeze, and then after a couple of minutes she would come back out of it and seem to be fine. But after a couple of months, she began to whimper, and she would do it even when I was cradling her in my arms. She was in pain, but it was internal, she wasn't well, and life was no longer good for her. I was so torn. Wiggles was literally a miracle that had been given to me when I needed her most. I was in deep depression after a horrible rejection, and God provided a little companion who loved me unconditionally. I was everything to her, and she to me. How could I let her go? But she was in so much pain. I realized that keeping her in pain was being selfish, knowing that keeping her was less painful to me than letting her go, but I couldn't let her go on like that and suffer.

I called my vet and arranged to bring her in. I was so broken up over having to do this that I called a friend to meet me there because, well, I needed a friend. When I arrived, I carried her in. She had been to the vet before, and no, she didn't like going there for any reason. She was shaking because she always shakes when we go, but this time I was in so much turmoil myself—second guessing if I was doing the right thing or not. I had to wait a few minutes for the doctor, so I sat in a chair holding her, her curly white fur shaking with the rest of her, as I gently stroked her as if to say soon the pain will be gone my baby-girl.

The doctor came out and sat next to me to ask me if I wanted to be there in the room. He described what it would be like, how she may appear to be in pain, but she wouldn't be. That's all I needed to hear to know that I didn't want to be there—I couldn't. He understood, and I gently handed her to the doctor. He headed for the room, and all I could do is head out the door, my friend had her arm around me as I cried. On the way home, all I could do is cry out loud saying, "I'm sorry Wiggles." By far THIS was the hardest thing I've ever had to do (writing about it hasn't been a piece of cake either based on the empty tissue box sitting next to my keyboard).

Now I'm completely alone. Wiggles was so small I never heard her coming, so I had put a little bell on her collar. Sometimes I would think I heard her bell off in another room, but of course, I didn't. It took a good week or two to get over the grief of having to put Wiggles to sleep, but we all have to move forward. Maybe it's time I should try checking out a church, but I need a SAFE way to do it.

David, his wife, and two daughters, were members of a church nearby. It had been a few years since I had even gone to church, and though I did want to go, I couldn't do it on my own—so I asked David if I could go to church with his family on Easter. He said of course and so that Sunday I met them at their home and followed them in my car. It's a pretty big church, must seat 1,000 or so, and I know they have several services. David loves to talk to people, when we arrived he went off to see someone. David's wife wasn't feeling well, so she wanted to sit near the back and close to the exit, "just in case."

The worship was fine, I wasn't overly inspired by it and maybe it was because I wasn't familiar with the songs, but I guess you might say "I wasn't feeling it." The pastor got up to give his message, and it was all good until maybe two-thirds of the way through when suddenly he took a left turn.

Out of the blue he totally changed the subject—not sure I've ever seen a pastor do this in the middle before, especially in an Easter sermon. He began to talk about how the church needed to embrace those in the gay community and welcome them into the church. Now, he didn't say a word about those who are transgender, he didn't say "LGBT," but everyone pretty much knows what the general public applies to the gay community gets applied to those who are transgender whether that's right or not (usually not).

He spoke of welcoming people who are gay to the church, how the church has made it difficult for them to feel welcome, and I was in awe—this is EXACTLY what should be coming out of more pulpits in more churches. This church was rather conservative, and one that I could easily like and attend, so to hear him say what he did had me sitting there it total amazement.

I'm thinking to myself, "Wow, after all these years and thanks to having friends I love and trust I was able to get up this morning and come to a church where perhaps I can give, where I can serve and where I can stand tall."

Then came the smackdown. The punch in the gut you didn't see coming.

He spoke of how important it was to get them into church so that they could experience the "healing" power of God, how they needed God so that they could get away from homosexuality. Right then and there I felt it all coming back. The pain, the judgment, the rejection. Like I said, if this is how he feels about people who are gay, I have absolutely no reason at all to believe his opinion about my being transgender would be any different. My heart started pounding, and it was getting hard to breathe, my eyes began to water up, and I could feel a full-on panic attack coming. I was thrown back to what had happened all those years ago in Sacramento—I had to get out of there.

I leaned over to David's wife and whispered, "I'm sorry, I have to leave," and with that I got up and got out. I would have got up and left had we been in the front row—but glad I didn't have to. It wasn't an act of protest, it was an act of self-preservation. At the same time, their youngest daughter who was a freshman in high school, also got up and left the room. She is the sweetest thing, a bit Bohemian and very much her own person and I love her to death.

We both stood around outside for a minute visibly upset but didn't say anything; at the time she didn't even know I was transgender. David then came out and gave each of us a hug, he apologized to me saying he had no idea that the pastor was going to talk about that.

I said something like, "Whatever—I need to go." He knew I wasn't blaming him, but he also knew I was hurting and couldn't stick around to go out to lunch with them as we had planned.

174

Apparently, there were many people at the church surprised by the pastor as well, and from what I hear there were many discussions about it after the service. David called a little later that day; he explained that his daughter had a friend at school who was gay and was bothered by what had been said, and that's why she left the room the same time I did. After all it took for me to ask my friends to let me go to church with them, for that pastor to say those words on that day was all it took. That did it—no more church for me. The fact that I loved my Lord but couldn't trust His people ate at me. It took a lot for me to go to church with my friends for the first time in years, and all it took was this one visit to keep me away from church for a long time.

So, I buried my head and focused on work. No church on Sunday—no problem for me. I was glad I wasn't going. Nothing but bad is waiting for me there, and since people assume I take Sundays off I can sleep in—PERFECT! Except it wasn't. It wasn't perfect because I knew down deep where I wanted to be, I wanted to be in church, I wanted to be with other Christians, I wanted to take part in awesome worship, I wanted to hear God's Word taught. I couldn't even open my Bible, I couldn't watch any Christian show on television, I couldn't listen to Christian music. ALL of it reminded me of pain and suffering. I was such a mess I couldn't ever listen to the prayer at the beginning of a NASCAR race on television, I would fast forward past it every time. EVERYTHING reminded me of church, and when I thought of church, I thought of pain.

Having said that, I NEVER doubted or didn't trust God. There would be times when I would be driving from one client to another, and it would be such a beautiful day I couldn't help but say, "Thank you Lord," thanking Him for the beauty of His creation. It was all I could do, but it was my way of just letting the Lord know that I hadn't gone away, I was still here and that maybe, someday, I'd be around more often.

So, what's the next awesome thing to happen? My best friend, Janine with whom we've cried together and laughed together is moving to Denver. Her husband has a job opportunity with a company there. Just when you think you can't possibly be more alone, your best friend moves out of town. If David's family was my second family, then Janine's family was my third, and she was like a sister. I had spent Christmas with them, babysat her kids, celebrated their birthdays with them, and now poof! Gone.

I'm beginning to develop a pattern here, void in life—try going to church. Since the last one was such a train wreck, I needed something safe. I mean REALLY safe. So, I went online to see if there were churches that were known to be LGBT friendly or "affirming." Surprise, there are sites that will tell you just that. I found one that was further than I would have preferred, a solid 45 minutes across town but what the heck, it can't hurt to visit can it? And it didn't hurt. It was a small church, maybe 30 or 40 people there in a commercial complex. I didn't have high expectations in going, pretty much as long as it wasn't about being gay. I figure if we can get through a service without a mention of being gay, just focus on the Lord, then we're on the right track.

But, apparently, we couldn't do that one simple thing. I appreciated the worship, it seemed genuine and heartfelt. But we couldn't get through the message without mentioning being gay a couple of times. I don't want to go to a church were gayness is celebrated anymore than transgenderness (I believe I may have just invented a new word) is celebrated. Jesus should be celebrated, we should celebrate those who serve and those who get baptized—certainly. We celebrate who we are in Christ; I don't want to go to a church where being gay is celebrated. I don't want to go to a church where being transgender is celebrated. I want to go to a church where Jesus is celebrated, worshipping the Father and yes, where ALL are welcomed and loved—period. You'd think that would be easy, but that word ALL keeps getting in the way. Even for those churches that if you ask if everyone is welcome that would say "yes, of course" I'm finding it's more like "well, yes… sorta."

I couldn't even find a sense of belonging in an LGBT affirming church. I was beaten and bruised, bleeding and broken—I have been hit from all sides in the arena of my life. There I was, face down in the dirt. The Church had beat me up, and my family (literally and spiritually) had walked away leaving me for dead. I would try to get up but before I could stand, I would get knocked down again. Why did it have to be so hard to find a community of Christians to be a part of that loves Jesus, loves worship and where all are welcomed unconditionally? If you're not someone who is transgender you're probably thinking to yourself, they're EVERYWHERE. As someone who is transgender I can absolutely say to the contrary, no, they're not.

It's now spring 2015, and I'm about as low as I've ever been. Since I don't have the luxury of taking medical leave (being self-employed), I still force myself to get up and work—I put on my happy face with my clients and my friends, but at home, even on the way home the sadness takes over, the loneliness, the exhaustion. All my energy is used up being the happy and helpful Laurie to others.

In desperation, I send a message to my spiritual mom Sharon telling her how I hurt, how I'm lonely, how not being able to trust Christians saddens me and frankly, how I was pretty much DONE. I wasn't suicidal to the point. I was when I wanted to drive my car into that tree in northern California, but I wasn't too far from that either. What she replied with was the beginning of a turnaround in my life…

Laurie Suzanne Scott

"My darling Laurie,

I wish I had words that would make the anger and hurt go away. We both know that there aren't any. I'm angry for you for all the things you listed. You deserve love, respect, acceptance, compassion, companionship, joy, love, laughter... every good thing comes by the way of the Father's hands. Sadly, those He first chose to love you substituted their prejudice and ignorance for His Love and Wisdom. God loves you just as you are. He knows what you went through. He knows the torture and the torment that riddled your life before you sought to be free from the wrong gender identity. He knows your desires and pursuits were from a pure and good heart. Your family sees perversion, but your FATHER sees perfection.

As unfair as it is that your family let you down, it's time to recognize that what they have to offer is labeled with a Skull and Crossbones on it. It's poison. It will always be poison. No matter how desperate you get, it will still be poison. Unless and until they allow God's heart to fill their own hearts it won't change. They are steeped in an indoctrination that has them convinced that they are sacrificially "hating" their daughter/sister in order to follow Christ. In reality, they all love you. They love the version of you that they think has been destroyed. I bet they'd give anything to have you back—so long as you embodied what they have been taught to believe is "right." Of course, they are dreadfully wrong. God will tell them to their faces on that day. Then they will have to deal with the sorrow and regret for what they've put you through for so long. Meanwhile, your Father in heaven will continue to lift you up if you let Him. You have to look to Him for love, protection, validation, encouragement, provision.... And stop returning to the same bottle of poison you've been drinking out of for years.

As unfair as it is that your church family at Awaken let you down, we know that they did (and probably still do) love you truly. They acted

178

out of fear, ignorance and failed diplomacy. But not malice. I'm sure it was really painful deliberations that led to their hurtful decisions. But please know that their choices weren't about YOU so much as their fear over the reactions of others. I remember how I planned in advance what I would say and do to anyone who insulted or hurt you at Shadow Ridge. But I had the advantage of seeing just how badly the leaders at Awaken had hurt you so I was able to learn a little bit from their mistakes. I'd like to think that I would have done all the right things anyway, but in all honesty, they had already charted the territory and revealed the perils of a wrong turn. I would never want to be guilty of making a stupid decision that caused someone a boatload of pain, but I'm as flawed and fallible as the next gal.

"Father, forgive them, for they don't understand what they're doing."

What happened to our Jesus wasn't right or fair. He certainly didn't deserve it. But He did it for YOU, so that you could have freedom in His name.

I pray freedom over your life. I ask our Father to bring companionship to you. I pray that He would show you what you must do to receive all that He longs to give you. I pray that He would erase the pain. I pray He would replace your anger with forgiveness. I pray He would end your loneliness. I pray you would FEEL His loving presence, His joyful acceptance and healing touch right now. I pray He would give you the wisdom to look forward and not backward. I pray His Holy Spirit would overwhelm you with tears of joy over being set free!!! I ask it all in the name of our precious Savior, Jesus Christ. May all the glory be His! Amen.

I love you sister."

It took several days for me to absorb all that Sharon had said (depression will slow your roll a bit). Did the skies suddenly open up with bright light streaming down? Did the heavens sing? Did I suddenly wake up the next morning and see blue skies with birds chirping and squirrels playing out my window? Nope.

What I did have somehow was hope. The hope that almost had died in me. Her prayer was heard, and God began to move in my life. The flame had been flickering and frankly was about out, but what she wrote gave the flame enough oxygen to begin to burn a little brighter, and that flame began what I called Laurie 2.0.

13

LAURIE 2.0

"He gives strength to those who are tired and more power to those who are weak. Even children become tired and need to rest, and young people trip and fall. But the people who trust the Lord will become strong again. They will rise up as an eagle in the sky; they will run and not need rest; they will walk and not become tired."

Isaiah 40:29-31 (NCV)

YOU HAVE TO GET BACK ON THE HORSE: We all know what that expression means. When something bad happens, when you fail, you don't let it defeat you—instead, you go back and try again. If you don't then you'll spend the rest of your life afraid to try again—I almost was, and I see it in the lives of others who have been hurt by the Church, and not only have they not wanted to go back to church, they don't want anything to do with God. And this breaks my heart. It's so apparent how Satan is able to manipulate Christians to forsake Christ. He does it through other Christians. You call someone a sinner, that they must change or they're not welcome. If you're born transgender, that's not something you can change because it's just the way you are. Being told the way you are, the way you know God made you is a sin has left a wake of people off to the side while the Church marches on. And you know what—many if not most are unable to get back on the horse or even want to. That son of a bitch Satan will try to turn that pain into festering anger. As a Church, we should be trying to help people who need it get back on the horse, feel welcome to join us. The only person Jesus ever turned away was Satan. If you feel the need to fix someone, start with the mirror. If someone does need your help "fixing" their life, they'll ask.

As summer begins something within me is telling me it's time for a change—a big change. I don't mean moving to another town and starting all over again. I mean a change that begins with me—I called it Laurie 2.0. Part one of Laurie 2.0: I'm pretty tall, when I had my surgery all those years ago I weighed 185 pounds (I refer to that as my "fighting weight," which for my height was about right). Throughout all those years of depression, I had ONE friend who was always there, always ready to help me anytime I needed it with an unlimited amount of comfort. And that friend was food.

I called upon that friend rather frequently over the years and it shows (wow does it show!). Another effect of depression is that you don't care—you don't care much about anything. So, I gained almost two hundred pounds over the years—and I didn't care. Well, if I'm going to make a change, this is an obvious place to start, and one that with enough determination, I can do myself.

My food of choice when depressed is pretty much anything with lots of carbs (to be honest I must say, that I pretty much love carbs even when I'm not depressed). Seldom would my foods of choice qualify as "health food." So, if I could cut out most of the carbs in my diet, I would lose weight just from the sheer fact I would be eating less.

Part two of Laurie 2.0 is to start wearing makeup again and look a little nicer when I go out. For years I wouldn't bother with makeup (again—I just didn't care,) I would go out plain-Jane style, lipstick was the only thing I wore.

Part three of Laurie 2.0 is to change the way I wear my hair. For years I would wear my hair in a ponytail—ten seconds in the morning and I was done. During this time, I decided to let my bangs grow out and start wearing my hair down more often.

Finally, part 4, after eleven years in the "wilderness" here in Austin, I decide it's time to find a church (yes, one more time). But it's different this time. This time I feel more motivated and for some reason, I'm ready to put more emotional energy and effort into it this time to fight against my depression. I'm now treating my life as a project (hence the Laurie 2.0 description).

So, after scouring the web for churches in my area, visiting their websites, watching any videos they may have, I narrowed it down to two churches. One was only fifteen minutes away, and as it happens, I've been driving past it for years and didn't even know it was there (it's tucked back off the highway). The other was also appealing, but a good 40 minutes away and I'm thinking that with a church closer to home, there will be folks that live in my area and it will be easier to connect with people. All things being equal, I would want a church closer to home, so that's the one I decided to visit first—Austin Transformation Church.

In order to even get myself there, I followed the same advice I was given following the disaster in Sacramento; I would drive to the church and pull into the parking lot the day before. Simple, easy, with no one there—theoretically there is no threat, right? But this is when theory and reality collided.

It's the Saturday before Labor Day, time for my "dry run." As I drove down the highway getting closer to the church, I could feel the nerves kicking in. By the time I pulled into the church entrance my hands were sweating on the steering wheel, and my heart was pounding. As I drove into the parking lot I was so nervous; I was really feeling the strain—I had to take deep breaths just to control it and this was in an empty parking lot! Fortunately, I survived the moment and I headed out, back to the safety and comfort of home.

The next morning my alarm wakes me up. I actually slept much better than I expected. As I realize this is the big morning, I start to feel the nerves churning in my stomach, kind of like soup simmering on the stove—not boiling out of control, just a slow, steady and gentle rumble of anxiety. It's time to leave, and I grab my Bible as I head out the door. I'd like to say I was feeling spiritual and looking forward to cracking open the Bible during the service, but in truth, it was something for me to hold onto and the fabric cover on it would keep my clammy hands dry. And with that, I'm off to church.

Wow, am I scared! It has been a long time since I've been to church, and the few churches I've been to the last eleven years have not been terribly successful experiences. To avoid having to talk to anyone, I purposely arrive five minutes late for the service. I pull into the parking lot just as I did the day before and park my car. I follow other people toward the building figuring they know where they are headed. My heart is pounding. A greeter is at the door, she smiles and says hello to me, I manage to form a weak smile as I walk through the doors. I can hear the worship music spilling into the lobby as I walk in. With my Bible in hand, I walk into the sanctuary.

Yay! There is a seat at the end of the aisle in the very last row, closest to the exit so I can curl around and if necessary, make a quick escape—perfect! Though everyone is standing, I sit down in my chair for a moment to put down my purse, gather myself together with a deep breath, and then stand back up and take part in the worship.

Austin Transformation Church (ATC for short) is fairly big, with probably 800 seats on the floor, and a mezzanine behind me that probably seats another couple hundred. The worship is extremely good, the professionalism of the musicians, the depth of the lyrics, the quality of the sound—it is even better than I had hoped. Most importantly they aren't going through the motions; this—was—worship. I had missed it so much it's bringing me to the edge of tears. It is so amazing and touches me so deeply I have to try HARD not to break out crying, because if I do, I'll probably melt down and make a scene right here. But at the same time, I'm near panic and SO want to get out and get some air—I feel almost as if the walls of the church are closing in on me. I hold onto my Bible, squeezing it like a security blanket, and stay put—how else will I know if I want to attend this church if I don't stay to the end to find out? That's why I came in the first place, to see if this church might be a place I can call home!

The pastor's name is Jack, and his message was excellent as well—a great combination of humor and truth. I'm starting to choke up a couple of times because what he says is speaking to me at this moment and I can feel the tears wanting to come. Now, I REALLY want to get out that door, but I sit tight and grip that Bible (if the cover had been made of metal it would have had a dent in it by now). When the service is over, I immediately head out and there are more smiling, happy faces wishing me a good day as I walk out the doors and straight to my car. The open outdoors, the bright sunshine and fresh air are welcome friends and whew, I finally make it to the solace and safety of the interior of my car. On my way home it strikes me that there is NOTHING about this church that I don't like. It meets and exceeds every hope and expectation I have for a church. It's not just a good church, it's exceptional in every way!

As I pull into my driveway and into my garage, I turn off my car and in the quiet serenity, I think to myself "this is the church I want to go to," followed by "oh crap… THIS is the church I want to go to!"

This is first church since moving to Austin that I want to be a part of, but one thing I do know is as sure as there is a God in Heaven, I CAN'T survive another episode like Awaken Fellowship in Sacramento. I definitely don't have it within me to invest myself emotionally into this church and have it go south. I can't live through that again.

I need to communicate with Pastor Jack about my experience at Awaken, how badly I was hurt, and how I truly believe I couldn't live through it again before I commit to being a part of ATC. I spend the afternoon with a knot in my stomach trying to figure out how to do this. How do I explain myself without looking like someone who's unstable or a wacko, but someone who loves Jesus, yet feels beaten down by the Church, fearful of Christians, and afraid that it could all happen again?

One thing I know about myself is, I can't just go to church on Sunday morning and think I've "paid my spiritual dues" for the week. I need to serve. I need to contribute—I've always done so in the past, and I don't see myself changing in that respect. So, I need to communicate with Pastor Jack before moving forward. My emotions are so raw right now, that I don't see how I can sit down and have a conversation with him like I did with Pastor Frank at Awaken. Back then, I already knew some of the people, including Pastor Frank and they knew me a bit. Here I don't know them at all, and they don't know me. If I sit down with him in a room I'm pretty sure I will sit there, cry, and only get a few words out—I'm just too fragile to talk to him in person.

I can only see one way to communicate my thoughts and ensure that it is "for his eyes only." I'm going to have to hand it to him personally. This thought adds to my already nervous existence. But it does have the added benefit of at least he will see me in person when I do, and he will know when he reads it that the woman he saw standing before him at church is the transgender woman spoken of in the letter.

So, my project for the week is to craft together a letter that as briefly as possible conveys the depth of my hurt as a result of trust given to a church and then seeing that trust destroyed. I start the letter by introducing myself and stating that I am the one who handed him this letter. I explain how I attended the previous week, that I loved it so much that most of the time I was having a panic attack and part of me wanted to get out, but I needed to be sure this was a place I wanted to set roots. I told him about how I was raised in a Christian home, accepted Christ and how the Church and a church family has always been important to me. I then talked about Awaken, that the letter they sent me was humbling and yet I didn't want my being there to be a problem, and the reason for that was because I'm transgender.

Boom! At this point, I don't know if Pastor Jack is going to read on or wad the letter into a ball and toss it into the trash, but at least all my cards are on the table—and FACE UP!

So, he gets my whole story in a two-page letter. The letter is in the envelope of a card I bought, and the envelope is in a pocket of my Bible because I'm going to need my "security blanket" yet again this weekend. I'm almost as nervous this week as I was last week. Last week I didn't even put my toe in the water—all I did was go to the pool and LOOK at the water. This week I'm taking a step that I haven't done in over a decade, this time the toe is definitely in the water. So this week I take my favorite seat—last row on the end of the aisle closest to the exit. If last week my anxiety level was at a ten, this week maybe it's a five. Now, church SHOULD be at an anxiety level of zero, so I still have a way to go at this point, but this week was almost bearable. If the service is lousy, I have an out and can walk away thinking the previous week was a fluke and I'm dodging a bullet.

Nope—this week is awesome, again. Amazing worship and a great message. When the service is over, I now have to navigate my way to the front where Pastor Jack is while everyone else is heading out. I eventually get there and nervously wait while he's talking to some other people. He sees me and comes over and asks for my name; I tell him "Laurie."

Then he surprises me with his next question; he says, "What's your last name?" I didn't expect someone with such a large church to genuinely want to know specifically who they were talking to. I expected him to say "Hi Laurie, welcome" or something generic and not unexpected. I get the impression he actually cares about people enough to even ask for the last name and isn't just going through the motions.

So, I tell him. He then asks how long I've been coming and how I found out about the church.

I tell him last week was my first week and that I really liked it. At this point, I reach into my Bible (you know—my security blanket) and pull out the red envelope. I'm sure my voice sounds a little nervous when I say, "This is for you and well, it's a little private" as I hand it to him.

As he slides the card into his message notes, he looks into my eyes and simply asks, "How can I pray for you, Laurie?" With that, I can feel my eyes watering up and a lump building up in my throat. All the pain, all the hurt I experienced years ago is trying to surface again. I'm risking going through it all again.

I barely choke out the words, "It's all in there," as I nodded toward the card I had given him. And with that, I turn around and quickly head for the exit. I need air fast, and again am welcomed as I exit the building by the beautiful Texas hill country, bright sunshine and yes—an unlimited amount of air. I put on my sunglasses to hide what I'm sure are my red eyes from being at the point of tears and head for that sweet, sweet cocoon of safety and serenity that is the inside of my car. After sitting in the Texas sun for over an hour, it felt like a warm blanket wrapped around me as I settled into it.

Later that week, I call his assistant and ask for an appointment to meet with Pastor Jack. I get there a little early the day of our meeting and tell the woman at the information desk my name and that I'm there to meet with the pastor. She informs his assistant I'm here and asks me to have a seat. As I nervously sit there, a couple of minutes later, his assistant Jennifer comes down and says the pastor is running a little late and hasn't arrived yet.

Jennifer sits down next to me and we start talking. As it turns out, she used to live in southern California, and for the next fifteen minutes, we talk about things like toll roads in southern California—which were unheard of and something I never thought I would see when I lived there. We laugh and I feel like

I have an instant friend. Pastor Jack then arrives, and so he and I head upstairs to his office.

As we enter his office his wife joined us—now I'm having déjà vu! The first time I sat down to talk with a pastor and his wife it ended badly months later, I'm hoping this will be the start of a different story. I have one singular goal for our meeting, that if indeed I am welcome to be a part of the church, I don't want there to be any "misunderstandings" in the future. Thankfully, since he has read my letter (probably more than once), I didn't have to start from the beginning, so I decided to make it an "AMA" (Ask Me Anything) opportunity for him.

In his office was a small round table, barely big enough for the three of us to sit around. There is a box of tissues off to the side, so I reach over to move them closer and say to them with a nervous smile, "just in case."

He has what I would call the "usual" questions when encountering someone like me, he does seem a little surprised when I mentioned that I had been married, and after maybe 30 or 45 minutes of discussion, he kind of shook his head with a slight grin and said, "well, this is a first for me."

I laughed, sensing both his kindness and his probable feeling of, "Oh Lord, what have you brought to my doorstep?"

I explain that it's possible I might tell someone at the church of my history if we become close enough friends, but I had no intention of going "public," and telling strangers that I was transgender wasn't something I would do. I wasn't an activist or even an advocate; I only wanted to be a part of the church family. Throughout our conversation, I mention that it is important to me that he understands I don't want this to be an issue at the church—so much so that I feel it's important that he knows about it now, so he won't have it surprise him later if it ever comes up. Not realizing it, I say it again several times, and when he has heard me say it enough, he reaches out across the table, touches my arm, and says words that I'll never forget hearing.

He says "Stop—the church is fine, the church is solid. I just want to make sure you don't get hurt again."

That brings me as close to tears as I can be. Hearing those words are so healing and comforting to me. It is like he wrapped one big Band-Aid around my heart. At the same time, we both know that even if he is welcoming, that there probably are folks at church who, not knowing me, might be "troubled" that someone who is transgender is not just a member of the church, but serving there as well.

Pastor Jack is acutely aware of this possibility, and simply asks that if I am going to tell anyone about my history, to check with him first. It makes sense to me, because he might know them better than me at that time and can provide some insights as to why I might or might not want to tell someone about my history, and I agree it's a good thing to do.

So, feeling great after meeting with Pastor Jack and his wife, and seeing as how I'm now standing on the high-dive, all I have to do now is take the leap "into the pool." As it turns out, it is going to be much deeper than I ever expected.

14

BACK IN THE SADDLE

"When all these things have happened to you—the blessings and the curses I have listed—you will meditate upon them as you are living among the nations where the Lord your God will have driven you. If at that time you want to return to the Lord your God, and you and your children have begun wholeheartedly to obey all of the commandments I have given you today, then the Lord your God will rescue you from your captivity! He will have mercy upon you and come and gather you out of all the nations where he will have scattered you. Though you are at the ends of the earth, he will go and find you and bring you back again to the land of your ancestors. You shall possess the land again, and he will do you good and bless you even more than he did your ancestors! He will cleanse your hearts and the hearts of your children and of your children's children so that you will love the Lord your God with all your hearts and souls, and Israel shall come alive again!"

Deuteronomy 30:1-6 (TLB)

FAITH IS HARD: I'm not saying it should be, I wish it was always easy to hold onto. I've learned that faith isn't automatic, and it's not an all or nothing concept. In fact, in Matthew 8:25 when on the lake during a storm, the disciples in fear woke up Jesus who had been sleeping, and he said to them, "You of little faith, why are you so afraid?" (NIV) He didn't say you of NO faith, he said you of LITTLE faith. Faith is something like a muscle, and as you use it, as you exercise it, it becomes stronger, it grows. It's so easy to have faith in God during the good times, the easy times. But as things get tougher, that's when our faith in God is challenged. It's when we can continue to have faith during those tougher times that we learn (and actually believe as a result) that yes, God will come through. This allows us to have faith in Him when faced with even greater challenges. I see that in my friend Sande, who at the time of this writing is being treated for cancer. Never have I seen her less than joyful nor heard her less than thankful for God's goodness. She's an inspiration and role model of faith when things are hard, and I'm glad someone I can call a friend. Her life is a lesson on faith.

Not knowing how my meeting was going to go with the pastor, I had already scheduled an appointment with Lin for the next day. So, I'm talking to her (via Skype) and when I told her about what Pastor Jack said about not wanting to see me get hurt again, she started to tear up. I've seen her happy, I've seen her sad, and I've seen her angry over some of the things I've endured, but I had never seen her get emotional like that before, so of course, I got emotional too, and we both cried happy tears a little.

Sunday arrives and I'm ready for church! A few weeks ago, I was a panicked mess, and now I'm excited and can't wait to get there. No more sweaty hands, no more "don't look me in the eye because I'm scared" running through my head. Now as I walk from the parking lot to the building I'm smiling, saying hello to people, and looking forward to a great morning. Did I cry during the service—of course! It was so good; I felt so free and grateful to the Lord for bringing me to this church. I was able to fully enjoy it and enjoy a peaceful feeling in church for the first time in years.

After a couple of weeks at my new church and listening to past messages online, I'm feeling good about it. I'm feeling a peace, feeling settled—like this is where I belong for the first time since attending Awaken. And that's when it began to weigh on me— that I needed some closure with what happened at Awaken.

And so, I began to write. I began a letter to Pastor Frank at Awaken Fellowship. I had completely cut myself off from them when I drove away that day 15 years earlier. No one there had any idea what happened to me after that, how I was hurt to a debilitating point, and how I wasn't even able to go to church for years.

I began to write to Pastor Frank. And I wrote, and I wrote, and I wrote. There was so much pain in my words as I reminded him of my first coming to the church, how the letter sent to me asking me to become part of Leadership Training led me to tell him about my history. How when I left that meeting with him and Beverly, I felt confident that he would "stand by me" if things got dicey at church for some reason.

I explained to him all that I went through since that last day at Awaken, the depression, the time off work, the fear of going to church and being judged by Christians, how it crippled my walk with Christ. I was adamant that there was NOTHING wrong with me, just that I was "wired" differently and didn't understand why he felt I needed to be "re-wired." I told him that a couple of people who I had told my story to described what happened to me as "spiritual rape," and though I didn't believe it was his intent, that it wasn't an unreasonable assessment of the result. I explained that all this made me feel like I was of NO value to the Lord or His Church, and that God had no purpose for me— what more could one do to destroy a person.

From there, I told him about how after years and years of floundering, I was finally able to seek out a church home, how it wasn't easy, how my hands were sweating, and my heart was pounding just driving into an empty parking lot. Then the next day—how scared I was and at the same time, blessed. And finally, my meeting with Pastor Jack and him wanting to make sure I didn't get hurt again.

I closed the letter telling him I didn't need to be fixed because I wasn't broken—God doesn't make mistakes, and I was grateful that He doesn't, that I am exactly who He made me to be. And finally, I thanked him. I thanked him because Awaken was where I discovered what it was to worship, what it was to serve, and where I received the gift of tongues. I told him that I didn't need to say, "I forgive you," because I knew they meant no harm; that I knew they meant it all in love, but at the same time to give me a place and accept me into their body, and then strip it away piece by humiliating piece nearly killed me.

After FOUR pages of pouring my heart out, reliving all the pain and getting it all out, what do I do now? Do I mail it? Do I just tuck it away? It was rather therapeutic to write it all out, and it did help to get out all the things that had been just sitting there inside me. But how does it help anyone else? How does it help Pastor Frank avoid the same thing happening again?

If all I do is read it to myself and leave it at that—it doesn't help anyone else. So, I printed out the four pages, put them into an envelope, addressed it (marking it "private"), and feeling a little trepidation, I popped the envelope into the slot at my post office, and that was that. But I was immediately surprised—I suddenly felt as if a weight had been lifted from me. I know that's a common and probably overused phrase, but it is how it felt.

It's now the first of November, and a new four-week membership class is beginning at church. So, I go to the class during one service and then actually go to the last service right after that. All-in-all that was almost four hours at the church, and later that day it suddenly occurs to me—I didn't think about Awaken once! No panic, no stress, no fear. It was my BEST SUNDAY EVER since I had moved to Austin 11 years earlier.

All of the classes were informative, the third week especially. We would take a personality assessment and also a spiritual gifts assessment, and they had an interesting way of combining the two to determine where you would find a good fit within the church as a place to serve (assuming you wanted a place to serve).

I definitely was about serving. Not surprisingly, I was found to be a fit in the Worship and the IT areas. I wasn't all that interested in doing IT, after all, that was my day job, and I loved music, so I wanted to serve in the audio area.

The fourth and final week of the classes they brought in people from all areas of service, so we could talk with them, get acquainted and learn more about serving in their areas. No one from sound or IT was there, but a gal who helped in the worship area was there and saw how I would be a good fit in the sound area, and said that she would pass my information along.

As I was about to leave the room, a big guy comes rushing into the room. Steve came straight over to me and introduced himself as the leader of the IT volunteer team. Clearly, someone had found him and told him there was this tall, geeky girl with IT skills in the other room who wanted to serve. He was really nice, and I told him a little about my tech background. We arranged to talk more another time about how I might be able to help in the area.

A few days later, I'm coming home after working with a few clients, and I stop at my mailbox like I normally do. As I pull the mail out of the mailbox I see a familiar logo on one envelope—it says Awaken. All of a sudden, my heart starts pounding. It had been a month since I sent that letter to Pastor Frank, and to be honest, I had pretty much resigned myself to the fact that either he didn't get it, hasn't read it, or after reading it had set it aside or tossed it. I didn't expect a response of any kind. But here it was in my hand, I got back into my car and didn't even wait until I got home—I opened it and read it right there…

"Dear Laurie, Thank you for your kind, gracious and thoughtful letter. I can hardly imagine how difficult it was for you to write, but thank you for extending yourself and taking the time to share your heart. It truly did remind us of the wonderful person we met so long ago, which only made the pain we read about even more heartbreaking. My heart hurts for the complexity of your life and all you went through, as well as the inadvertent pain you felt by some of the words we shared and decisions we made. As you expressed so beautifully, our intentions were never to hurt you, but obviously, that intent was never realized. We are very, very saddened that you were hurt so deeply by the whole situation and sincerely ask your forgiveness for the pain we caused you. It truly did bless our hearts to hear that you are in a healthy church environment and that your relational roots will be able to go down into the soil of the church

family. You will remain in our prayers and thoughts. I love you, Laurie, and sincerely hope and pray that you have a wonderful life, dear one."

Well (and I'm sure you're beginning to see a pattern here), I just started to cry. Though mailing my letter to him did lift a weight from me—there was something so healing to my heart when I read that letter. I couldn't share it fast enough with Lin and Sharon. After all these years, after all the pain—closure. I somehow felt "released" to move forward with my life, that the last of the baggage was gone.

As Christmas approached, I had friended a few people at church on Facebook, including a couple of the pastors. One pastor had "liked" a post that someone he knew posted referring to an article about the global sexual revolution, specific to gender identity and how it would result in a "new totalitarian regime by the state." Now I'm a little nervous; is THIS what a pastor believes at my church? If it is, then I have a bumpy road ahead. I sent a message to the lead pastor's wife asking her what am I supposed to do with this information, because it bothered me. She encouraged me to talk directly with that pastor. And that's what I did.

It was the Christmas holiday, so I had to wait until the first week in January to meet with him. On Monday before meeting with this pastor, I sent him the letter I had given to Pastor Jack about my background, so I didn't have to start from scratch.

On that same day, I heard from Steve on the IT team asking if I was ready to go, and that they would need my SSN and Driver's License number, so they could do a background check. GREAT! A background check! I have no idea what shows up on one of these, and I don't know who is going to see it. I don't know if there is an "AKA" part with my old name or not. Oh well, I sent a message to Pastor Jack saying if he needs to give anyone a "head's up" over my situation, to go ahead.

Wednesday evening, I met with the executive pastor who had liked the Facebook post that concerned me. We talked for maybe 10 minutes; he wanted to assure me that what he liked was the comment his friend had made about how parents need to pay attention to what their kids are being taught, and that he hadn't even read the article that it linked to. As for me—he had no issues. We spent the rest of the time talking about some of the church's systems and also about high-end audio, since I noticed he had some nice gear in his office. It was a good meeting.

When I got home, I was sitting in my office going over my meeting with the pastor, and suddenly I started to cry. What is going on? I had a great meeting with a second pastor at the church, so life is good, isn't it? If tonight's meeting hadn't gone well, then it would have been easy to walk away from this church. I had met a few people, but I wasn't that heavily invested in it yet, and rather than struggle with pastors, I could just leave.

Thank the good Lord, it DIDN'T go badly. Actually, it went great. And now I was out of excuses. It was the trust issue raising its ugly head. How can I trust that what happened at Awaken wouldn't happen here? How do I trust the people here to not turn against me? And THAT's when it hit me (those 25 years of therapy were finally paying off) that I was trusting people and I wasn't trusting God. Putting your faith and trust in people is asking for disaster—and I know that! But I guess it was that little voice of fear that was whispering to me that "it could happen all over again" that gave me pause. So, I had to make the conscious choice that I WASN'T going to put my trust in the pastors or the church, I was going to remember my life verse and trust that the Lord had my back. And from that moment on, I was "all-in" at my new church.

My heart was feeling so good that I wanted to share it with my friends in northern California, so I planned a trip for the end of the month. I didn't realize it at the time, but it had been eight years since I had been back there to see anyone. My, how time flies when you're not having fun. I contacted friends, including Sharon, and was so excited at the opportunity to see everybody again. And then, I had a thought. This was an opportunity to put that final nail in the coffin and bury it. So, I sent an email message to Pastor Frank with the subject line "Got Time for a Hug?" letting him know I would like to give him a hug the Sunday morning I would be in town.

He replied that he was returning late the night before from a conference, but that he would be there for the third service and looked forward to this "divine opportunity."

Pastor Karen was the Women's pastor at my church and needed help with her printer at home. I hadn't yet met her, but we hit it off when we did. We talked, and I told her about my experience doing sound. Since she had a background in radio and television as well as recording audio books, she mentioned maybe connecting me with people she knows who could use my expertise in that area.

I didn't want her recommending me for something and having my being transgender ever be an issue or tarnish her reputation, so I check with the lead pastor about telling her—and while I'm at it, in the same message, I asked about telling Steve and his wife, Laura. We were becoming good friends, and I wanted to let him know that time for "the talk" with them may soon come. He had no issue with my talking to Pastor Karen, but to hold off with Steve and Laura as he was "uncomfortable" with me telling them.

So, the next week I talked with Pastor Karen, and after all of five minutes she was like "is there anything else?" It was the most uneventful conversation I have ever had with someone. She was totally fine. That made three, count them three, pastors on staff that knew my story and it didn't seem to bother them. After my experience where as far as I knew only the senior pastor in Sacramento knew, this was comforting and uplifting.

Finally, my trip to northern California comes up. It's a Thursday and I fly into San Francisco because I scheduled an appointment with Lin since I was going to be in town.

I didn't have much to talk to her about in the way of needing help with something. In reality, I was doing extremely well. I got there a little early, and once again was sitting in that familiar chair in the waiting room with what seemed like the same old magazines. When Lin came out of her office to get me, she had this big smile on her face. I walked into her office and she gave me a big hug. I didn't remember her as being much of a hugger, but it felt good and I was happy to reciprocate. We had a great talk, I told her about my upcoming visit to Awaken, and she was amazed and impressed that I would go back to the lion's den. I had already shared with her the letters that I sent and received from Pastor Frank, and this was the frosting on the cake.

I was staying with my friend Kim in Sacramento and arrived at her house mid-evening. We had a little time to catch up, but it had been a long day, so I called it quits pretty early and headed for bed. The next day, I got to spend time with Kim and took her and her husband to dinner to thank them for letting me stay with them during my visit.

Saturday, before heading over to spend the afternoon with my "sister" Andrea, I thought I would take the time to find out exactly where the new building was for Awaken as they had moved to a new place since I left. I had the address on my phone and quickly found it. Surprisingly I didn't feel any nerves of any kind—it was a building I had never seen before in a location I had never been to before. But since I was in the neighborhood, I went over to the old building that they still used for other purposes. It looked exactly the same, and oddly enough it's almost as if all those ghosts were still there at the building ready to call my name. It was an eerie feeling—how just seeing that building brought back those memories and feeling.

I spent Saturday afternoon with Andrea. That evening, I met up with Sharon at the church she had been attending at the time. Afterward, we went back to her home where her husband had prepared dinner (what a nice guy!). We spent the evening talking, some about our time when I lived in Sacramento, and some about tomorrow when I would hopefully get to see Pastor Frank.

So here it is—Sunday morning. I'm feeling a little anxious even though I know this is going to be a good day. The last time I had walked into Awaken was over 15 years ago, and I ran out crying, went into a deep depression, and at times didn't think I would ever have a purpose or reason even to live. So yeah, I was a little anxious.

He knew I was coming, and I knew he was going to be there—so there were no surprises, yet I didn't know for sure how I was going to feel when I actually saw him. As I drove to the church, I'm ever so thankful I took the time yesterday to nail down the location. I find a place to park and get there as the previous service has ended.

Sharon had agreed to meet me there as moral support. After I arrived she sent me a text that she was almost there. Since I had a little time to kill but didn't want to go into the sanctuary and take a seat until she got there, I spent some time in the lobby. I'm looking around to see if there is anyone I know. I look, and I look, and I look some more—no one. Not a single person do I recognize. THEN, I saw a gentleman that used to be on staff that I recognized. I was standing in front of one of their bulletin boards and he came over and introduced himself—he didn't recognize me, had no clue who I was. He came over thinking I was a visitor (which I guess I was). I introduced myself "Hi, I'm Laurie" and still nothing, no sense of recognition. He introduced himself, welcomed me, and I left it at that.

When Sharon arrived, I was able to breathe a little better. Yay! A friend! We went inside and found a couple of seats.

Once we sat down—Sharon poked me in the leg and pointed to our left. In the row in front of us at the end of the aisle was Pastor Frank, sitting in a chair and talking with someone. I decided to sit tight and wait until he finished his conversation. When he did, he got up and walked toward the front. He never saw me, so I got up and went to the left side of our aisle and followed him.

So, then Pastor Frank walks across the front to the far right side—I looked at Sharon and gave her a shrug with the "I guess I'll follow him around" look. So, I followed him across the front, then he stopped and started talking with someone sitting in the front row. I'm standing behind him—politely waiting for him to finish so I can say hello. He didn't even know I was there. When he finished, I wanted him to be sure he knew I was there, so I said in a loud enough voice, "Hello Pastor."

He turned around and smiled and said "Laurie! Hello!" He immediately gave me a big hug and into my ear he whispered, "Laurie, I'm so sorry."

I whispered back, "It's ok." We talked briefly for maybe another minute, and then we gave each other another hug as the service was about to start.

Sharon was watching this all go on and was in such suspense and anticipation of what would happen she was frozen at first. Then as Pastor and I were talking, she realized this is a once in a lifetime photo opportunity and scrambled for her phone just in time to get some shots of our second hug.

Those are pictures I will always cherish. They signify the closure of an extremely painful time of my life—yet they also serve to remind me that God will make the best of ANY situation in one's life. I emailed one of the photos Sharon took to my pastors in Austin with the subject line, "It is Finished!"

One wrote back saying, "This is what redemption looks like. My heart is full..." and another wrote "Wow, wow, wow! Thankful. Healing and hope, all in one image."

The rest of my trip was great visiting with my friends, but one story I have to include here is winding down Sunday evening with Andrea as I was telling her about my day. I'm over at her place in her living room—she lives with her (real) sister and her three-year-old nephew. We were relaxing on the sofa and she suddenly sneezed. I instinctively said, "Bless you." Then I saw this as a teaching opportunity for her nephew, so I turned to him and said, "When someone sneezes, we say God bless you."

And in a totally straight and ever so innocent face, he says to me, "I say excuse me when I fart!" Andrea and I busted out laughing! Ah, from the mouths of babes!

So, I return home to Austin. I've finally closed that painful chapter of my life. Now, I can settle in, REST in the fact that

Laurie Suzanne Scott

I have total closure over what happened at Awaken and can be a normal woman serving and worshipping at my church—just living life.

Yeah well, that's what I was thinking, but no, God had to get me this far before I could move forward and discover what His continuing plan for me was.

15

AM I CALLED, OR CRAZY?

"Therefore do not be ashamed of the testimony of our Lord, nor of me His prisoner, but share with me in the sufferings for the gospel according to the power of God, who has saved us and called us with a holy calling, not according to our works, but according to His own purpose and grace which was given to us in Christ Jesus before time began."

2 Timothy 1:8-9 (NKJV)

WHO, ME? I never thought of myself as someone who would be "called" by God to do, well, much of anything. I had resigned myself to the fact that life in the shadows was going to be my life. Oh sure, maybe I could serve on a sound team at this church or another church, but it was never what I felt was a "calling." In reality, it was just part of my defense mechanism, to be in a safe place where I didn't have to sit with other people and get to know them, just me safely ensconced behind my good friend, the sound board, and getting some musical gratification

Laurie Suzanne Scott

at the same time. A calling? No. It was more of using a talent I had which fed my need to serve, and yet I didn't have to expose myself emotionally to others. And then it started, it was just a thought that maybe I could be of help to people who were transgender in a rather anonymous way. Then perhaps maybe a not so anonymous way. And then next thing you know I'm thinking that "someone" needs to do something! But when I thought that I might be that someone, the wheels practically fell off. That is when I came to realize not just the importance, but the necessity of having godly people around me who can speak openly and honestly into my life. I had been going it alone for so long that I didn't think to consult anyone until I had about driven myself crazy. The importance of having people you trust, godly people who can speak truth into your life is necessary if you're going to be willing to do what God asks of you.

A couple of weeks before my trip to Sacramento, I coincidentally had reconnected with a friend from Sacramento on Facebook. Melissa was the worship leader and her husband Jon played drums at Discovery Church, the last church I went to in Sacramento before moving to Austin. Melissa and Jon were newly married at the time with no kids, and Jon and I worked for the same company at the time. We weren't what you would call close friends, but good friends through church. After I moved to Austin we lost touch. About three years after moving to Austin, I got a note in my work email from her husband Jon just to say "hi" and that they were now going to Awaken, and that Melissa was on the worship team. This was during my time of wandering in the desert, and this note was that son of a bitch (Satan) kicking sand in my eye.

A friend I knew in Sacramento is now going to Awaken? The very word "Awaken" brought back all kinds of dreadful feelings, my fight or flight response was kicked into gear by merely seeing the word. And the snarky side of me was trying to emerge. What would I say? "I'm so glad the church that hurt me deeper than I've ever been hurt is a place you're happy and call home!" Maybe I could say, "If you like Awaken then you should stay at Awaken, but please leave me alone!" I didn't fight, nor did I have to flee. I simply went stealth.

They didn't know my background (as far as I knew), and so I ignored it and didn't respond as if I never saw it (well, at least that's the impression I was hoping to leave). Now here it is eight years later in January 2016, and I get a message on Facebook saying, "Hey Laurie, how are you?" from Melissa. We shared pleasantries, I learned she now has four children and had moved to the Chicago area about five years earlier.

After my trip to Sacramento, she saw the posts of me and Pastor Frank hugging, and she casually mentioned that he had referred to me (not mentioning me by name at any time) in a couple of messages and that she loved me anyway.

I was taken aback a little. I asked Melissa, "Do you KNOW my story?"

She told me that a mutual friend had told her after I had left Sacramento, then she said "I can't even begin to understand, but please know you are very much loved. Your walk is hand in hand with the Lord, and that's the truth. My job is to love." And then she told me, "You are a very unique Christian...." which made me chuckle—like tell me something I DON'T know!

Suddenly, out of the blue, someone that I thought I probably would never hear from again is telling me she knows my history and still loves me. I've always been so careful to introduce that information to others myself—I figure if it comes from a third party it may not be communicated well (let's just say I have information control issues).

After that, we caught up via email and in one email shortly after connecting, she said, "*I want to be honest with you... I don't know what to think about your change... you're the only person I know who has done this. A small part of me is sad for you, for the struggles that you've had to face, but a big part of me knows that you are an amazing, giving, creative, loving, and needing love kind of person. That is what I focus on. You are just... you.*"

And that's all I could be—just me, yet we remained friends, and she would soon be God's affirmation of a ministry I didn't know I was about to embark upon.

Something that helped with my uneasiness at church was my growing friendship with Steve and Laura. Steve and I had talked a little bit regarding computer issues at church, but I hadn't had much chance to get to know his wife Laura, so we went to his favorite barbecue spot in town one Saturday. He was an obvious frequent flyer there, because the staff all waved at him when he walked in the door.

Now if you're not from Texas, you need to understand that when you order barbecue, one thing you're going to get is bread. Nothing fancy (hey! It's barbecue). Just plain, sliced, white bread. At this restaurant, they have it out for you to help yourself while in line. Steve and his family were in front of me since they knew what they were going to get. As this was my first time at this place, I wanted to check out the menu. As we moved forward in line, Steve reached for the bread and offered it to me. I was still trying to be good on my low-carb diet and I said, "No thank you, no carbs for Laurie 2.0."

It seemed like such a simple and innocent thing to say, if anything I thought he might say, "Oh, what's that?" and I would explain my diet, coming to church, trying to look a little nicer with makeup, etc. Did he ask that question, of course not! I spent my entire life keeping most of my relationships with people on a relatively superficial level—that was my safe space. If no one really knows me, then no one can really hurt me (made sense to me). But Steve is not one for superficial relationships, so what comes out of his mouth after I mention Laurie 2.0?

He says, "Then you're just going to have to tell me all about Laurie 1.0."

What? That's like my entire life! Suddenly my barbecue lunch was looking like an afternoon inquisition. Being home alone with a large deep dish pizza and a bottle of wine all to myself quickly became a much more appealing way to spend my lunch—to heck with the carbs, but I was standing right there next to him with a tray in hand—I was stuck. So, I just smiled and shrugged back at him.

We got our food and grabbed a table. We prayed and as we started to eat, Steve launched with, "So, what brought you to ATC?"

And so, it begins. Everything in my LIFE is what brought me to Austin Transformation Church, and he wanted to hear it all?

"Were you going somewhere else before?"

Really? Why don't you ask me if I'm transgender, so I can skip avoiding it?

So, this started the most carefully edited version of my life I had ever told anyone. I began saying that it had been years of

211

no church before coming to ATC. I mentioned I moved here from California, Laura mentioned they moved here as well from the Bay Area, I said that I had a "bad experience" at a church in Sacramento, blah, blah, blah. Told them (almost) the whole story—I told them I grew up in California, where my parents live and that I had two brothers. I told them I had been married (I always use the term "ex," a nice safe gender-neutral word) and I told them about grandpa and then Awaken and the hurt. I simply didn't tell them what the bad experience was or why.

They knew I was deeply wounded, because I couldn't tell them about it without choking up a little—I didn't mean to or want to but the wound was deep, and the scar will always be there as a reminder of the pain. It's a lesson that I'm continuing to learn. Even though Pastor Frank and I had that moment at Awaken a couple of months ago, and even though I hold absolutely no bad feelings today toward Pastor Frank or his church, talking about the experience does tend to make my eyes water a little bit—what can I say, tears come easy with me.

I guess I monopolized most of the conversation, but they did get a few words and questions in from time to time, mostly when I was taking a bite of my barbecue (the burnt ends and sauce is a special, off-the-menu item that's awesome if you can stand the heat). We had a very enjoyable time together. Eventually, we wrapped it up, cleared the table and as we were walking out, I looked at the time. NOT POSSIBLE! We had been sitting there talking for almost three hours! This was one of those "where did the time go" moments. But it was from there that my friendship with Laura grew into her becoming one of my good friends.

Starting to feel at ease with Christians at my church, I'm sensing I can maybe just relax. But then something began to come over me.

Sharon was in the middle of working on a documentary about the Church, and I was beginning to feel as if maybe I could help her. She was already writing about me in the companion book, and maybe I could offer to be in the video documentary if it would help make it better.

This would mean I was putting my FACE onscreen talking about being a Christian and transgender. Not even a month earlier would I have ever thought such a thing. I was pretty happy to hang in the shadows and be pleased with my life as is. But there was a tug, something telling me, "You can do more, you can do this."

So, I put it out there and offered it to Sharon in an email, the subject line: "I SOOOO Do Not Know About This..." I read and re-read the message before I even sent it. I knew that in a way I would be "outing" myself, but since no one was expecting her documentary to be the next Star Wars movie, I felt that even if I were in it—no one I knew would probably see it, and if they did, they already knew my history. It was a safe way to help someone I cared deeply for.

She replied a couple of days later saying how she thought it was a great idea, and how she would only position it to show my pain and hurt and not in a way of letting me become an object of ridicule. Now, I don't know why, but I guess deep down I thought she would simply thank me and say no. But now I'm having second thoughts because she thinks it's a good idea. Really? What does all this mean? As it turns out this was the beginning of getting me to places I never thought I would go—ever!

A week is way too much time for me to think about things, and boy did I think and pray about it a lot during the week after Sharon told me being in the documentary would be a good idea.

But something began to stir up inside me.

There was an anxiety and butterflies in my stomach about all this that I couldn't shake. It wasn't an anxiety in the sense that I thought something bad was GOING to happen, but more like a nervousness about what COULD happen. This little "tug" that I had earlier felt was beginning to be a stronger pull. What I knew was that I had things to say to the Christian and transgender communities that no one else was saying.

I never knew, but had recently come to learn how high the attempted suicide rate among people who are transgender—an insane 41%. And if 0.3% (that's three in a thousand) of the population is transgender, then I probably wasn't the only transgender person at my own church! And not just that, but they may currently be at a point I used to be, in the shadows and suicidal. That swirling pool of numbers in my head triggered something within me.

Suddenly it wasn't enough that I was serving in the IT area within the church. It wasn't enough that pastors at my church knew about MY history and were accepting me into the church. I felt like all that wasn't enough—that in some way maybe God was calling me saying more needs to be done.

Well, I took that ball and ran with it (another way of saying that's when I went off the rails).

Do you remember that scene in Forrest Gump when the college football coach put Forrest on the team because he could run so fast? The other team kicked off, and Forrest Gump is standing back on the goal line staring off into the distance as if he's thinking about what he might have for dinner that night. The ball is caught by the other player who runs it over to Forrest

Gump, puts the ball into Forrest's hands and yells "Run! Run!" Forrest Gump starts to run and is running down the football field past everyone. Suddenly, he takes a left turn and is heading straight toward his team's sideline. Everyone on the sideline is shouting and waving to redirect him toward the end zone. No one can catch Forrest. He reaches the end zone and the team scored—the crowd erupts in wild cheers!

But Forrest Gump kept running. He kept running, knocked over a few band members who were standing outside of the end zone cheering in celebration, and then kept on going into the tunnel and right out of the stadium.

My problem is I ran (and ran fast) in the direction I thought I was supposed to go, because, well, why else would God call me if I didn't know what He wanted? So I went the direction of "how can the church let this go on?" SOMEBODY has to DO SOMETHING!!!

And with that, I began to spiral out of control. I'm feeling this calling that seemingly never existed before—who was going to do it if I didn't?

I sent an email to Sharon and also Pastor Karen at my church with the subject "Am I Called or Crazy?" I told them about how I felt I was being called to "some kind of something," something that I couldn't even describe at the time. I talked about how appalling the attempted suicide rate is among those who are transgender and how based on the numbers, I probably wasn't the only transgender person at my church. If those people were going through what I had gone through in my life, how could I ignore that? Someone had to do something; I HAD to do something!

But at the same time, I didn't want to jeopardize my relationship with my church, I couldn't leave it now. I was bouncing back and forth as if I was inside a pinball machine.

I got what amounts to the same advice from both of them: "Breathe." "Slow your roll." "Rest." "Just BE where God has placed you at this time," meaning just settling in at church. I realized in their messages that, yes, I needed to take a breath, slow down, and wait upon God. I had begun to take over in the driver's seat. I mean if God has called me, He must want me to drive, right? And boy did I take the wheel!

Both of them were right of course, and yes, I needed to back off, so that's what I did. These are two wonderful women of God I love and trust, and I'm not going to begin to ignore the counsel they give me. After sleeping on their advice, I felt better the next day and told them so.

Sharon said "Whew!"

I asked her if she felt like she dodged a bullet.

She replied, "I feel like I caught one out of the air aimed at your heart."

When I met with Pastor Karen, she explained how she had a similar experience in her own life at one time and totally understood how with this sudden realization of mine, I had compressed what might be the next few (or even several) years of my life into just a couple of weeks, and felt like I had to fix everything with everybody right now. And that's what I had done. I wound it down. I took the time to breathe. And it worked… for about a week.

It's a funny thing about depression, it can sneak up on you at any time. I hadn't been taking anti-depressants for a couple of years now, and I was, for the most part, doing fine (didn't feel much different when I was taking them). So it doesn't take much of a push by that son of a bitch (you know who I'm talking about) to take you from feeling fine to feeling desperate.

I'm sure there are doctors out there who can tell you all about how the brain chemistry changes, blah blah blah. All I do know is that you can slide downhill in a hurry—and that's what happened. One week after being okay with the solid advice given me, I suddenly found myself at a whole new low-point.

"What happened?" I'm asking myself. I was fine, and now, I'm not.

That son of a bitch found a new vector of attack for me—loneliness. Being alone is not an atypical situation for those who are transgender, and it can be even lonelier for Christians who are transgender. Many of us live in the shadows of the Church, we're there but all you see is the outside and whatever little bit about ourselves we may choose to divulge to you. You see a man or a woman, we may have transitioned already, or we may be hoping for the day that we can—but you see only the part of us we allow you to see. You know, the "shiny" part. The part that looks good on the outside.

Within us there is pain. Pain perhaps from the loss of loved ones, not because of death but because of our existence and the distancing that comes after transitioning. The pain may be from the knowledge you're not the gender that biology gave your body and yet you feel stuck, like there is nothing you can do about it and the life of duplicity you're leading is slowly eating you up inside. The pain may come from the fact that you love the Lord God with all your heart, all your soul, and all your mind, and yet Christians in your life who otherwise like and even love you would suddenly find you unacceptable in their presence and an "abomination to the Lord."

And the pain may come from the knowledge that you may well spend the rest of your life alone, and that's the angle that son a bitch came at me with. Being a heterosexual woman, I find men attractive. Being Christian, I would only want a Christian man to be that one special person in my life. The rub comes when I think, "What Christian man would want someone like me?" And before you say, "Oh Laurie, there's someone out there for you," think about it.

Let's take a poll of all single church-going Christian men, pass a piece of paper out to each one of them and ask them this question: "Would you want to have a relationship with a woman if you knew she had been born a boy?" How many pieces of paper would have the word "yes" on it? I don't see anyone writing "yes" down. Not out of 1,000. Out of 10,000? Not sure. Out of 100,000? Okay, maybe one or two. I'll concede that—maybe.

So, I go into this emotional death spiral over being lonely. So again, I'm writing to my spiritual lifeguard Sharon, telling her that "I'm done," and that she should probably "let me go" because I wasn't feeling like I was worth her investing any more of her life into. I told her that after being out and about all day working with clients, that I needed more to come home to than just my dogs.

I then went into (while having my own private pity party) how if I did unplug from people, it takes a LONG time for anyone to miss me and say, "Hey, where have you been?" And I talked about how even though going to my new church is wonderful and every Sunday the service is amazing, that I find myself coming home feeling empty and isolated. I was feeling like I had nothing to lose by just blowing up my life. Come out to the world all at once and let the chips fall where they may.

If it's a problem at church, well then, I guess I have to move on. But at least then I would know who my true friends and supporters were and wouldn't have to walk on eggshells around people.

I told Sharon not to even respond for a few days, because I probably would not want to read it anyway. Now, there was no way she wasn't going to respond immediately, but it did take me a couple of days to gather myself up to read her response, and even then, a few days to completely go through it—I had to take it in small doses, I was still pretty fragile.

She went through each point I had written and addressed each one, understanding that some were that son of a bitch poking me and others were things that just have to take time.

But all this started with my "Am I Called, or Crazy" email, feeling like God might have something in store for me.

Sharon added this to her response: "*I agree with you that God is doing something with YOU. The reason I think this is because A) you're a devoted Christian and always have been. B) You're not gay. C) You've been celibate all these years and make for a great spokesperson. No one can point to your wild, indiscriminate sex life and say that you don't have any morals thereby disqualifying you from being "used" by God as a messenger. D) You're the perfect example of [being] transgender NOT being about sex. This has been your burden but is also your testimony.*"

She then ended the email with a prayer, and in it, she said something that at the time I took as just words in her prayer, but didn't expect a literal answer to… "*Jesus, You have reached out and touched me before. I felt Your hand on the back of my head. It was the most amazing moment of my life. Do that for Laurie. Touch her in a way that she knows it's You. Show her that You are near and that YOU'VE got this. Help her see what is depression and what is the scheme of her enemy. Lead her to the right kind of help."*

For a few days, I didn't even read her email—I just let it sit in my inbox. At the same time, I was feeling the need to "work through" all this with some professional help. Not so much about being transgender, I'm at peace with that. But navigating this feeling of being called and its effect on my relationship with other Christians, both present and in the future. For that, I felt I needed a Christian therapist to help me.

It wasn't a decision I came to easily. Inside I almost felt like I was betraying Lin after all the years we had put in together. Lin had been my therapist for 26 years at this point, I loved her. She helped me understand myself as someone who is transgender and most importantly helped me as I transitioned into a new role in society, and helped me through my trial at Awaken. But this was different—and it required someone different.

I asked Pastor Karen at church about a Christian therapist. Since there was a member of the church who headed a Christian counseling center here in Austin, I asked her about him—she recommended one of his associates, Roma. I made the call, and in no time, I had an appointment to meet with her the next week.

But something amazing happened before my appointment. It wasn't an hour AFTER I had made my appointment with Roma that I read the prayer in Sharon's email where she asked the Lord to "Lead her to the right kind of help." THIS! This was God at work! She prayed, He answered, and I didn't even know it at the time.

The next Sunday morning, Sharon shared on Facebook one of Ralph Marston's posts titled "Activate Opportunity." In talking about opportunity he said, "It is a starting point, and going forward from that starting point requires work."

That same morning at church, the youth pastor gave the message, and he talked about "Breaking Through," and it started with "What if our greatest obstacles became our greatest opportunities?"

It was in that moment I knew God was saying, "Did you hear that Laurie? Are you paying attention?" And yes, I was. I realized that my challenge of being Christian, conservative, and transgender was also the opportunity God wanted me to embrace and yes, to do the work. I suddenly felt energized. I was beginning to put the pieces together.

I was so excited that I wrote to Sharon, "You know, sometimes I can be a little thick, I may not always be able to hear God's soft voice whispering in my ear, so He shouts to be sure I'm paying attention, this morning was one of those times."

One thing I was dreading about starting with a new therapist was getting her up to speed on my history. I didn't want to take weeks and weeks bringing her current about my life, so I assembled a collection of the letters I had given to Pastors Jack and Frank along with some recent emails between me, Sharon, and Pastor Karen and sent them all to Roma. Even though she hadn't read all of it (it was a lot) by the time we first met, she knew pretty much where I was at, certainly enough that we were able to quickly move forward.

In our first meeting (having already read all my "prep work"), she asked, "How can I help you?"

I had to stop and think. And all I could say is that I didn't know exactly, except that now that I've opened myself up, there's all this "stuff" starting to come out about me, my relationship with others (as in guys), and my relationship with "the church," and I need help managing it. It seemed I sometimes got overwhelmed and would spin out of control (you think?). I didn't think my answers were helpful to her, I thought she was expecting or hoping for something specific—as if after all those years of therapy I should have my problems identified, if not already answered.

Rather, she smiled and said, "I can help you with that." Roma has truly been a blessing. Each time we meet, she opens it with prayer, and when we're done she closes our time with prayer.

It was in our second meeting after she had read the last of the "introductory" material I had given her, when she commented on how much she enjoyed how I write (go figure, there's no accounting for taste). So, I joked how the subject line of one of the emails "Am I Called, or Crazy" would be a good title for a book and she said, "You've already started it."

Me? Write a book? Now THAT'S crazy! (It's ironic that the "crazy" idea came from my therapist.) I don't know squat about writing a book, and besides, then everyone would know about me, and I have a hard enough time with rejection without putting my whole life out there, forget about it. But a funny thing happened, it planted a seed—and that seed began to sprout.

16

FRIENDSHIPS AND DISCIPLESHIP

"Two are better than one because they have a good return for their hard work. If either should fall, one can pick up the other. But how miserable are those who fall and don't have a companion to help them up!"

Ecclesiastes 4:9-10 (CEB)

THE JOY AND FEAR OF NEW RELATIONSHIPS: For most people, making new friends is a good thing—and simple. It's not complicated, it doesn't involve a lot of thinking, nor a lot of worry. If you had concerns about the person, you probably wouldn't enter into a friendship in the first place. Easy. For someone who is transgender, maybe not so easy. If this person finds out I'm transgender will they reject me? Will they say or do things to hurt me? This gets magnified at places like work or church where you're around the same group of people. We all want relationships with other people, we're wired needing relationships. But Christians don't have the greatest track record of showing Christ's love and compassion when faced with someone who is transgender. And that's a shame, because you might otherwise discover that the shy guy or gal sitting alone in church really isn't shy, just afraid. Afraid of what you might say. Afraid of how you might act. And what you're missing is a person who loves and cares deeply about other people, people like yourself. A person who loves the Lord as much as anyone in your church. A person who wants to serve the Lord and be among His people, people like you.

I've been going to my new church over six months now, and even though several pastors at my church know my background and are welcoming and loving, I still feel a little uneasy at times. I still have trust issues. I wasn't sure within myself that leadership at my church was okay with the fact that I was transgender. Tolerant maybe, but okay? I'm not sure. Some Sunday mornings at church I would feel a little uneasy, nervous. I knew my trust belonged with God, but in looking back, it was that son of a bitch Satan at it again trying to convince me that I couldn't trust the awesome people God had led me to. You can almost hear that SOB whispering in your ear, "Don't trust them, they'll do it to you just like Awaken did."

Sharon had been such a positive influence on my life as a pastor and friend, that one day I was poking around the Internet and ran across an interview she had done on a Christian television show near Sacramento. It was a rather low budget production, but that didn't matter. The conversation was about her documentary and book, and what struck me was something she said. Everywhere she and her crew went, the same question was asked of regular people attending the church... "What does it mean to be a disciple?"

Only one person understood it about being a true follower of Jesus, to learn from Him in order to be more like Him to the world in which we live. ONE person—out of over 50 churches! That astounded me! The most common answer she got was "inviting other people to church." I was almost as surprised as she was. Really? Inviting people to church is discipleship? Even I knew there was more to it than that. I know for a fact Jesus never said, "Come, follow me so that we can go hear someone else talk about God." But I also have to admit that I might not have added being Jesus to the world to my own definition.

I grew up in a "Have you heard of the Four Spiritual Laws" pamphlet culture, where we learned about the Bible with the goal of telling people about Jesus and how they can be saved. It was an "ask Jesus into your heart and to forgive you, don't sin, go to church, and read your Bible" culture. Sound familiar?

Paying attention to HOW Jesus treated other people, WHO He chose to have close to Him, and WHAT His relationship to the Father is wasn't ingrained in me. In the last couple of decades, I had come to learn about the awesomeness of a more intimate worship experience, of sensing His presence in worship. But discipleship, true discipleship as it was meant in Jesus' day, had never found its way into me.

So, I asked Sharon for some suggested reading on discipleship. Preferring audio books myself, I found some on the topic and asked if she was familiar with any. She was with one: *The Great Omission* by Dallas Willard, so I bought it. I didn't even make it to the beginning of chapter one. I hadn't finished the introduction, and I already realized that I and so many other Christians are missing the mark.

Jesus told us to go out and make DISCIPLES of others, not to go out and make people say the sinner's prayer or a multitude of other things that would be the result of our being a disciple of Jesus. One of the words that Willard used in describing a disciple is "apprentice."

We all know what an apprentice is. That's someone who is learning hands-on with the guidance of a master—until the day comes when the apprentice is no longer an apprentice but is equipped to go out on his or her own. In Jesus' day, the rabbi was the master. A disciple was a follower of the rabbi and would follow the rabbi wherever the rabbi went, as an apprentice. And Jesus was a rabbi. When the rabbi ate the disciple would eat. When the rabbi would pray, the disciple would pray. When the rabbi slept, the disciple slept. Day after day after day, until the day came when the disciple is ready to become a rabbi himself.

Realizing that I personally had a lot of work to do in this area, changed how I saw myself as a Christian. I realized that Jesus would never turn me away as a disciple because I'm transgender, nor did He ever allow any of His disciples to push someone aside because they weren't the "right kind of person." When Samaritans refused to welcome Jesus as they headed toward Jerusalem, James and John offered to call down fire from Heaven to destroy the Samaritans, and Jesus rebuked them for it. Bringing people closer to Jesus is impossible if you're pushing them away from Jesus. You can't have it both ways.

As Christians, we're not called to tell people, "You're not welcome here, maybe you should leave. We hope you find Jesus, just please find Him somewhere else."

Does that sound like Jesus? Does that sound like the kind of Church God wants us to be? The church I grew up in, everyone dressed nicely on Sunday. These days, many churches are fine with casual attire, realizing clothes don't make the Christian. At what point does a church say to someone, "You don't fit in," "You're not like us and it doesn't matter if you're a Christian," or maybe, "You need to change before we'll accept you here."

These are the messages those who are transgender get from the Church. Now I'll grant you that's not necessarily the message the Church intends to send, but that's how it's being received.

When Christian organizations stand up vehemently against legislation allowing transgender people to use the bathroom of their gender as opposed to their biological sex, the transgender folks take that as an attack against them. The argument that it's for the protection of women and children stops there, with no proposal for equally protecting those who are transgender from similar attacks when they use the restroom (I guess if you think they are sinning, they don't need to be protected). It would be so easy for Christians to put out their hands in kindness, friendship, and love to those who are transgender if they could see how their actions appear. And that's when I realized someone has to do something.

The message is simple, but people are so busy fighting their social wars that they don't stop for a minute to look for a solution. It's all about the war. Defeating the other side is more important than a solution, and a victory for both sides is never even considered. I MUST win, and you MUST lose.

I didn't see myself currently as someone to join that brawl. I took the time to read more about being a disciple first, because that's where God wants us all to be and I knew I needed to start there.

Good Friday was coming, and it was going to be a big event. Churches from all over town were getting together, and we were going to hold a city-wide service in the large arena downtown, big enough to handle over 12,000 people.

I wanted to go, and I was trying to work it out for friends to go along. The tickets were free, but you still needed to reserve them. While I was waiting to hear back from friends, the tickets were all "sold" out. I checked with the gal at our church who did all the heavy lifting in getting the whole event put together, and she told me she was sure I would be able to go down there and get in.

But here's the deal—I didn't want to be alone among thousands of people. Oh sure, there would be several people there that I knew, but I would probably never see them there or be able to sit with them. We're talking the largest arena in Austin; you're not just going to "bump" into someone from your church, especially when you don't know many people there.

When the evening came, I stayed home, sad that I wasn't able to go. Staying home did more than make me sad though, it brought up even more within me. I wanted to get connected with others at my church, but even on Sunday mornings sitting in a room with 1,000 or so others, I felt alone. I felt alone because my life, my WHOLE life was a secret. It was a secret to my friends Steve and Laura sitting next to me at church, never mind everybody else sitting in the room.

Letting others at my church know that I'm transgender risked causing at the very least a "commotion" at the church, and at the most, could cause an all-out fight and division within the church. I certainly didn't want that, that's not my purpose for going to my church. I LOVE my church and wouldn't want to do anything that would cause disruption, but feeling isolated because I couldn't get close to people and develop deeper friendships was beginning to wear on me.

Because of my decision to be a disciple of Jesus, I chose to start by carefully reading the WORDS of Jesus, and I couldn't think of a better place to start than the book of John. In reading the first chapter in John, I realized that being a Christian who is transgender is kind of like being from Nazareth.

After Jesus called out to Phillip and said, "Follow me," (calling Phillip to be a disciple), Phillip went out to find his friend Nathanael. In John 1:45 Phillip says to Nathanael, "We have found the one Moses wrote about in the Law, and about whom the prophets also wrote—Jesus of Nazareth, the son of Joseph." Nathanael had quite the response in verse 46: "Nazareth! Can anything good come from there?"

When I read that passage, I made the realization "I'm from Nazareth too!" I imagine Nathanael's response was similar to my own pastor's response when he realized there was a Christian who was transgender, who not only wanted to attend his church but be involved and serve at his church.

He was probably thinking, "Can anything good come from a Christian who says they're transgender?" I'm sure he prayed, "Lord, I know I've asked you to bring those to our church who need you and can find your transformational power here, but this wasn't exactly what I was thinking! You know I love you, but what am I supposed to do with this? My church isn't ready for this!"

If he hadn't prayed this when I introduced myself to him in that letter, then surely he had prayed it at an earlier point in his life, because clearly God had given him the answer: "Just love her." And that has been my pastor's approach with me since day one. Just love. For him it's simple. I think for most on staff at the church who know my background, it's just as simple. At the same time, for some (and maybe only a relative few) of the four thousand or so who go to my church, it's not simple.

But I realize that information like this in the dark can be tough for some people. People who have had the chance to get to know me before I tell them about my history almost universally accept me.

All these new realizations came at the same time as an upcoming event at our church. Four times a year on a Sunday night we celebrate baby and child dedications, new members, and those who wish to be baptized. I was baptized when I was eleven, I kinda sorta knew what it was all about back then, I had been told but gee, I was eleven—I did it because that's what I was SUPPOSED to do. And doing (and being) what I was supposed to do (and be) growing up was something I was good at.

In the new member's class when I first started attending ATC, as well as in Sunday morning services, Pastor Jack said that he would love to baptize folks as adults, with them fully appreciating the significance of what it means. In the back of my mind ever since I transitioned some 24 years earlier, I had wanted to be baptized as "Laurie."

With Pastor's encouragement, I decided this was the time. I sent an email telling my friends about getting baptized, and the outpouring of support was nothing short of amazing. Sharon said she wished she could be here for it, so I came right out and asked her, "So what on your calendar is preventing you from coming out?" I wanted her to be here after all the love and support she had given me. The next day she was booked on a flight to Austin to arrive the day before my baptism.

In anticipation of getting baptized, an interesting side-story began to develop. Pastor Jack had decided to do a series called "Hot

Topics," basically a series of messages that maybe some churches wouldn't tackle, and he asked the congregation for suggestions on topics he should talk about. Well, I wasn't going to let this opportunity pass without getting a word or two in.

As the series approached, he said it was looking like four or five buckets, including politics (it was the presidential primary season in full force), and he also intimated that social issues such as gay marriage could be a part. I thought that if he was going to talk about gay marriage, how much harder would it be to introduce the topic of Christians who are transgender? It was a five-week series, but I never knew what the topic that week was going to be until Sunday. As each week went by, no social issues.

As it turned out, the last Sunday of the series was the same Sunday that I was getting baptized and Sharon would be here. Could it possibly be that he would talk about it the same day I get baptized? I kept Sharon informed each week, and each week, we got closer and closer to my baptism day with only hints that "social issues" would be covered. I was so excited that she was coming and able to have the opportunity to meet the important people in my life here and vice versa. But during all this anticipation of a great weekend of celebration and friends, God was pressing something upon me, and I was feeling it.

17

GOD DOES HAVE A SENSE OF HUMOR

"The wicked plot against the godly; they snarl at them in defiance. But the Lord just laughs, for he sees their day of judgment coming."
Psalm 37:12-13 (NLT)

WILLING VS. TRUSTING: Have you ever played that game where all you have to do is close your eyes or be blindfolded, stand up straight, then fall backward and let your friends catch you on the way down? Would you? Right now you're reading this and maybe thinking to yourself, "Sure, I'd do it—they're my friends." That's being WILLING. Now imagine yourself at that moment when you're standing there in a room, blindfolded. Your friends are around you laughing—you're not sure WHY they're laughing. You start to laugh, but it's a nervous laugh. Before you start to lean backward—your heart starts to beat a little faster. You maybe clench your fists a little bit. You

233

take a very deep breath. You start to wonder if your "friends" will really catch you as you fall. Maybe you decide to lean back; maybe at the last second, you change your mind. THAT'S the difference between being willing and trusting. It's one thing to be willing to be called to serve God. But what happens when you actually feel called, and it's not what you thought that calling would look like? It takes both willingness to follow it and trust in God that He knows what's best for you (eventually you'll see He's right). People often think of God as some powerful and yet terrifying figure to be frightened of. Yet, we were all made in His image; we are able to love because God loves. We are able to cry because God cries. And we are able to laugh because God laughs.

I had been going to a women's Bible study at church on Monday nights for a couple of weeks now; it was a study of Nehemiah. It was difficult to attend, because I so related to the story of Nehemiah being called, yet at first, because he didn't tell anyone at the beginning what it was about. I couldn't even share that I had that in common with Nehemiah, much less what I thought I was being called to—I wasn't even sure exactly what it was I was feeling called to, but clearly it had something to do with being Christian and transgender, and that wasn't a topic I felt free to share at my table with the other gals.

One Monday night when I got home after Bible study, I deeply felt God's calling, He was tugging at my heart. I felt a need to help Christians like me who are transgender, and a burden to inform those within His Church who would condemn others with no understanding of what it is to be transgender. I started to pray, and I did something I don't normally do when alone at home, I prayed out loud—and I started to cry.

In my tears I said, "Lord, there must be someone else. I'm unprepared—I'm unqualified. Of all the people out there, surely there must be someone who can do this rather than me."

And suddenly, for the second time in my life, I HEARD God's voice. In the middle of my tears our Father in Heaven, the Creator of the universe said the following to me, "No, there isn't—but you'll do."

What? "You'll do?" And like that my crying turned into laughter. God had found my funny bone.

"You'll do?" The Lord certainly didn't have to worry about me feeling all full of myself and thinking how great I am being "called by God" with the ringing endorsement of "but you'll do."

I wiped away the tears as I was still chuckling at how God knew how to stop my crying, and that He apparently agreed with me that I am unprepared and unqualified—yet he had a plan for me. I didn't even know what the plan was. I described it at the time as being "some kind of something," because I had no idea what it was. I settled down and went to bed wondering what does all this mean and where would my life be heading.

The next day I wrote a post on Facebook, and I titled it "God Has a Cruel Sense of Humor." I realized that Moses was a HORRIBLE spokesperson for God—he stuttered. Abraham was WAY too old to be the father of a nation. The only qualification Lazarus had was that he was DEAD! Yet God still found a way to use these and others in the scriptures. God can use us REGARDLESS of our qualifications, but we have to be willing (and I'm not even sure Lazarus had a say in the matter). And yes, willing and scared qualifies as "willing."

I was now willing (I mean, if God says, "You'll do," then that pretty much settles it, right?) But I was still scared. For me to do what I think He's calling me to do means I'm no longer "in the shadows." I didn't know which was worse, the pain and isolation of not being able to share my whole life with others, or the fear of what will happen if I DO put it out there for all the world to see.

So now I'm forced back into that area where I have LOTS of issues… TRUST. I have to say, it is easier to trust God than it is to trust man, but now we're talking about MY life. It's so easy when helping others to say "trust God, He has it all planned" until it's YOUR life that needs to show that same kind of trust and faith.

I had sent that email to all my friends telling them that as part of wanting to be a disciple of Jesus, I was getting baptized at the end of the month, inviting my local friends (and Pastor Sharon) to come and share the occasion with me. The response was overwhelming. Everyone was SO supportive. Everyone knew my history and the struggle of my life, so I was able to explain how important this was to me—being baptized as Laurie. Everyone that is, except Steve and Laura. For them, my best friends at church and becoming my best friends in Austin, I had to create an edited email just for them. I cried doing it. There were going to be people coming who had never been to my church, they were coming for me, and they all knew the special significance of it in my life, but Steve and Laura were in the dark. They were, of course, happy and rejoicing with me in my decision to be baptized; I wished I could have shared with them what made it all the more special for me, but alas I couldn't.

Laura replied to my email saying "Wow. What a message. Can't wait. Such an awakening and turning point in your life. I really feel honored to be included." Then she continued "I hope someday you'll feel comfortable enough to share with me what happened to you. It hurts me knowing the obvious depth of your suffering. I'm not one to be shocked or dwell in the past, but I feel like there's a puzzle piece that's missing or at best blurry. Just know if you ever feel safe telling me, it would not go beyond me unless you told me it should." It was becoming harder and harder as our friendship grew to not share about my life with her, it was starting to get awkward and straining our friendship.

I decided it was time to communicate with Pastor Jack about all I was feeling, and I started crafting an email to send him. I started it days before getting baptized—I would run versions past Sharon to see what she thought. She had always been so helpful in providing me wisdom from her perspective as a pastor herself to help me understand Pastor Jack. I wanted to be sure I was making my points clearly. It became a work in progress that continued even when Sharon was here. And finally, that day came.

I was so excited to see her. I had told Pastor Jack that Sharon was coming out and she hoped to stand beside me as I got baptized, and he had the idea that she do it. Then Sharon suggested they BOTH do it together, which made her being here even more special. She had never been to Austin before, so after picking her up at the airport, I gave her a quick tour and a taste of Austin before heading home to settle in for the evening. I was eagerly anticipating church the next morning, because we were now at the last message of the Hot Topics series and everything he had indicated in the past pointed to pastor covering social issues. I was thinking, "What if he talks about how the Church needs to love more, especially those who are gay or transgender?" I was sure I would start to cry if he did, which would probably tell everyone sitting around me that it somehow applied to me.

So here it is, Sunday morning. For breakfast, I made a Texas staple for Sharon, breakfast tacos, and then we headed for church. There were people I wanted to introduce her to, including some of the pastors as well as my therapist who also attended the church at the time. So I walked her around introducing her to everyone I could, I was so happy to have her here. I wanted her to meet as many of the great people at my church as possible.

We sat up close to the front with Steve and Laura. Worship was great—always a blessing. Finally, the time came for Pastor's message. I was nervous as could be. I reached over and gave Sharon's leg a squeeze, the anticipation was killing me. Here it comes—what I thought I might never hear from a church that I belonged to was about to be said. Pastor started with a brief review of the previous weeks, and then he said it… "And this week, the topic you wanted me to talk about is… Islam."

You know that "huh" sound that Scooby Doo makes when something isn't what he expected? Well, that's what my mind was doing. Sharon and I glanced at each other with the "I guess he's not talking about it" word bubbles hanging over our heads. I didn't feel so much like my balloon had been popped, but more like all the air was slowly allowed to escape while my brain recalibrated to the fact that social issues were not going to be discussed, at least not today.

When the service was over, we headed to a local barbecue with Steve and Laura. I wanted them to get acquainted since they were all so important to me.

After lunch, Sharon and I headed back to my home to chill until it was time to go back to the church for the evening service. Now that she had "experienced" my church, we talked more about it, and she could see how wonderful of a place I had landed. It did her heart good to see it and mine to share it with her. I didn't go to just a church, I went to an EXCEPTIONAL church, with an exceptional pastor who deeply loves and cares about everyone who goes there.

One thing Sharon and I talked about was my necessary (well, in MY mind it was) talk with pastor about me, and trying to express to him how important it was to be FULLY known by those I considered close friends—I mean after all, they aren't "close" friends if they don't know my background, at least in part.

As Sharon and I talked, I can only explain it as, this must have been a little what it was like to be a disciple at the feet of Jesus. Now, I DON'T worship Sharon, but I do love her and how God had given her such amazing wisdom. I soaked in as much as I could. She understood exactly what I was feeling and was able to help me understand what Pastor Jack might be feeling.

But time was short, and it was necessary to head back for the evening Celebration Service. When we arrived they had shorts and t-shirts for those of us getting baptized to change into. Once I changed, we got seats up near the front. I was looking around for Pastor so I could help Sharon know when to come up, but alas he was nowhere to be found. I had told all my friends in town, even those who didn't go to my church about my baptism and was amazed at how many people showed up. Some brought flowers, but them just coming was a huge blessing.

Much to my surprise, one friend (Lisa) came as well—and I didn't even send her an email. She was a client of mine, and we had talked about church a little in the past, so we knew each other were Christians, and I always had fun joking with her about her "imaginary" husband, because it seemed he was never home whenever I was over there to help with her computer. So in that regard, we were friends but had never got together outside of my coming over and getting paid to help with her technology. But the week before my baptism, I had run into Lisa at the supermarket. We stopped right there in the store and started talking, and I told her that I was getting baptized the following Sunday.

She asked about the when and where, so I told her—not thinking she would actually come. You can imagine my joyful surprise when I turned around that evening and there she was. We hugged and I thanked her for coming—she, along with Steve and Laura were the only ones there who didn't know my FULL story, which was in one way a sad thing because they couldn't appreciate how extra special an occasion this was to me. But in spite of not knowing, they were there for me because of our friendship, which in another way was equally special to me. As my friends came by to say hi and let me know they were there, I made sure to introduce them to Sharon and each other.

The service started with some worship and then the baby dedication. There must have been 30-40 babies and small children being dedicated to the Lord that evening. Pastor LOVES dedicating babies, and these days, now with his eldest daughter recently married, he keeps throwing out hints about wanting to become a grandpa—which I'm sure embarrasses his daughter.

Then, came time for those of us getting baptized—pastor asked us all to come onto the platform. During the baby dedications, since we hadn't been able to catch up with Pastor as to how Sharon would join in, we planned it ourselves, and that's why we sat at the end of the row near the baptismal, easy access. So, everyone getting baptized comes up to the platform, and kept coming and coming. We all barely fit up there, by my count there were almost 40 of us! I was near the back of the line, and as pastor one by one welcomed each person into the water, I was trying to catch Sharon's eye as if to say, "I guess we're winging it from here."

She was wearing a light jacket over her top, and I knew she wasn't going to get wet with that jacket on. As I got closer to the head of the line, Sharon started to remove her jacket, so I knew she already had a plan (after all, this wasn't her first rodeo when it came to baptisms). There were many wonderful moments among the baptisms. The first ones to get baptized were a husband and wife who had recently lost their five-week-old baby, and it was a way of renewing their vow to God to follow Him through it all (tell me THAT doesn't make you want to cry!) Before my turn arrived, a young boy, maybe 10 years old got to be baptized by his own mother. His father, her husband, had passed away so raising him was her job alone.

Finally, it was my turn. As the boy was leaving the water, Sharon got up from her seat in the second row and came up the platform and down beside the baptismal next to Pastor. He was ready to step back and let Sharon do it, but Sharon had already told me that as he was now my pastor and my covering before God, that he should do it; she just wanted to be there and lay her hand on me as I went through the water, which she did. When I came up, I started to cry with happiness, I gave Sharon a hug right there, and yes, it got her wet, and she didn't care. Apparently, a lot of people cheered for me when I came up but I didn't notice it being all caught up in the moment. Being baptized as Laurie had been a dream of mine since I transitioned some 24 years earlier, and finally, after all the years and tears, it finally happened and is a moment I'll never forget.

After the service I changed clothes, then Sharon and I went to dinner with my second family, my "brother" David, his wife and their girls at the second largest restaurant in Texas—the Oasis.

Now, this is Texas we're talking about, so being the second largest is saying something. The Oasis sits some 450 feet above Lake Travis with the perfect location for a Texas sunset, and seats some 2,500 people. And when it comes to sunsets, this one was made to order for a visitor from California. We arrived just in time to get to the patio and see the red and orange hues reflecting off the lake as the sun slowly set behind the hills beyond Lake Travis. And as they do every evening just as the sun sets, they ring a bell announcing the start of evening, which is welcomed with cheers from the people there.

David and his family have been so wonderful to me, and I've mentioned them more than once to Sharon, as I have her to them, so it was only right we get to spend some time together before her flight home in the morning. But morning did come, and the fleeting 40 hours or so of Sharon's visit had come to an end as I drove her to the airport. But what a wonderful 40 hours it had been. She got a taste of Austin the city, my church, and my friends. And we had some good times just sharing with each other. It was the day after she left when I was struck with how lucky I was to be able to spend that kind of time with her. I mean how much would someone PAY to be able to spend that kind of time with their pastor? Sharon has always been a voice of reason and source of incredible wisdom in my life, and to be able to hang out with that for almost 48 hours? THAT's a blessing!

18

THERE'S A CRACK IN THE CLOSET DOOR

"Do not lie to one another, for you have put off the old self with its habits and have put on the new self. This is the new being which God, its Creator, is constantly renewing in his own image, in order to bring you to a full knowledge of himself. As a result, there is no longer any distinction between Gentiles and Jews, circumcised and uncircumcised, barbarians, savages, slaves, and free, but Christ is all, Christ is in all."

Colossians 3:9-11 (GNB)

A LIFETIME IN THE SHADOWS: I had spent my entire life in the shadows. For the first half of my life, virtually no one knew of my being transgender. I was so fearful. Between thinking either there must be something wrong with me, or I was sinning by even thinking I might be different, I kept my mouth shut and maintained the illusion that I was nothing more than a normal guy. Even after transitioning and having surgery, with few exceptions, no one knew my history since I lived in a new neighborhood and had a new job. For someone with a lifetime fear of rejection because I'm transgender, it would seem unlikely that I would be the one God would want to use to reach out to others about Christians who are transgender, yet here I am. And just as the slightest amount of light shatters the darkness in a room, hearing God tell me that "I'll do" was enough to let me know that my being in the shadows was going to be a thing of the past. God said in Jeremiah 7:23 "…Obey me, and I will be your God, and you will be my people. Live the way I told you to live so that things will go well for you." (GW) And this is when it comes down to nothing more than faith and obedience.

One area God seemed to be sending me was in the way of writing. Up until now, I haven't been much of a writer or certainly never thought of myself as one. I had a blog for my business that I had been posting to for six years, but I never considered it "writing" so much as giving general information to my clients and anyone else who might stumble upon it. Once in a blue moon, someone might say "I enjoyed reading your article," but I always attributed it to the fact I probably said something stupid or funny that gave them a chuckle.

But God was laying things on my heart to say, and it was time to start saying it. The obvious place was Facebook, but there were many friends who didn't know I was transgender, including those at my church, so I needed to tread lightly.

I wrote an article asking, "Why Are We Christians at War with Each Other?" The term "evangelical Christians" is used pejoratively by some who would be considered more progressive or liberal, and those more on the right see "liberal Christians" as picking and choosing what they want to be true and ignoring the rest. All the while, each side is asking how the others could even be considered Christian believing what they do, and in doing so, both are acting in the most self-righteous and un-Christian way possible.

No one seems to take the time to appreciate what the "other side" is doing in serving the Lord the way they've been called to serve. It's as if "our calling" is the ONLY calling the Lord has for His Church, and if some other churches aren't doing what our church is doing, then they must be serving Him wrong. They aren't hearing His voice; they're not following His path.

How arrogant we are, thinking God has given our church or denomination His complete calling for ministry to others here on Earth. It's as if Paul never wrote what he did in 1st Corinthians, when he talks about the body of Christ and mocks how silly it would be for the foot to say, "because I'm not a hand, I don't belong to the body," or the ear to say, "I'm not an eye, so I don't belong to the body."

And yes, it does get difficult for me when I see friends of mine make a negative comment online about something transgender-related, either as a joke or as political commentary—mainly because I think they would have thought twice about posting or commenting if they knew I was transgender and would see it. Or if they do know me, that they didn't think about how I might feel seeing what they wrote.

This is what prompted me to tell a friend on Facebook about my background. I had known him for probably 15 years. We first met when I was part of a new group at the company I used to work for, and he was my manager. Later as groups morph (as they frequently do in the tech industry), we were co-workers in a similar group (anyone who has worked in the tech industry is well familiar with the term "re-org," as an almost annual ritual).

Tom was a devout Mormon, and that made me just as nervous about telling him about my background as it would had he been a conservative, evangelical Protestant. But even though I had left the company eight years prior to starting my own company, and he retired from there two years earlier, we had remained friends, and I would help him with his household technology issues from afar. It was even a standing joke of his, whenever he called I would answer the phone, and the first thing out of his mouth was, "Oh great one," usually followed by, "I have a problem," and then laughter.

Since it was inevitable that he would one day find out if we were to stay friends, I decided this was as good a time as any to tell him. I put together an email, and didn't go into detail because I told him that if he would like to know more, I would gladly talk to him about it, but I did give him the gist—that the Laurie he knew at work and when he first opened the email is the same Laurie now at the end of the email, only that he knew more about me than he did before, and I hoped we could still be friends going forward.

What he sent back stunned me. It was simple, direct and to the point... "Laurie, we love you! You are our close friend and the best tech chick this side of the Mississippi. We appreciate your honesty. Absolutely no impact to our relationship."

I was overwhelmed with happiness that my friend and I were still friends. I was also a little bothered that he thought there might be someone on the OTHER side of the Mississippi that might be better than I at what I do, but since he was trying to pay me a compliment, I took it as such and smiled inside.

Having now come out to Tom, it was time to come out to the world—at least the world outside my personal sphere of close friends. As for my church, that would take some time.

It was time to get a website up and to start saying some of the things God had placed on my heart, both for Christians who are transgender and the Church at large. Sharon had the idea that at the top it should say in big letters, "I Am a Christian," harkening to the scene in Elephant Man when he says, "I am not an animal." And I got it. But knowing the habits of people on the Internet, just saying, "I am a Christian" at the top wasn't going to grab anyone's attention, because at first blush they wouldn't know that the topic of the site was about being a Christian AND transgender, so I made it plain as day… "I Am a Christian & I Am Transgender." Now THAT will make some people plant their foot firmly on the brake and stick around to see how this is even possible. So with a little time and effort and a huge prayer, I launched my site in May of 2016. Along with the header of, "I Am a Christian & I Am Transgender" was my picture—right there for all the world to see. Hello world—I'm transgender. And with that—I was officially OUT.

But that didn't mean I'm suddenly posting a banner on my business site that says I'm transgender, or waving a flag at church to make sure everybody knew it. I didn't even post it on Facebook. Just the website. I've never felt that throwing something like this in the face of people is the right thing to do. An attitude of "well if YOU have a problem with it, the problem is with YOU" shows a tremendous lack of consideration for others, and pretty self-defeating if you wish to have a meaningful dialog with them. All that being said, I did feel like I needed to talk more with my pastor. He wasn't so uneasy with me as much as he was with how the church would react, if like a grenade it was thrown out there that "hey, there's a transgender person here with us!" Not to mention that churches like mine are part of what God has called me to and who to reach out to. Not with a big stick but with love and words of understanding—shouting at people doesn't convey love (unless maybe you're on the Titanic and it's going down).

So, for the next couple of days, I worked on crafting an email for my pastor. I already had an appointment with him later in the week, but I wanted to precede it with some of what was on my mind. I told him about feeling "alone." How on the previous Sunday he had talked about how people could be all alone in a marriage, people could be all alone in a huge arena, and people could be all alone at church. And that really hit home for me, because I DID feel alone at church. I had my friends Steve and Laura, but they didn't know about my background—and these were my BEST friends at church. I couldn't tell them about how significant my baptism was. About hearing God's voice and what he had called me to do. How ironically, the church where the amazing transformation of my life has taken place is the only place I CAN'T share my story.

I sent the email to Pastor Jack, and in the meantime, I went to a class being held on Wednesday night at church talking about the foundational aspects of Christianity, as well as things like how we got the Bible we have today. I went to the class with much on my mind, thinking about all that had happened in the last two months and what God has placed on my heart. Pastor taught the class this week, and he was talking about the value of generosity, and he talked about some of the organizations that the church locally helps, and he got to the point he wanted to make, which was "humility is not thinking of yourself less, it's thinking of others MORE."

And that's EXACTLY what started all this in the last few months for me, the "Called or Crazy" moment, when I felt like something needed to be done. All I care about is helping others who are transgender and those in the Church that need help understanding those who are transgender. I have plenty of good friends who know my full background, and I could easily go back into the woodwork and into the shadows, but that's not why God created me. He created me for this very time, for this moment of my life. Everything I've endured, everything I've gone through both good and bad, has been preparation, getting me ready so that I COULD do this. Six months earlier, I would have told anyone they were crazy to say I would be doing what I am. And yet, here I am.

It was time to talk to Pastor Jack about Steve and Laura. I don't know about you, but sitting in my pastor's office is intimidating to me. He's not a scary guy at all, but I'm not very good at difficult, personal conversations. It's hard when you've spent a lifetime developing defense mechanisms protecting yourself from "personal" conversations. Some people thrive on challenging conversations; it's like giving spinach to Popeye—it makes them ready for more. That wouldn't be me. I don't like confrontation at all. I don't even like disagreement, but we all have to encounter it at some point.

When I met with my pastor, it was difficult for me, mainly because I so wanted him to understand, but I left not feeling much progress had been made. He didn't understand the "need" to tell people close to me; I failed to communicate how isolated I feel, how it's lonely fearing I can't get close to people. We also talked more about Steve and Laura, how I would like his "blessing" as it were to go ahead and tell them. They were my best friends at church. It wasn't a "balanced" relationship; Laura had shared deeply personal things with me KNOWING there were things about my life I hadn't told her (she felt like I didn't trust her, which wasn't true, but that was her perception).

Now you have to understand, Steve and Laura are very conservative by any measure, and Pastor Jack knew this well. Steve, being in charge of the IT volunteers, is often in the office and he and Pastor talk frequently. Pastor is sure someone as conservative as Steve and Laura couldn't possibly handle the truth of my history.

But the BEST part of our conversation was after telling Pastor how hard it was to have a "normal" friendship with them and NOT include my history, he leaned forward at the little round table we were sitting at and said in a somewhat hushed tone, "But they like Ted Cruz."

And without skipping a beat, I leaned forward toward him, and looking him straight in the eye, I said in a similar hushed tone, "So do I." I guess he was expecting it to bother me and he certainly didn't expect me to be a fan of Ted Cruz. The only thing that bothered me was that Ted didn't end up getting the nomination, but that's water under the bridge now.

Pastor did end it, however, saying how I could really be risking getting hurt by telling Steve and Laura, and that it could spill over into the church, but that I should talk to Sharon about it and pray about it, then do what I thought I should. At the time (mostly because of my current sensitive frame of mind), I took it to almost mean tell them if I want, but it would be selfish, and I'm risking causing a division in the church by doing so (in hindsight, I think he genuinely was more concerned that I didn't get hurt by additional rejection).

At the same time, he did support my reaching out to those who are transgender. On the drive home, I was trying to reconcile all we talked about and the fact that he had baptized me a couple of weeks prior. My only conclusion was that we have an unspoken rule at church, a "don't ask, don't tell" policy. I sent Sharon an email telling her how everything seemed out of sorts. Why did God lay all this on me only to have me in a place that doesn't want me talking about His calling?

Sharon reminded me, not for the first time and it wouldn't be the last, of how much has happened in a very short time. In less than two months I committed to discipleship, heard God's voice, built a website and ministry I never thought I would, and was baptized. Yep—less than eight weeks. Have I truly learned that lesson of patience that God tried to teach me back in the "Called or Crazy" moment? Um, apparently not, at least not well.

What I wasn't realizing is that God wasn't turning me loose yet, because He knew I wasn't ready yet—He was trying to help me expand and grow. But I took off like a dog let loose off a leash, until I abruptly found out that no, I haven't been given free reign. It wasn't that long ago God taught me to let Him drive, that when I let Him drive the road was smooth, the route was correct, and the destination was easily reached, even if I myself didn't know exactly what that destination was. God had made it clear to Sharon that I was precisely where He wanted me to be, under the protection and covering of my pastor. She explained to me that it was obvious that my pastor loved me, cared about me, supported me, and had my back—if not, he wouldn't have baptized me. But being a pastor herself, she helped me understand how difficult this is for any pastor to navigate. She had spoken with Pastor Jack and assured me that his heart is in agreement with mine; that it shouldn't matter to folks.

But the reality is that to some people, it does—and he's not just my pastor, but everyone's pastor who calls my church home. He is leading the church to be a church where one day this won't be an issue. But until that time, people can get hurt in the crossfire, and he needs to guard against that as well—and I understood. It's not up to me to change everyone's hearts. In fact, it's not up to me to change ANYONE'S heart. My job is to do what God has asked me to do, which is to avail myself to Christians who are transgender and be an example to Christians within the church—that because someone is transgender, it doesn't mean they don't love the Lord or shouldn't be allowed to be a part of His family.

The next day, I was at the supermarket and thinking about what Sharon had told me—and it all made sense. I started to think to myself, "I don't have to tell Laura, I can keep everything to myself for the sake of my church." Yeah well, that thought lasted about five seconds as I went through the ramifications of what that meant. That meant I couldn't tell my best friend at church WHY I don't talk to my family today or WHY I haven't seen them in 24 years. I can't tell her WHY I got divorced. I can't tell her HOW I was hurt at that church in Sacramento and why it led to my 11 years "in the wilderness" here in Austin. I can't answer the question, "What is God doing in your life," because I can't tell her about hearing God's voice. I can't tell her about my ministry or my website. I can't tell my best friend ANYTHING that is really going on in my life, how I find application in Pastor's messages to my own ministry, how when I read God's word it speaks to me, and how when I'm inspired to write something on my website I can't share it with her.

And of course, right when I'm feeling a little sensitive about pretty much everything, a good friend of mine, a friend who loves me and knows my history, "liked" a cartoon on Facebook. It was late at night and I was in bed. I set the alarm for the morning and thought, what the heck, one last peek at Facebook to see any last minute posts. The cartoon showed three bathroom doors. The door on the left said "Men," the door on the right "Women," and the door in the middle said "Confused?" I just stared at my screen in disbelief. How could she do that? Does she think I'm confused? I went to her name in my "Friends" list and immediately unfriended her, after which I remembered something said in a message at church earlier in the year... When it comes to anger, our first response is our worst response.

If you're angry, adrenaline is going through your system, and no one makes thoughtful, rational decisions on adrenaline. Anger and adrenaline make you want to scream, anger and adrenaline make you want to throw something. For some, it makes them want to punch a hole in the wall (I'll take their word for it on that one). But even when I had somewhat calmed down, I was still dazed by my friend's action. If my good Christian friends think being transgender is a state of confusion, then I have even more work than I thought set out for me. Maybe I'm in over my head. How do I go into this battle so disadvantaged that my friends believe I'm "confused"? How do I change the hearts of strangers when my friends don't believe it? Maybe I AM wasting my time at my church and should move on.

These are all the thoughts of a woman new in ministry. These are the thoughts of someone so excited about being called by the Lord, but not experienced enough yet to understand how that son of a bitch Satan keeps finding a soft spot in me to push to bring doubt and uncertainty about my ministry to my mind. The truth about my friend liking that cartoon is that she didn't even think about me being transgender, and that's something I forget about people. It's a fact that I'm transgender. Nothing changes that. But people who know me see me simply as a woman. Even when they know I'm transgender, they forget. When I visit them, I don't go into their home and say, "Now don't forget, I'm your transgender friend."

Likewise, when I walk in the door they don't say, "Oh good, our transgender friend Laurie is here." They don't even remember that I'm transgender unless it comes up in conversation, as in something happening with my family or some other related thing in my life. When she saw the cartoon, she didn't think I was confused, actually she was so sure I wasn't confused it didn't occur to her to think about me and how I might react, or more accurately OVERreact.

It reminded me of the time when I was new at the tech company, and a gal Debbie (who trained me and who knew my history) asked me if I had an extra tampon with me.

I gave her my best "really?" look and said, "Debbie, think about it."

It took her a second, and then she laughed and said, "Oh, I totally forgot about that!"

So here I am, new in my ministry, being bamboozled by that son of a bitch Satan and thinking maybe I should leave my church and start afresh somewhere else. Sharon (once again) tells me to breathe and reminds me that it's that SOB that's trying to wreck everything. God has a plan, and Satan isn't one bit happy about it, he's attacking me at my weak points, which at the time were plentiful, because I was insecure and frankly wasn't fully trusting the God that I had previously trusted to work all this out.

I realized that it was probably inevitable that I would at some point tell Laura, and when that time came, if things went south in that conversation, then I would probably have to leave the church rather than allow it to become a problem. And the time for our talk turned out to be sooner rather than later.

19

THE LUNCH THAT CHANGED
EVERYTHING

"When we give thanks and share the cup of blessing, are we not sharing in the blood of the Anointed One? When we give thanks and break bread, are we not sharing in His body? Because there is one bread, we, though many, are also one body since we all share one bread."

1 Corinthians 10:16-17 (The Voice)

THE REALITY OF REJECTION: Experiencing rejection from people close to me in the past was like burning my hand on a hot stove. I knew how much it hurt, and I didn't want it to happen again. However, there seemed to be an impending and unavoidable collision of my desire to protect the church I love from a major bru-ha-ha, and the desire to be able to share about my life with my good friend Laura. If things go bad, they could go VERY bad. Bad for my pastor who allowed a transgender woman to serve (albeit as a volunteer) at the church and bad for me, as I would undoubtedly lose my best friend at church and need to leave in order to protect my pastor and not bring strife into the church. I know there are activists who would say I SHOULD shake it all up, that it would be a good thing. But 1 Corinthians 16:14 tells us, "Do everything in love." Intentionally causing a disruption within the church is not a loving act. People's HEARTS need to change; you can't just change laws and think people are going to go along. As people's hearts change, laws become less necessary. I know my pastor felt like the church membership (as a single body) wasn't quite ready to be okay with those who are transgender having membership and serving at the church (even though I was already both a member and serving). It was going to take some time. At the same time, I am called to a ministry, and my own church seemed to be part of my mission field.

A couple of months earlier, the women's ministry at church held a "glamping" event (glamorous camping for you uninitiated) at the church. The time it started was clearly spelled out in the emails and online, 6:30 pm on a Thursday. Unfortunately, in most places, the time it ended was omitted, and it was the source of some confusion. When I called Laura to see if she was going, she said she wasn't into camping and indicated her boys would need her in the morning.

I chuckled and said, "Laura, it's only two and a half hours, you can do that."

"What?" she said. "I thought it was an overnight thing."

I explained it was only a couple of hours and would be fun to hang out. Everyone was going to be in pajamas and pearls and slippers, you know—just having fun (and oh yes, LOTS of food!).

I said "C'mon, it'll be fun," and she gave in. She lived about a mile from me, I told her I'd swing by around 6:00 and pick her up and if she wanted to leave early we could, because I'm not so big on social events with mostly strangers, but it was a way of meeting some of the other women at church.

Thursday rolls around, and I put on my PJ bottoms, a long pink sleep-shirt that went to almost my knees, and my furry sheepskin slippers. I was a sight to behold—something akin to a freakishly tall Oompa Loompa with extremely short legs. What the heck, everyone was dressing silly! So I swing by Laura's home and knock on the door—her husband Steve opens it, and I say "ta-da!" (showing off my exquisite taste in camping attire). I'm pretty sure at that moment he was reconsidering his decision to allow me onto the IT volunteer team at church.

Steve laughs and says, "Oh, wow!" and leaves it at that. Laura comes to the door, and off we go.

No sooner had we got into my car and closed the doors then Laura says, "Can I tell you something?" I could see she was becoming upset, not in a mad way, but something was bothering her. She seemed fine 60 seconds ago at the door, but clearly, something was up that she needed to get out.

She then said, "I know you feel like you can't trust me with whatever it is about your past..."

Whoa. Let's stop right there for a minute. It killed me to hear Laura say that. The TRUTH was the opposite, I TRUSTED

Laura and wanted to tell her about my past, but navigating it all has been difficult, and apparently even for her, because I know she considered me a friend, and I was about to learn JUST how good a friend.

Laura continued, "I know you feel like you can't trust me with whatever it is about your past, but I need to talk to someone, and I trust you even if you don't feel you can trust me."

This is EXACTLY what I mean about relationships getting weird when you can't fully share your life with a good friend.

Her words were more daggers into my heart. Then her eyes started to water up. Something was wrong, and whatever it was she needed to get it out. She started by saying NO ONE else in her family knew about this and it needed to be kept that way, but she needed to talk to someone because it was killing her.

I had no idea what was going on inside her, but I let her talk. She began to tell me the backstory, and 20 minutes later as we pulled into the church parking lot, she was still building up the story but hadn't told me what it was that she wanted to tell me.

By now my deep concern for what was bothering her was intermixed with some internal chuckling, because it SO reminded me of the many times when I would be telling my full history to someone I knew for the first time. There always seemed to be this long preamble, as if to make the bomb I was going to drop hopefully a little less destructive.

We pulled into a parking spot at the church, and leaving the car running I put my hand on her shoulder and said, "Laura, you can tell me. What is it you want to say?"

She finally told me what it was. It involved a disappointment by someone close to her and was a BIG deal to her, and I understood. She was pretty devastated, and it confirmed to me how good of friends we were. We both were willing to share deep "secrets" with each other. But my willingness couldn't be realized at the time, because I was walking a high wire between friendship and honoring my pastor's request to hold off.

She thanked me for listening, we gave each other a big hug, and walked down to the event. We had fun, ate food, sang worship songs by a campfire, and even took pictures next to a life-size bear (stuffed - the bear that is and for that matter, so were we with all that food). Afterward, I drove her home and told her I would be praying for her.

Later that night, I wrote her an email letting her know that I would be praying for her and what she shared with me. I explained how bad I felt that she thought I couldn't trust her. I told her that I had trust issues with the Church at large and not with her, but at the same time I had agreed not to talk about it (I didn't say with whom the agreement was with), but was looking forward to the day when I could, and when that day comes we'd do lunch.

A couple of weeks later, after the weekend of my baptism and our lunch with Pastor Sharon, I sent a message to both Steve and Laura letting them know how badly I feel not being able to share more about myself. I said it hurts me as much as I'm sure it confuses them, that they've been so wonderful and patient—and though they have never brought it up themselves, that I knew they were wondering what all the mystery was about. I did say that I was "working on it" and looking forward to the day when I could spill the beans and remove the veil of mystery, and that having my best friends from church meet Sharon was the highlight of the weekend (well, after the actual baptism that is).

Several weeks pass. Each week I sit with Steve and Laura up front at church and we worship together (usually in the second or third row) and on occasion, we'd go to lunch together after church and have a nice talk about their family, or if it went there—politics. Now I'm just as conservative as they are, so it never was a problem, and one thing for sure you can always bet Steve has something to say on any political topic—not because he likes to talk a lot, but because he is well informed.

Finally, I'm at a point where it doesn't make sense to keep my history a secret from them. The depth of our friendship was becoming a little one-sided. I was learning things about their family, their lives, where and how they grew up, school, etc., and for me, it was pretty much left to talking about my work, because I couldn't tell them about all the other GREAT stuff that was going on. Finally, I had had enough. Either this was going to work, or it wasn't. Either we were good friends, or we weren't. This was going to create a problem at church and with Pastor, or it wasn't.

So, I sent an email, an email to my pastor.

I let him know that after thinking about and praying about it, that I was going to tell Laura. I was SURE she was going to be okay, though it may rock her world for a moment while the dust settled in her mind. I was sure our friendship was beyond whatever issue she might have with my being transgender. I was less sure about Steve, but if I felt Laura was 80 percent or more to the good, then I put Steve at maybe a little better than 50 percent.

I told Pastor that if things went south and it created a stir within the church, I would leave. If I was wrong about my friends, if my judgment was so off that things blew up, then I would walk away and not be a source of disunity at the church. At the same time, I had called Laura and asked if we could meet for lunch. There must have been something in my voice or the way I said it, because she got the idea that this was THE lunch I had referred to a couple of months earlier. We planned to get together on Monday at a Chinese restaurant in a little shopping center near our homes.

The day before our lunch was a different day for me. It was Sunday, but my mind was on Monday. As I pulled into the church parking lot, all I could think about was that after nine months at Austin Transformation Church, this might be the last time I make this drive to church. I tried to be cheery and smile to the greeters as I entered the doors. The lobby was swirling with people leaving the previous service and arriving for the next. People were standing around talking and drinking coffee. Some were laughing. There was a group of three or four off to the side praying for someone. It had a bit of a surreal feel to it. I was taking mental pictures of everything, because I wanted to remember it.

I arrived before Steve and Laura, and I didn't want to run into anyone else who I knew, because I was worried my "life is good" facade might be too easy to see through. I went into the sanctuary and got us seats up front in our usual area.

Just as the music was starting, Steve and Laura arrived. Laura gave me a hug, and I leaned over and gave Steve a hug. Worship was a bit of a struggle for me this morning, because all I could think about is that this could be my last week. The last time to enjoy this awesome worship. I looked around the building and up into the rafters. I tried to take it all in, the sound, the people, the surrounding, the spirit. If this was to be my last week, then I wanted to absorb and remember as much as possible about it.

I could tell my eyes were starting to water up. It would have been so easy to start crying, but I then didn't want to have to explain WHY I was crying. No matter where I looked or who I saw, the theme that kept running through my mind was "this might be it." I don't think I even heard the pastor's message that morning. Oh, the sound waves left the speakers and reached my ears, but getting processed by my brain as words to be pondered? Nope, he might as well have been speaking in Japanese and teaching how to make origami animals. When church was over, I said goodbye to Steve, "See you tomorrow" to Laura, and headed for my car not knowing if I would ever come back. I didn't feel like hanging around and talking to anyone. Tomorrow would come, and I'd then find out what my future looked like, with Laura and Steve and my church in my life—or not.

And indeed, tomorrow did come. I made sure I didn't schedule any clients for the day. I didn't know if I would be feeling happy, concerned, shocked, depressed, or what! No clue, and if I was going to be a depressed basket case, I didn't want to have to call clients to reschedule.

Our lunch was at noon, and it sure made for a long morning waiting for time to leave, to get in my car and make that long five-minute trip to the restaurant. In hindsight, I probably should have scheduled a client so I'd have something to take my mind off the upcoming lunch. I had given a lot of thought about how I was going to tell her. It's not like this was the first time I'd done it, but this time was different. I wasn't just risking a dear friendship, I was risking any relationship I had with anyone from my church. If there was a way I could tell her and help her try to understand, then I had to give it my VERY best attempt.

As I drove toward the restaurant from home, my thoughts were "how will Laura react?" It was almost like watching a movie in my head—I'd play out the scene where I tell her and then would come her reaction. I'd play the scene in my head again, and it would be a different reaction. As I was driving up the small street close to the little strip center where the restaurant was located, the last scene that played in my head, is that when I told her I was transgender, her reply was, "I thought so." Did she already know? Was I all worked up, including worrying about my church and my pastor for nothing?

We both pulled up to the restaurant about the same time. Was I nervous? Oh, you bet. I met her outside the restaurant with a smile and hug as she did me. It was a cute little restaurant. Though it was only a few minutes away from my home, I had never been there. It's one of those places that you go, "Oh, I had no idea there was a restaurant there!"

We walked in, and it wasn't very busy. Normally that would raise a red flag with me. If a restaurant isn't busy at noon and dinner, I wonder why—but I had checked it out online and it had great reviews, so I didn't let it bother me. But of course, where did we get seated? Right there at a table in the middle of the room! If you're going to open your soul up to someone who may in the next moment reject you and try to cast you out of her life as if you were Satan himself, don't you think you'd want a table a bit more private? I was so consumed with telling Laura that I didn't even have the wherewithal to ask for a different table.

The hostess seated us and handed us our menus, and I plastered together the most pleasant "thank you" smile on my face as I could. Laura knew that THIS was the lunch, and I KNEW that she knew—so I said, "Let's figure out what to order." I didn't want to get into some heavy conversation only to have a server walk up and say (do you know what you want to order?) So we both politely ignored each other and threw in a little small talk as we figured out what we wanted to order. I DO love Chinese food, so something spicy was what I was looking for. Eventually, we both figured out what we wanted, the server came over, took our order and left. So there we were—just the two us with our iced teas and this huge secret that we both knew I was about to reveal.

There were a few seconds of silence, then Laura looked at me and said, "Are you going to tell me what you've been holding back?" knowing that the answer was yes. She wasn't demanding; she was breaking the ice because someone had to do it.

I muttered out a soft "yes" as my eyes watered up. I was so scared. I didn't want to lose my friend Laura, but this was a bridge I had to cross—I'd either make it to the other side or it would blow up and take me with it midway, and I had no way of knowing which way it would go.

I started with this… "Remember when I picked you up for the glamping event and you told me something private in the car?"

She said, "Yes, of course."

I said, "And then you spent the next 20 minutes until we finally got into the parking space before you could finally tell me what it was you wanted to actually tell me?"

She chuckled and said, "Yes, I do."

That's when I said, "Well, this is probably going to be a lot like that 20-minute preamble you gave me before getting to the punch line, but bear with me and we'll get there." She nodded yes, and so I started to tell her my story.

But before starting my story, I told her I thought our conversation could go with her having one of four different reactions... I told her this could go as I see it four different ways... one being "no big problem—I get it, and we're okay." In which case, I pick up the check.

The second being, "Oh, okay I need to think about this and can we talk about it later?" Laura gets up, and I pick up the check.

The third possible response being, "I have a big problem with this, I'm going to need some time, but I'll contact you when we should talk," she gets up, leaves the table, and I pick up the check.

And the final option is, "Get thee behind me Satan, never contact me again and never let me see your face in my presence for the duration of my life!" And yes, she gets up, and yes, I pick up the check. Those were pretty much the four options the way I saw it.

By this time I'm pretty sure Laura must have thought I was some kind of ax murderer.

I talked about how growing up, I knew there were certain expectations, expectations that people take for granted. I told her about how I tried everything, including getting married to have a "normal" life. I spend the next 15 minutes telling her all the marginal stuff, but I didn't get down to the punchline. Just before that, we were served our egg drop soup. So it was time. Tell her now or wimp out and pray Jesus returns in the next day or two.

As much as I believe in prayer, I didn't think I was going to pray my way into the second coming happening within 48 hours, so I decided to tell her. I told her that back in April I heard God's voice. That it wasn't like, "God when I open my Bible show me what you want me to see," kind of voice—this was HIS voice. I told her about how I had felt a calling—and on that particular evening it was laying heavy on me, and I asked the Lord in tears if there wasn't someone else who could do the job—and the Lord said "No, but you'll do." How from that I began what could only be called a ministry.

What I said to Laura in a slow and deliberate manner was, "I've been called to minister to Christians who are evangelical and conservative... people like me." She nodded her head acknowledging that knowing me as she did, I was a conservative Christian, and this was not a newsflash. She probably thought that something really noble in a conservative Christian way was about to follow.

I then continued, saying, "And also to minister to Christians who are transgender..."

And as I paused there was a glimmer in her eye, as if she was thinking what an amazing thing this must be as a ministry.

But then I continued with the punchline as she raised a spoonful of egg drop soup toward her lips... "People like me."

And it was at THAT very second her spoon stopped moving as if frozen in time three inches from her lips. If this were a movie, you couldn't have scripted her response better. A Christian? A conservative? AND transgender? I could almost hear all the gears grinding around in her head as she tried to reconcile what she knew about me as a person and as her friend with what I had just told her.

It took maybe five or ten seconds in real life, but at the time it felt like an eternity. She put the spoon, still full of her egg drop soup

266

back into the bowl, and the first word out of her mouth was, "Okay." That was it, not, "Okay what kind of freak are you?" Not, "What kind of horrible person are you that you would deceive me after all these months?" Just, "Okay." And almost right on cue, our server came back out with our main course meals.

Laura looked up at her and just laughed, saying, "I'll just need this to go." It might have been the funniest thing I've ever heard someone say in my presence. At this point, Laura was "all-in" to our conversation and the food be damned, but since I'm paying for it—go ahead and box it up!

I was pretty much with her at this point and told the server with a smile, "Same for me—I'll need a box."

With both our meals nicely encapsulated in hardy foam containers, we continued to talk right there at the table. One of the first things Laura said to me was, "I thought that maybe that was it, but wasn't sure."

After all, what could I have done? Killed my ex-husband and served timed in prison for murder? Embezzled millions of dollars from some Wall Street firm? She knew me well enough to think those things couldn't be true, so she listened to my story. I filled in all the blank spaces that she needed to have filled in to understand the WHOLE picture of my life. For the next two hours, I talked. And when I was done, her response was the same as the moment I first told her - "Okay." She knew who I was before today's talk. She knew my heart. She knew I was genuine. She also knew that there was something missing to fill in the blanks in her information, and now that she had it—and it all made sense to her.

We talked and talked until the restaurant informed us they close for the afternoon at three o'clock until dinner. We both were pretty much surprised—we've done it again, talked for hours over a meal. But this time, I was filling in all the blanks that I had left out when we had our long barbecue lunch months back.

As we walked out, I was so euphoric that my friend hadn't run out of the room screaming as if her hair was on fire, that I wasn't thinking about much else. This was a HUGE hurdle to cross, and it had been done. We hadn't even gotten outside the doors to the restaurant when Laura asked, "What about the elephant in the room?"

I didn't get it. So being clueless to what she was talking about I said, "Huh?"

Laura said, "Steve, what about Steve?"

Yes, what about Steve? I left that to her. I said, "Go ahead and tell him when you think the time is right."

Apparently, the time was right about 30 seconds after she got home. I could have asked Laura how she told Steve and what she said, but I almost have more fun imagining what it might have been like.

I can imagine her driving home saying to herself, "He won't believe it. He won't believe it. He just won't believe it." She was probably tempted to call him from her car but decided to wait because she wanted to do it in person.

You know that feeling when you're in your car and you really, really need to go to the bathroom, you're so close to home you don't stop, and the closer you get to your home, the more you need to go. That's what I'm thinking Laura was feeling with this new knowledge she had. I picture her pulling into her driveway, and as soon as she walks in the door she goes over to Steve, and since they home-school their youngest son, she grabs Steve by his shirt and pulls him into their bedroom and closes the door behind them, and in an intense but soft voice says, "You WON'T believe this!" Followed by a pause to make sure their boys wouldn't hear, "Laurie was born a boy!"

What I wouldn't pay to have been able to see the expression on his face. I'm sure they had both talked about me saying things like, "Did she kill someone? Is she in the witness protection program?" For all I know there actually may have been a degree of disappointment with the revelation that I was transgender. Nothing so exciting as I might have once testified against the mob, or I had to shoot my husband because he tried to kill me.

Whatever his reaction, it didn't take long before I got a text from him. It said, "Hey—would you like to sit down and talk for a bit on my way to the airport this evening?" I had left Laura about an hour earlier, WHAT did THIS mean? Was he going to question everything I knew about myself to be true? Was he going to accuse me of being someone "deceived" by Satan who needed the healing powers of Christ? He asked if we could meet at another hole-in-the-wall restaurant, this time a Greek restaurant close to home that, yes, I never knew was even there (hey, I don't get out much!).

He had a flight out on business, so we got together around 5:00, only hours after Laura and I had met. Steve makes me nervous. He's really smart. I mean nuclear scientist kind of smart and analytical as well, and I wasn't sure my "I always knew I was a girl inside" emotional plea would carry much weight with him. He could easily be one of those who believes that whatever your biology is (as in genitals) when you're born determines who you are—black and white, pure and simple. None of this grey area baloney.

But I didn't have to plead my own case, because whatever Laura told him when she got home before the text to me more than did the job—that or the job never needed to be done within his heart. We met and ordered something for dinner and sat down. He started sharing that he loved me as much today as he did yesterday, and nothing had changed.

He then shared things about his life that he doesn't share with many people. He understood what it's like to be a Christian that isn't necessarily understood by other Christians. I had NO idea. His own life experiences gave him the heart that tries to understand the lives of others without jumping to judgment. As smart and as dogmatic at times he might have appeared to be, God had used his life experience as lessons to learn and to live by. And this was one of those moments.

As Steve was telling me about his past, I was sitting there thinking to myself, "Hey Steve, you don't need to be telling me all this—I'm just wondering if you're okay with what you've learned about me."

The bottom line is, yes, he was. But just as I want people to know the WHOLE me when we're talking to each other at this level, he wanted me to know HIM at a similar level, which deepened our friendship all the more. I was honored that he shared what he did about his life. Not many people would—but Steve is an exceptional and genuine person, and I am BLESSED to be able to call him a friend.

A funny thing he shared with me is that my pastor, my dear pastor whom I love with all my heart, apparently was shall we say, "fretting," about my telling Steve and Laura for weeks. Steve's job gives him the freedom to work from pretty much anywhere, which allows him to swing by the church frequently and chat with folks between phone calls. Steve loves to chat, and I don't mean with his fingers on a smartphone, but old school—face to face using his voice. He's talked a lot with Pastor Jack over the years, and they're pretty close. So whenever Pastor saw Steve in the office, he would ask something to the effect of, "Has Laurie said anything to you?"

Steve, knowing that there was "something" I hadn't shared with him and Laura would answer with "No, nothing" and leave it at that. I do feel bad that I was putting my pastor through the wringer like that. He was stressing even before I sent him that email informing him that I WOULD be telling Laura and Steve.

After Laura told Steve at home, he sent Pastor a text letting him know that he now had my backstory.

Apparently, Pastor responded with, "You okay?" I guess Pastor Jack figured he'd feel the earth quake when Steve found out.

Steve responded saying all was fine, that he's called to love unconditionally and that's what he was going to do. And the funniest part of all is that he then asked Pastor, "I understand you may have some concerns, how can I help you?"

And just like that, I had my friends. I had my church. And I probably had a somewhat relieved pastor who felt like he had dodged a bullet (or maybe a small landmine).

As it turned out, keeping my friends Steve and Laura, and just as importantly, keeping my church, proved to be a pivotal point in my journey, a journey that was just beginning.

20

AND SO IT BEGINS

"God has given each of you some special abilities; be sure to use them to help each other, passing on to others God's many kinds of blessings. Are you called to preach? Then preach as though God himself were speaking through you. Are you called to help others? Do it with all the strength and energy that God supplies so that God will be glorified through Jesus Christ—to him be glory and power forever and ever. Amen."

1 Peter 4:10-11 (TLB)

The following Sunday, after Steve and Laura learned my background, was no different than any other Sunday. Except for one little difference. On more than one occasion, we caught our pastor's wife looking over, seemingly in disbelief that the two most conservative members of the church were sitting with me just as we had for months. I think (or at least I like to hope) it was the beginning of a recalibration of sorts in how she and Pastor Jack perceived the feelings other church members might

273

have about the whole transgender issue. That it IS possible that even conservative evangelical Christians can be kind, loving, and accepting toward others who are transgender—and maybe even friends.

Around the same time as the suspense with telling Laura was going on, I got an email from my worship leader friend Melissa, whom I had reconnected with a few months earlier. She had told me back then in a message, "I want to be honest with you... I don't know what to think about your change..." She didn't know how to feel about my being transgender, but she loved me because that's what Christ taught.

The months passed with us staying in touch on Facebook and the occasional phone call. I had recently gone live with my website and had sent out a message to about 40 friends letting them know about my calling and the website. She had been reading my posts and articles. And then one day the most amazing, touching message from her showed up in my email, more proof of God's goodness and timing.

"Dear Laurie,
I was just thinking the other night that when I die, I want to know that my life mattered, that I left the world a better place than when I entered it. That is what I hope to know when the time comes for me to meet my Savior. You, on the other hand, have the proof of a life purposefully lived right now. You are going to literally save lives with your testimony. Your testimony will bring many to life through Christ as well. You will also be attacked, slandered, and misunderstood. Nothing new under the sun. I will be praying for God's protection over your life. I definitely don't understand how it feels to be you, but I know my heart and mind have been changed because of knowing you. Be blessed and follow after God. He won't lead you astray.
Love,
Melissa"

I cried at how faithful God is. How MUCH He must love me, to keep bringing encouragement to me when He knows I need it most. And even more importantly, this was an affirmation of the ministry He was calling me to. Melissa is living proof that people's hearts can change when they are willing to look at your life and heart, and not judge based on what they might think or hear. If I was going to have to reach people one person at a time, then so be it. God didn't call me to meet a quota, He just called me—the rest is up to Him.

The website was up and running, and this book was started. Eventually, people I know who aren't aware of my history are probably going to find out. The question I was faced with was, do I let them find out for themselves, or do I tell them? Letting friends know who don't know... ugh! Facing potential rejection is never fun, and I'm a little gun shy each time I have to tell someone.

But if they're friends, they're friends. It's time to start letting them know and hope for the best. While I didn't go on a coming out binge, I did selectively tell people, and universally they were all fine and thanked me for sharing that part of my life with them. Whew! Again, what a difference people's thinking can be when they actually know someone in a given situation, rather than just what they read and hear about a group of people.

Working on my website and getting started with a book did leave me with another problem—publicity. I had a pretty good feel with Facebook, so I thought about how I could make that work to build an audience.

Here was my problem. I had many friends, mostly from church, that didn't know I was transgender. I was committed to keeping my word to Pastor Frank and not just toss the grenade of, "Hey everybody, I'm transgender" into the church.

I discovered a neat little trick on Facebook. You can break your friends into smaller groups. So I created a sub-group of friends consisting only of those who knew my history. Simple. And I also created my author page, so when I posted there, I could share it on my personal page only to my special group of friends. Now I could post and share on Facebook and insulate my church at the same time. And it was perfect! Until...

In early August, I added a post to my website, linked to it on my Facebook author page, and then shared it from my personal page. Except for one little boo-boo. I forgot to assign it to my "special" group of friends. Instead, it was assigned "PUBLIC," as in everyone I knew and the other one billion users on Facebook! I didn't notice it until 30 minutes later when a Facebook friend, who was also a client of mine and who didn't know my history, LIKED my post!

The post was titled, "Rejected by Your Family? Go Get a New One!" It was about creating a "family" of your own from relationships you have with friends. Below the title was the name of my website in nice large letters, "I Am a Christian & I Am Transgender," along with a big picture of my face (right about then, it seemed more like a highway billboard).

There was nowhere to hide. My client knew my name, and she certainly knew my face. Is it possible for your heart-rate to suddenly double in one second? It seemed mine did. I didn't plan on telling her yet. But more than that, what was driving me into full-on panic mode, was wondering who else had seen it. Maybe other clients who didn't know. What if someone from church saw it? I immediately changed the post so that only my special group would see it, hoping that would be enough to limit the damage.

I was a total mess over what might happen if those at church who didn't know my history had seen it and were disturbed by it. I had promised my pastor that I would do nothing to cause a disruption at church—and I may have very well done just that. There is no undo button on Facebook. I could have deleted the post, but if someone had already seen it, the damage was done.

I put an email together for Pastor Jack's wife and Pastor Karen at church, letting them know what happened, that it was an accident, and I didn't know if anyone from church had seen it. There were seventeen people at church I was friends with on Facebook at the time, including a few on staff that, as far as I knew, were not aware of my full backstory. So I sent the two pastors the list of people.

I then checked with my client/friend who saw the post and asked if we were okay. She was just fine, and in fact, has a sister who is gay and had been shunned by the Catholic Church years ago, so she was sympathetic. And fortunately, no one from church saw it (apparently).

Since then, the friends I've told have been okay with it. But telling my friends at church is a much slower process, because it can impact the church negatively if I'm careless in who and how I tell them.

There was a period of time following that "Facebook faux pas" when I was so fearful about developing new friendships that might lead to "the talk," that I shut down the chance of it happening again. I resigned from my volunteering position, and I didn't participate in any of the home groups or Bible studies.

Did it work? If the goal was to make myself miserable, then it was a phenomenal success, because I was not a happy camper. I'm not the kind of person who can just show up at church on Sunday, make my appearance, shake hands when we're told to, listen to the message, and then go home until the following week satisfied that I've fulfilled my weekly Christian obligation. I realized God made me someone who values people and friendships, He gave me the heart to serve, and He gave me a need to be connected. When I tried NOT to be the person He made me to be, it was a spectacular fail! You would think I would have learned that lesson years ago when I was suicidal. Sometimes, we need to be reminded that fighting against who God made us to be does not bring peace to our lives. Lesson learned.

How blessed I am continues to amaze me. God is so good. With trepidation, I tell my story and with arms wide open, time and time again, my friends tell me they love me, that they know who I am, and that's enough. My pastor loves and welcomes me, and the same can be said for the other pastors and staff. As time has gone on, my circle of friends at church who know I'm a Christian AND transgender slowly continues to grow.

I spent the first half of my life in fear of someone finding out my secret. I allowed the bigotry I perceived from the world around me to convince me that there was something wrong with me; what I knew about myself couldn't possibly be in keeping with God's plan for me. That eventually lead to seeing that big oak tree and starting to plan how I could end it all right there. The pain was so deep. And I didn't know any other way to end the pain.

But God didn't let go of me, just as He promised in His Word. The tree that Christ was nailed to, the tree that gives us life, is stronger than the tree that could take my life. It was the call to my friend Joy that God used to save my life, and in the months that followed, I learned there was another way to end that pain, and it was simply to be the person I was created to be. What was once unthinkable became my salvation. And in a single moment of God talking to His child at 65 miles per hour on Interstate 80, that pain was taken away. Completely. Never to return.

Of course, that created a new complication in my life. The hesitation of people to embrace my having surgery and living as Laurie was now the hesitation of people to embrace me, knowing that I wasn't born female. The fear of my "truth" being discovered didn't go away, it just flipped.

Now I was happy with me, but the fear of discovery was still my concern. Having to tell my employers was brutal, because either state law for real estate or a background check for the tech company would involve the question, "Are there any other names you have been known by?" Fortunately, their response was okay, fine. But a lifetime of fear having your secret known becomes ingrained in you. My family rejecting me as they did was not a surprise to me. Disappointing and sad, yes, but not a surprise. The church that I loved and had opened up to, only to have the rug pulled out from under me nine months later—THAT is what devastated me and led to depression. I never knew a church could hurt someone so much.

I tried a couple of churches and eventually moved out of state to start over. That's when I discovered my fear and pain moved with me. I spent 11 years hiding at home from Christians. It was the prayers of one person, my spiritual mom, that got me to give Christ's Church another chance. That was the beginning of my transformation, which is also the one-word goal of my church for each member there.

Pastor Jack's unconditional love opened the door, and the Lord did the rest. When I first started attending ATC, telling others, much less building a website, writing a book and putting my entire life on display was not in my plan. But that's why Jeremiah 29:11 is my life verse, because God knows the plans He has for me. It took genuine transformation of my life and being willing to do whatever God wants me to do—whether I wanted to or not, to get me to where I am today.

Do I ride off into the sunset and live happily ever after? My story is still being written. God isn't done with me, and I have no idea where He'll take me from here. Is there still bigotry toward people who are transgender? Yes, there is, and I step forward trusting God that there is more He wants me to do. I hear of that unfortunate bigotry almost daily online and have had to face it myself—from Christians!

My church is a work in progress as are many, if not most churches. Christians are not perfect, and we all know it. My circle of friends at church who know my full story is slowly growing. Some of my Christian friends go to other churches, so those churches are being touched as well, if only by one person. It's going to take time for people to understand that being transgender is not a choice, is not a sin. Everybody will need to exercise patience (a fruit of the spirit I might add – Galatians 5:22) if hearts are to change.

SO WHAT'S MY POINT?

I'm nobody special. God didn't call me because I'm someone super holy (far from it) or have some special connection with the Lord. I'm a mess, but I'm a mess before the Lord God. I depend on Him for my today and tomorrow. I wasn't prepared for what God had for me when He called. I didn't WANT Him to call me—but I said, "Yes Lord, whatever you want." A disciple listens to the words of her teacher, and though it can be hard, that's what I'm trying to do.

I'm not transgender because something unfortunate happened to me when I was young. I'm not transgender because I chose it later in life. Having lived it, why anyone would choose this is beyond my comprehension. There is some science to suggest there are actual brain differences in those who are transgender compared to those who aren't. Honestly? It doesn't matter to me whether science has the answer to the question or not, because I already know that it's just how I was wired. God doesn't make mistakes, and He didn't with me, nor did He with you—however you're wired.

If you're a Christian who isn't transgender, I would hope that you would welcome anyone who would want to join your church, be a part of your community, and want to serve beside you. They see Jesus in you; they sense His presence in the service, that's why they've come. Do you really want to turn them away? For any reason? If you knew the person was transgender, would you avoid sitting next to them or shaking their hand? Do you think you're honoring our Lord if you do? I'm sure Jesus would have no problem taking a seat next to them.

You have no idea how hard it is to muster up the strength as a Christian who is transgender, especially if they're looking for an evangelical or conservative church, to actually show up at church. Despite what you see on the evening news or online, not all who are transgender are liberals, activists, and use the word evangelical in a derogatory way. But the evangelical church (and others) can make it hard at times to feel welcome. There are many, many people like me still in the shadows of our churches. I'm not saying someone who is transgender should be celebrated, as if to say, "Look at us, how wonderful our church is that we accept people different than us." I'm not even saying that you have to go out of your way to make them your next best friend. But there is making someone feel welcomed, and then there is making someone feel unwelcomed.

We are all called to love. It's the proof that we are disciples of Jesus. John 13:34-35 says, "*A new command I give you: Love one another. As I have loved you, so you must love one another. By this everyone will know that you are my disciples, if you love one another."* (NIV) And let's be honest here, some of you can be a little hard to love. So can I. But I looked through 55 translations of that verse, and not one said to only love the ones who are easy to love.

Don't you think that even with the twelve men who dropped everything to follow Him, Jesus didn't get a little exasperated during those three years together? When Peter cut the ear off of the priest's servant in the garden, can't you imagine Jesus looking not too surprised and thinking to Himself, "Peter, really?" He knew Judas was going to betray Him, but that didn't stop Him from loving Judas. When the soldiers were driving nails through His hands and through His feet, Jesus still loved them. And even while He hung on the cross with His life slowly draining from Him, He asked the Father to forgive them. THAT was unconditional love—THAT was Christ's love.

Ultimately, is it your decision if someone loves God and they are saved? And if you think that maybe, just maybe it isn't your call to make, is it your call to decide if they're welcome into your community? And I'm not talking about just someone who may be transgender. What if they are gay and tell you they love the Lord and want to be a part of your community? What if they are homeless, are dressed in rags, and don't smell very nice. Would you turn them away? They may not look like you, they may not dress like you, they may not smell like you. They may not hang out at the same places as you or associate with people of your economic level. If your church says, "Come as you are," does it really mean "Come as you are as long as we don't find you offensive"? Or maybe "Come as you are once you've gotten yourself straightened out to our satisfaction"? Perhaps it's "Come as you are, but you have to stop doing what we call sin."

We do have a heart problem within the Church in spots, and I have no doubt that eventually, the Church will get there—it may be one heart at a time, but Christ's Church will get there.

Being transgender is such a fact of a person's existence, it's hard to develop close friendships and fellowship when you have to constantly dodge this fact about your life fearing rejection and ostracization at every turn. Look, I understand if you did something when you were younger like rob a bank or sold drugs and went to prison. Maybe you had an abortion. These are things that you might be ashamed of and wish to keep private—I get that. Or, it may be part of your amazing spiritual story, and you're fine sharing it. That's wonderful.

I'm not ashamed of the fact that I was born male and subsequently had surgery, because being transgender is not wrong, it's not a sin. It is what it is. I love our Lord. I want to serve Him in any way He asks me. Being transgender is not a reflection of my walk with the Lord. If someone I don't know at my church should ask, "What is the Lord doing in your life these days?" it's sad that I don't feel the freedom yet to tell them. As excited as I am about what He has me doing, as amazed as I am that He even chose me to do this work, I can't tell them.

It's a work in progress and part of what He's called me to do. He didn't call me to point fingers and shame them into acceptance. They need to see Jesus and His love in me so that they can only conclude that, yes, you can be a Christian and transgender. That their Christian brothers and sisters who are transgender are just, well, their Christian brothers and sisters—period.

If you're a Christian and you're transgender and are struggling to find a church community, I'm here to tell you right now—it's not always easy, but it can be done. Granted, I live in a large city in Texas. There are lots of churches to choose from in any flavor not too far from my home. If you're in a smaller town, your choices narrow and that can make things more difficult. I know you want to be liked, you want to be loved. You would like people to agree with you. Are you likable? Are you lovable? Are you agreeable? Or do you make it hard for others to like you or love you? Do you walk into a church with an attitude of, "I'm transgender, and you have to like it, dammit!"? That's not coming across as agreeable and certainly not likable for most folks, myself included.

That son of a bitch Satan is happiest when we Christians find ways to criticize each other and divide ourselves into smaller groups so we don't have to associate with each other. I hope and pray for Christ's Church, that when we say, "Come as you are," and "All are welcome," that we mean it.

My story isn't over. This is just the beginning of whatever "some kind of something" God has in store for me. I hope whether you're transgender or not that you'll join me on my journey. My website at TransfiguredHearts.com is where you'll find me. I've got articles and blog posts there, where I'll continue to describe my journey and reach out to Christians, transgender or not. I'm also on Facebook as Laurie S. Scott. I'd like to hear about your journey, your experiences. Feel free to message me on Facebook or write to me at Laurie@TransfiguredHearts.com.

God doesn't make mistakes. You and I, ALL of us are fearfully and wonderfully made. Praise God!

May our Father in Heaven bless you as you discover the path and journey of that "some kind of something" He has laid out for you to follow.

GRATITUDE

Scott Lawson, Greg and Susan Lear, Kim Mogan and Carrie Siegel: Without your generous help in getting the book to the finish line it would be nothing more than a document sitting on my computer's hard drive – thank you so very much!

Morgan Gist MacDonald: I had a story to tell and not the slightest clue how. Your expertise combined with your boundless encouragement made turning a life story into a finished book, it would never have happened without you.

My awesome Pastor Jack and other pastors at Austin Transformation Church: From day one you've been nothing but loving and gracious toward me. I would have no ministry nor this book if it weren't for the transformational love shown to me at ATC. I love you all.

My "sister from another mister" Andrea: You've been there to love and support me from the day we met. You drove out to Austin with me, so I wouldn't have to drive alone and helped me move into my home. You encouraged me to write this book. You are everything I could ask for in a sister—neither time nor distance can separate us. I love you, sis.

My "brother from another mother" David: I was barely limping along when we met, and you helped me begin to find my footing again with Christians by opening your heart and making me part of your loving family.

Dr. Lin Fraser: Who knew that 26 years after I first walked into your office, I'd be trying to find the words to express my deep appreciation of not just your professional guidance and honesty, but your genuine concern and care for my well-being? You were exactly who God knew I needed, and I can't imagine having a better person who could have helped me walk through that most difficult time of my life.

My dear friend Joy: You literally saved my life. I'm not sure I'd be around to write this book had it not been for your sensitivity to God's Spirit on the day I called, ready to end it all.

My dear friend Janice: God is just determined that we be lifelong friends, and I couldn't be happier about that. When I think about our friendship over the various stages of our lives, I can't help but smile. What a blessing you continue to be to me.

Mom and Dad: You gave me life—how can I not be thankful for that? I'm alive today because of the foundation of faith in God you instilled in me. But there is a huge hole inside me that misses you and longs to see you again. In heaven I know we'll get to give each other a big hug with tears of joy, I just hope I don't have to wait that long—I long for the day I can give you that hug right here on Earth. Tears? Guaranteed! I love and miss you with all my heart.

Sharon Bollum: Oh, my dear Sharon—You've been my pastor, my mentor, my spiritual mom, and most importantly, my friend. You saw the hurt in my heart, and when you learned my story you wrapped me in love. You've covered me in prayer, you've listened to my broken heart, shared my tears of anguish, defended me from my critics, laughed when I was being silly, flew all the way to Texas for my baptism, kept me grounded when I leaned toward lunacy, and celebrated my breakthroughs. There is no measure for the depth of my love for you.

To my Lord and Savior Jesus Christ: I am loved because of You. I have life because of You. Without You, nothing else in life matters.